Adventures in Research

Adventures in Research

Volume I
Latin America
and an Introduction into Europe

Howard J. Wiarda

iUniverse, Inc.
New York Lincoln Shanghai

Adventures in Research
Volume I
Latin America and an Introduction into Europe

Copyright © 2006 by Howard J. Wiarda

iUniverse books may be ordered through booksellers or by contacting:

iUniverse
2021 Pine Lake Road, Suite 100
Lincoln, NE 68512
www.iuniverse.com
1-800-Authors (1-800-288-4677)

ISBN-13: 978-0-595-39710-5 (pbk)
ISBN-13: 978-0-595-84116-5 (ebk)
ISBN-10: 0-595-39710-7 (pbk)
ISBN-10: 0-595-84116-3 (ebk)

Printed in the United States of America

TABLE OF CONTENTS

PREFACE

This is the first of a three-volume set entitled "Adventures in Research." I have written a large number (over sixty) of scholarly, academic books in my life dealing with American foreign policy, international relations, comparative politics, and Third World development; but somehow, these books don't tell the full story. They deal more with academic themes and issues but they don't entirely capture the excitement of research, travel, interviewing, and living abroad that go into the writing of these books.

Over the course of my academic-think tank-policy career, I have been fortunate to have traveled and/or lived in five continents and over sixty countries. My students tell me that my classes are fun and exciting precisely because I am able to weave personal stories and adventures into my academic lectures. At the urging of friends, colleagues, students, and family members, therefore, I have tried in these volumes to capture some of the sheer fun and excitement of doing original research in foreign countries.

But these books are not just about adventures abroad. They also show how scholars wrestle with complex issues, the difficulties of doing interviewing and living in foreign countries, and how ideas and theories get tested, rethought, and reformulated in ongoing research situations. Readers who are looking for stories of fun, adventures, and misadventures abroad will find plenty of them here; but serious readers will also find a large storehouse of information and ideas about the social sciences, foreign affairs, comparative politics, and how nations change and develop.

The three volumes are organized chronologically and cover a forty-year period. They begin in 1962 with my first trip to the Latin American part of the Third World and end in 2001 with an incredible sabbatical leave year that took me to Europe for the first six months, then Brazil and South Africa, and finally a trip all around Asia that ended in poor, bedraggled East Timor. The book is organized chronologically because that provides logic, order, and sequence to the story told here. Any other way of organizing the material (exclusively by geographical region, for example) would throw the logic and sequencing completely off and result in the narrative jumping back and forth unacceptably between time periods as well as different academic postings.

In general we can say that, for me, the 1960s was the period, in a research sense, of Latin America, the 1970s the period of Europe, and the 1980s and onward a period of expanding interest in global events and issues. But of course one does not abandon an earlier research terrain just because one's research interests have expanded into other, newer areas. That explains why, in Volume II devoted mainly to Europe, there are also chapters dealing with Latin America. For the facts are that even when I considered Europe my main research area, I continued to return to my research roots in Latin America; and when, later, I spent a lot of time in Asia and as a global traveler, I still maintained my interest in and frequently returned to both Latin America and Europe.

Volume I of this set deals with my initial forays into the foreign affairs research field. Almost all the chapters, 1-6, in the volume deal with Latin America. Chapter 7 on Portugal is also included in Volume I because at that time I considered Portugal and Spain part of a single culture area that I called the "Iberic-Latin Tradition."

Volume II, entitled "Europe and the Wider World," contains five chapters on Europe, reflecting the shift in my research interests during the 1970s from Latin America to Europe. The main focus in these chapters is my efforts to understand the differences between Northern and Southern Europe. But Volume II also contains a chapter on Israel and three chapters on Latin America, reflecting the wider range of my research interests and my continuing interest in Latin America.

Volume III is entitled "A Global Traveler." It contains chapters on Asia, Russia, Eastern Europe, and South Africa as well as on Europe and Latin America. This global perspective reflects not only my travels in parts of the world I'd not visited before, but also my broadened research and writing agenda to include international relations and comparative politics as seen from a worldwide perspective.

I have incurred many debts over the course of this four and a half decades of research, travel, and discovery. The institutions I have been associated with, the foundations that supported my work, and the many persons I've met and interviewed—all too many to name here—surely are at the top of my indebtedness list. Specifically in the preparation of this volume I wish to thank Meghan Morgan and Doris Holden who took on the huge task of typing the manuscript, and my research assistant Jennifer White whose technical skills in preparing a manuscript like this for publication far exceed my own. Dr Iêda Siqueira Wiarda has been an invaluable wife, mom, partner, and companion in all these endeavors, and our children Kristy, Howard E., and Jonathan all shared in the early adventures. To all of them I owe deep thanks.

Interested readers, depending on their areas of specialty, may wish to acquire any one of these three volumes or the complete set. It should be noted that chapters on Latin America and Europe appear in all three volumes, and this brief Preface appears in all three. However, only Volume I contains the Introduction to the set and only Volume III has the Conclusion.

Howard J. Wiarda
Athens, Georgia
Spring, 2006

INTRODUCTION

As a kid growing up in the 1940s and 1950s in the American mid-West, in Grand Rapids, Michigan, I never thought much about foreign travel. My parents were not poor, but they were not rich either; and the notion in those days was that only wealthy people traveled abroad. Even the term itself, "traveling abroad," conveys an air of mystery, of going to unknown and perhaps exotic places, and of upper-class status. Foreign travel was not something that one did, as today, quickly and easily. Such travel remained outside the realm of our experiences and expectations.

We did take family vacations, but those were limited to the U.S. and mainly to the mid-West. As a kid I remember going to Detroit and Chicago with my parents at least once a year, taking car tours around Lakes Michigan and Superior, and, before the era of interstate highways, going on longer leisurely trips to Boston, New York, and Florida. In those days crossing Canada, from Detroit to Buffalo, was a big adventure for me in new kinds of road signs, the absence of international motel chains, and a foreign currency that had to be converted into dollars. We took another trip once to Montreal and Quebec City, and I recall being intrigued both by the widespread use of the French language and the fact the people looked, dressed, and acted differently than they did in Grand Rapids, Michigan.

Part of it was money and affordability; the other part was the fact that, for mid-Westerners like me, study abroad was simply not contemplated. Nor were there, as now, student exchange or study abroad programs readily available and organized, and modern jet travel able to whisk you away. The kids I grew up with were nice, bright children from stable families and middle- or upper-middle-class backgrounds—many of them able to afford to travel abroad—but I do not remember from junior high or high school in the '50s a single family among our acquaintances or a single schoolmate spending a summer, a semester, let alone a full year abroad. By the time I went off to college in 1957 at the University of Michigan in Ann Arbor, some of this was beginning to change, and there were a handful of study-abroad programs; I recall, however, that the girl I was really in love with at that time went off for a junior year abroad in Paris and there must

1

have found another beau or maybe just someone with greater sophistication because, when she returned, the romance was never quite the same.

My father and mother were both very intelligent, and my dad, though not university educated, was especially interested in international affairs. At the age of seventeen, though Teddy Roosevelt "the rough-rider" was his hero, he had heeded Woodrow Wilson's call to go off to World War I "to make the world safe for democracy." Returning wounded and with a Purple Heart from the Great War, he had the opportunity to go to college but—a mistake he often regretted—turned it down to go into business and because he thought it would be demeaning, after his war experience, to go back to school with students a year younger and less sophisticated than he. Nevertheless, he always read the papers, maintained a lifetime interest in world politics, and frequently expressed his opinions to me on international affairs, blending both realist and idealist positions. He and my mother had in the 1920s sailed to Europe on their honeymoon both to see the sights and to visit my dad's old battlefields; during and immediately after World War II he was intensely interested in the plight of his cousins and their families in The Netherlands, German occupied and devastated by war and famine, writing to them regularly and sending boxful after boxful of food, blankets, and clothing. An independent who voted for both Republicans and Democrats, he supported Gerald Ford's reformist congressional campaign in Grand Rapids in the 1940s, and voted for peace activist Henry Wallace in 1948, a ballot that the rest of the family never allowed him to forget.

The one member of our family who did regularly travel and live extensively abroad was my Aunt Julia Wiarda, my father's younger sister. Aunt Julia had grown up in the '30s when few women went to college, but during the depression she had learned stenographic and typing skills and gotten a job in the Kent County (Grand Rapids) Registry of Deeds. But she was also bright, ambitious, and strikingly beautiful with blond, almost white (natural!) hair and deep, piercing blue eyes. During World War II she worked in war services and after the war parlayed that into jobs with Point Four (the early U.S. foreign aid program), the Agency for International Development (AID), and the State Department. She served in what were then all the world's hot trouble spots: China at the time of the 1940s communist revolution, Indonesia as it became independent from Dutch rule, Korea caught in civil war, Afghanistan when King Mohammed Daud was still in power, Europe during the Cold War.

Though only having a high school diploma, Aunt Julia, because she was smart (and pretty), rose up through the ranks and eventually secured a full foreign-service officer (FSO) position. She would regale her nephews with tales of her adventures and brought back wonderful gifts for the family: silk kimono nightgowns for my mother, an Afghan water pipe (seldom used) for my father, and a bejeweled Chinese sword for me. She was stationed in Shanghai when Mao's communists took over and gave me for my stamp collection a set of the last stamps minted in Nationalist China. I still have those stamps; and forty years later when I visited Taiwan for the first time and told this story, I recall my hosts being quite intrigued and offering to buy the whole set at a handsome price.

Aunt Julia received only brief annual vacations which she often spent in other exotic places; but on those occasions when she returned to Grand Rapids, maybe once every two or three years, the entire extended family of twenty or thirty persons would go out to the airport to greet her and to see her off. It was a big deal for us children and very exciting, especially knowing that she always brought exotic gifts. In those days it was only the now-defunct Capital Airlines that served Grand Rapids, shuttling passengers in on two-engine props from the bigger airports in Detroit or Chicago. Recall also this was the late 1940s, early 1950s, before the onset of modern jet travel when virtually every place in the world is now within one day's flying time. But on those old props it would take three or four days to get home from Afghanistan or Indonesia, with numerous refueling stops. So when someone like our well-traveled and sophisticated (she smoked, which women didn't do in those days) Aunt Julia came home, it was a major occasion.[*]

I had never before flown on a plane until I was seventeen years old and had gone off to university. At Thanksgiving of that freshman year I went to visit the house of my new best friend (and fraternity brother) Fred Koester, and we rode back to school on a flight from Chicago into Detroit's Willow Run Airport. By then, I was working on <u>The Michigan Daily</u> (Tom Hayden, of SDS and Jane Fonda fame and I were both freshman cub reporters), the Cuban Revolution was underway and profound changes were in the air in Latin America, and I was taking a variety of exciting, stimulating history and political science courses on European history, international relations, foreign policy, Latin America, France, and Spain, as well as a wonderful course on the philosophical bases of communism, fascism, and

---

[*]   Aunt Julia was also a gifted writer and every few months would send back a long missile to the entire family describing the country she was in and her adventures. These contained marvelous portraits of, for example, the raw beauty of mountainous Afghanistan or the Dutch exiting reluctantly from Indonesia, and at one point later in my career I thought seriously of collecting these letters for a volume I planned to call "A Liberated Woman in the American Foreign Service." But unfortunately some of the most interesting letters—of China in the midst of revolution, Korea in civil war—are missing, and so the project was never completed.

democracy taught by a young, enthused, dynamic professor, Carl Cohen.[1] Forty years later it would be the same Carl Cohen who achieved national prominence by raising the issue of the grid or point scheme used by the University of Michigan in determining affirmative action admissions.

It was not until I went to graduate school to study Latin America and international relations seriously and professionally that I had the desire, the opportunity, and now finally the means to travel abroad extensively and to live abroad for extended periods of time. At the University of Florida in Gainesville, 1961-65, there was then the country's best Latin American studies program, a particularly strong faculty in the history (Alva Curtis Wilgus, L. N. McAlister, Donald Worcester), comparative politics (Arnold Heidenheimer, René Lemarchand, Harry Kantor), and international relations (Fredrick Hartmann, John Spanier) programs, and a wealth of funding opportunities through major Rockefeller and National Defense Foreign Language and Area Studies grants to the University and its Latin American Studies Center.[2] I was quick to begin taking advantage of the travel and research opportunities these grants afforded.

Starting in 1962 I began this sojourn and travel odyssey abroad. Since then, in the intervening forty-four years, I have traveled abroad virtually every year, often several times a year and frequently to several countries on one trip. I have actually lived for extensive periods of time, in a dozen countries in Latin America and Europe, done extensive research (more than a week or two) in about two dozen more, and have traveled and engaged in shorter research projects in some thirty more. I have spent major research periods in Latin America, Western Europe, Israel and the Middle East, Russia, Eastern Europe, Asia, and South Africa. I have visited all the continents except Australia and Antarctica (a scheduled trip there was cancelled at the last minute). My C.V. and journal records show that I have spent time in no fewer than five continents and sixty-four countries.[*]

---

[*]   I thought that was a quite impressive number until one time I was in Freiburg, Germany, and a German academic colleague, Hans Illy, told me that he had visited 140 countries. He told me, which I had not known before, that there is actually an international association that keeps track of these things, decides when countries go in or out of existence (like the former Yugoslavia), and resolves disputes (e.g., are colonies or the Panama Canal Zone in earlier times to be treated as separate countries?). This association has determined that there are at present 240 "political entities" in the world; one member, a lawyer from Chicago, has visited 239. But "visiting" briefly for the sake of carving another notch on your belt of political entities dropped in on is not the same as working, researching, and living in a country to the point where you know it well.

As an academic, my fields of teaching and research interest include, geographically, Latin America, Western Europe, Eastern Europe, Israel and the Middle East, Russia, East Asia, and now South and Southeast Asia and southern Africa as well. Functionally or topically, I am a specialist in comparative politics, international relations, and foreign policy. <u>There is no doubt</u> that my <u>teaching and research</u> have been <u>enormously enriched</u> by all of this foreign travel and the opportunities to live and work abroad in so many places. When I write about foreign affairs and foreign countries, I now do it with a command and a self-assurance that can only come from having been there, seen that, experienced this, and <u>lived</u> there as only one with vast experience in an area can have. When I go to all these places, I am a seasoned, experienced traveler, "at home" in many cultures, and undoubtedly all this travel serves to enrich my teaching and writing.

But more than that, I am a walking storehouse of adventures, experiences, and stories from abroad that almost no one else has experienced. I try to weave these stories and adventures into my teaching on more serious and profound issues as a way of livening the discussion, waking up the students, and making the subject exciting and personal. The technique seems to work because every year my courses are ranked at or near the top of my department's and college's popularity charts. I get stunning responses from my students indicating that "Prof. Wiarda's course really turned me on to the subject" or "Prof. Wiarda's stories make the course more interesting" or "This prof. has had an incredible life." Years later I sometimes hear from students who, perhaps sadly, can't remember much of the intellectual content of the course but do remember the stories. Sometimes I even get the comment, though it's untrue, that "this prof. has been in so many exciting places and had so many adventures that he must be a CIA agent."

I have written a lot of academic books (over sixty) in my life, but I've never, outside of the classroom or at friendly dinners and cocktail receptions, told of the adventures and experiences abroad that lie behind all these books. For, in addition to the comments above, I have had numerous students who have written to me or said that I simply <u>must</u> put all my stories and adventures abroad in book form. That I have tried to do here in this volume entitled "Adventures in Research." For not only are the stories related entertaining as a kind of lifetime history of adventure, but they also—perhaps more importantly—serve to illustrate how research gets done, how theory and empirical research get blended, how one operates empathetically in foreign research locales, and how research in the fields of comparative politics, international relations, and foreign policy is carried out. It's been an exciting journey; I hope readers will enjoy coming along for the ride.

A note on sources: Over the past twenty-five years (1977-2003) I have been keeping a journal which records travel, adventures, impressions, interviews, and close, often insider comments on American foreign policy. There are now 150 of these journals, of 200 pages each, making a total of 30,000 pages or about 4,500,000 words—more or less! In addition, for each of these years, I have a volume or two of my "Collecting Writings"—memos, letters, reviews, notes, book outlines and proposals, invitations, guest lists—for that year. On top of that, I have files and boxes for virtually every research project in which I've been engaged over the last quarter century. So there are plenty of materials for these years. Materials on the earlier period (1962-77) are spottier, but I do have a complete collection of my own writings, some diary entries, letters and memos written, and boxes of research materials. It is these materials as well as the memories of friends, colleagues, and family members on which I draw. Not every date or fact will be entirely accurate, I suspect, and I apologize in advance for any mistakes made; this is the best that I can do. For those wishing to pursue these accounts further, all the records listed above will be available in the Richard Russell Library of the University of Georgia. The journals, especially, will provide a quite remarkable record and commentary on Washington policy-making over this twenty-five-year period, from Gerald Ford and Jimmy Carter through Ronald Reagan, George H. W. Bush, Bill Clinton, and George W. Bush.

NOTES

1. There is a chapter on the University of Michigan in my book, <u>Universities, Think Tanks, and War Colleges: The Main Institutions of American Educational Life— A Memoir</u> (Philadelphia: McGraw Hill/XLibris Corporation, 1999).

2. An account of graduate school experiences at Florida is in <u>ibid</u>, Chapter 3.

CHAPTER 1

THE DOMINICAN REPUBLIC AND HAITI

During my senior year in college, it began to dawn on me (and my parents) that I had no plans and no job lined up for after graduation. So I interviewed with several banks and junior executive training programs but still with no clear goals in mind. I had also become interested in Latin America, taken several courses on its history and culture, and paid a visit to my favorite teacher, Irving Leonard, to talk about graduate school prospects. He told me that the University of Florida had the best Latin American studies program in the country. So I applied there (and, perhaps naively, nowhere else, not to any of the more prestigious graduate schools), was accepted, and in the fall of 1961 drove down to Gainesville to start my graduate career.

I did very well in graduate school, taking an unprecedented five courses (fifteen credits) that first semester, working extremely hard, and getting "A" grades in all five. In the second semester I took three more courses (nine credits), signed up for six hours of Master's thesis credit, and worked as an editorial research assistant on the Hispanic American Historical Review, the journal for scholars of Latin American history. I took as many history as political science courses, but eventually declared political science to be my major field, and meanwhile won one of the prestigious National Defense Foreign Language and Area Studies fellowships which guaranteed funding for the next three years of my graduate school career, carrying me through Ph.D. course work and comprehensive exams, and providing a Fulbright-Hays award for a year abroad to write my doctoral dissertation.

During that first year in graduate school, I had fallen under the sway of a charismatic professor, Harry Kantor, who was the political science department's Latin American specialist. Kantor was a poor Jewish boy from Chicago, a product of a rough-and-tumble childhood, a socialist who had once worked in

Chicago's activist post office with Louis Untermeyer and novelist Richard Wright (Black Boy, Almos' a Man). Kantor made Latin America come dramatically alive in the classroom, painted a vivid picture of a continent polarized between traditional forces (Church, Army, oligarchy) and democratic ones, and was himself personally close to all the leaders of the Latin American democratic-left. It was a clear and attractive, if somewhat oversimplified portrait, but Kantor was a mesmerizing and enthusiastic teacher, and he took me under his wing.

In the early spring of 1962 I went to see Kantor about ideas for my Master's thesis. In those days you actually had to <u>write</u> an MA thesis before going on for the Ph.D.; it was not possible as now to go directly into a Ph.D. program. At that time I had not yet visited Latin America; my knowledge of the region was still very general and "academic"; and the specific information I had acquired about individual countries was quite vague. When Kantor asked me what country I was especially interested in, I had to say I wasn't sure. He then told me that the Latin America Center at Florida had a big Rockefeller grant for research in Central America and the Caribbean, that he had students working on or in every other country of the area, so why didn't I take the Dominican Republic? So that's how "the DR" became "my country," the "living laboratory" for my Latin America research and writing for the next decade.

My MA thesis (and first book—and "only good book," as Yale's Juan Linz once told me) hence focused on the dictatorship of Rafael Trujillo in the Dominican Republic. It was a study of the methods of dictatorial control used by Trujillo to stay in power for over thirty-one years, 1930-61, and, more theoretically, of the use of an authoritarian route to achieve national development as distinct from the democratic one. The thesis was quite comprehensive but, of necessity, based mainly on library materials from the University of Florida's rich Latin America collection—especially so on the Dominican Republic since the dictator made certain that <u>everything</u> published in the country during the "era de Trujillo" was sent to that depository. I did most of the research during the spring of 1962, finished the writing over the early summer, had the exam on the thesis in July, and received my MA degree in August. By then I was already en route to the DR.

Hugh Popenoe, father and son, in the University of Florida's school of agriculture, were the administrators of the Rockefeller grant for research on the Caribbean and Central America. The Popenoes had been working in Latin America for decades, owned a famous colonial house in the ancient Guatemalan capital of Antigua, and were pioneers in developing new strains of seed. They were also thought of as fair-minded administrators of the University's large Rockefeller money. I submitted a proposal indicating I wanted to do field work and interviews in the DR, both to supplement the library research that went into my Trujillo-era thesis and to begin preliminary research on my Ph.D. thesis, for which I planned to study the post-Trujillo transition to democracy and the emergence of a more pluralist society. I'm sure the way the system worked was that the Popenoes then checked back with Kantor, who gave them the good word about me and I got the grant.

A unique feature of the Rockefeller grant to Florida was that it called for faculty advisers to accompany their students into Latin America to give them the advantage of learning how to conduct research and how to "operate" in a foreign research setting. That was wonderful in giving me, a neophyte, an introduction to Latin America; I have never heard of any other grant program with such a feature. So in the first week of August 1962, Kantor and I headed down from Gainesville to Miami to catch a plane for the Dominican Republic.

The Dominican Republic

My then girlfriend, Barbara (Bobbie) Nichols, drove us to Miami in her little Volkswagen Beetle. She was a fellow graduate student at Florida working on her Master's degree in Spanish, a terrific dancer, and, because she was pretty and sexy and spoke perfect Spanish, a friend of many of the Latin American graduate students on campus. I think she was in awe of the fact I took five graduate courses there my first semester, had a perfect 4.0 grade point average, and—unheard of— had completed my Master's degree in a single year. She was from Fort Lauderdale and her family lived there, so at the end of the summer term in Gainesville, since she was going home for a few weeks anyway, she volunteered to take us to the airport.

In those days there were two airlines that flew between Miami and the Dominican Republic. The Compañía Dominicana de Aviación (CDA) was state-owned but had formerly belonged to Trujillo; it had a bad reputation for mechanical problems, late and unreliable arrivals, and frequent crashes. The other was Pan American World Airlines, then still owned by the legendary airline pioneer Juan Trippe. Both flew props. Pan Am had a "milk run" (many stops) flight that was a famous island hopper and that I would take many times in the next few years. In the morning it went Miami-Kingston (sometimes Montego Bay), Jamaica-Port au Prince, Haiti-Santo Domingo, the Dominican Republic-San Juan, Puerto Rico. In the afternoon it would turn around: San Juan-Santo Domingo-Port au Prince-Kingston-Miami. That way (and at no extra cost, as I recall), a passenger could stop off for a few days at each of the islands and sample the variety of the Caribbean, an opportunity that in the years ahead I would take full advantage of, spending time in all these countries. On this trip Kantor and I proposed to stop off for a few days in Haiti after spending the bulk of our time in the DR.

The plane sweeps down low over the dense, green, lush tropical island of Hispaniola, banks out over the blue Caribbean, and then lands at Punta Caucedo, the Dominican Republic's international airport. The first impression was of immense, stifling heat and humidity; after all, this is the tropics in August. The second impression is of soldiers everywhere, lounging, not looking very well trained or professional, but managing to swing the straps of their guns so they point in your direction. The third impression is of complete disorganization and utter confusion in the baggage area, with hordes of people standing around, lots of shouting and scampering to and fro, but nothing getting done. This was definitely not the clean, orderly, well-organized, Protestant/Calvinist society of my upbringing in Grand Rapids. Kantor, used to this, took it all in with a wry grin and much patience; I was barely in the country and already in culture shock. Plus, this was the old airplane terminal, not air-conditioned, and absolutely stifling. A waiter came by with a tray of rum and colas, two of which helped lift my already flagging spirits.

We hired a taxi into the city, proceeding west along the Avenida de las Americas, one of the DR's most spectacular coasts. It is a four-lane, divided highway constructed by Trujillo (everything it seemed in those days had been built by Trujillo) and laid out on the coral rock above the sea. There are palm trees and glorious tropical flowers, and the spray from the pounding sea squirts up through holes in the coral to make spectacular natural geysers. Along the way is the "tres ojos" ("three eyes"), pools of fresh, salt, and sulphur water in close proximity. Along this beautiful route I caught my first glimpse of Dominican poverty: run-down stick shacks along the road that Trujillo had torn down but now, in his absence, had reappeared, barefooted and tattered women carrying sticks of firewood or cans of water on their heads, and seemingly endless children with the bloated bellies of malnutrition, often with malformed limbs from the absence of medical care, and usually shoeless and even pantless—no need for diapers that way.

We cross the suspension bridge over the Ozama River into which Columbus sailed when he founded the city of Santo Domingo (recently renamed after it had been called, like everything else, after the late dictator Ciudad Trujillo or Trujillo City) in 1493. Then down into the narrow streets of the old colonial city.

Seemingly endless poor people on the sidewalks, much confusion and disorganization, everyone tooting their horns even though the traffic was going nowhere. But there were traffic policemen; things did move eventually; and I began to sense already that the Dominican Republic had its own rationality— even if it was not always my Protestant, North American rationality.

We round the corner of Avenida Isabela (named after the queen for whom Columbus sailed) and onto Calle El Conde, the main street of Santo Domingo. El Conde is a narrow street of only two lanes flowing one way to the west and lined with three- and four-story buildings (no skyscrapers here) that in 1962 constituted the central shopping area. Now, much of the shopping, businesses, and commercial activity has moved to the suburbs. El Conde runs for only nine blocks between the Parque Colon (Columbus Park) and the Parque Independencia; along this strip radios are blaring, cars are tooting, illegal power lines siphon off electricity to businesses and apartments, and a variety of bars and coffee shops serve as centers of intrigue and as launching pads for the turbas (disturbances) that rock the downtown area almost daily. Our hotel, the Comercial, is in the second block, with its entrance half a block off the main thoroughfare.

The Comercial had been recommended to Kantor by a colleague at Florida. It was centrally located—great for us as scholars—had a decent restaurant, and thankfully was air conditioned. But it lacked a pool—very welcome in the tropics—and had none of the "buzz" or intrigue of international visitors and conspiracy as was true at the capital's other two main hotels farther away from the center, the Jaragua and the Embajador. We stayed at the Comercial for our first week, later we moved to the Jaragua, and we played tennis, swam, and checked out the bar at the Embajador where all the CIA agents hung out.

Into the Maelstrom

So here we are in the Dominican Republic. It was then a country of five million persons, now it is seven or eight million. It is about the size of Vermont and New Hampshire combined. It was then a basically (90 percent) agricultural country with sugarcane the main crop and bringing in some 80 percent of export earnings. It was 80 percent illiterate, 80 percent rural, and one of the poorest countries in Latin America with a per capital income of under $400.00 per year. Predominantly mulatto (but with a small white elite), Spanish-speaking, Catholic, and Hispanic in its main cultural ties, the Dominican Republic shares the island of Hispaniola with Haiti, which it considers to be black, African, and barbaric. The DR takes up two-thirds of the island and Haiti one-third, but the proportions are reversed in terms of population, and the Dominicans have long feared that their Hispanic civilization will either be overrun (as happened in the nineteenth century) or submerged from below (by the black underclass) by the more numerous Haitians.

These were tense times in the Dominican Republic. Dictator Trujillo had been assassinated (while on the way home from seeing his mistress) a year earlier; the post-Trujillo transition had been violent and unstable; the country lacked institutions and infrastructure; an interim council of state was in power in part selected and organized by the United States; elections were scheduled for later in 1962; and riots and street demonstrations were occurring on an almost everyday basis. Staying at the Comercial (where none of the other Americans stayed), we were in the middle of the activity.

The United States was also vitally interested in the Dominican Republic. Recall that in the preceding three years in next-door Cuba, dictator Fulgencio Batista had been overthrown, Fidel Castro's revolution had come to power, Cuba had become a communist country allied with the Soviet Union, the Cubans were aiding like-minded groups in the DR, and the Soviets were bringing missiles into Cuba that two months after our visit to the DR would culminate in the October 1962 missile crisis, the closest the U.S. and the Soviets came to war in the entire Cold War period. The White House was extremely concerned that the DR situation was parallel to that of Cuba (silly and wrong; the two countries were vastly different) and that the DR might go the Cuban communist route. All U.S. Embassy activities in the DR were designed to, at all costs, prevent that from happening.

Kantor and I had checked into the Comercial by mid-afternoon; an hour later, refreshed from splashing cold water in my face, we were ready to head out again. It turned out that was precisely the hour (4:00-5:00 p.m.) when things start to heat up in downtown Santo Domingo. That is when politicians go from their regular jobs to their party headquarters, when the secretaries and shop girls start to sashay by in the afternoon paseo, and when the turbas begin. Kantor and I, going in search of the Dominican Revolutionary Party (PRD), proceeded east along El Conde, music blaring from every corner, to the Parque Colon. There, shoeshine boys scrambled to polish our shoes for 5 cents, older men played dominoes and dice, and politicians in white panama suits and hats gathered to slap backs and exchange chispes (gossip). On the south side of the square is the cathedral, the oldest in the Americas; on the east and west sides were the old military headquarters and the civilian administration now both converted to commercial purposes. On the north side was a bar and restaurant, the offices of the United States Information Agency (USIA) whose cars were often turned over and burned in the turbas, and the national headquarters of the PRD. We checked in at the USIA (which also housed the American Lincoln Library, a place where I later went often to borrow books, use the copier, and utilize—I'm sure, illegally—secretarial services), met the director Malcolm McLean, and then went next door to the PRD.

The PRD was a socialist or social-democratic party that was a member of the Latin American democratic-left. It had been founded in exile decades earlier by Juan Bosch, a charismatic intellectual and the DR's foremost writer, and his principal lieutenants Nicolás Silfa, Angel Miolán, and Ramón Castillo—all of whom had taken refuge abroad from Trujillo's bloody dictatorship. The party stood for democracy, social reform, and the raising up of the country's poorest, often forgotten peasant- and working-class elements. It believed in socialism but by democratic means.

Those positions were very close to Kantor's own ideology. He had also come to know well the PRD leadership (including Bosch who had stayed in Kantor's house) when he taught at a school for young Latin American democratic leaders financed by the CIA (occasionally the CIA does good things!) in San José, Costa Rica. That school had recently been transferred to Santo Domingo utilizing Argentine, Venezuelan, Cuban (exile), as well as Dominican professors, and had its own campus on the outskirts of the city. There it was training young labor, peasant, and party leaders in how to organize—and also how to resist communist incursions. The school in Costa Rica and now in Santo Domingo was headed by a mysterious Romanian, Sacha Volman, who worked for the CIA and was the U.S. embassy's link to the PRD, but whom Kantor suspected of being not just a double but a triple agent, maybe in the pay of the communists as well. Right from the beginning, thanks to Kantor, I was very well connected to the PRD.

As soon as we marched into the PRD headquarters, we were ushered into an upstairs room. As visiting Americans and honored guests, the air conditioner was turned on. One of the functionaries had been in Costa Rica and recognized the Kantor name. Soon party secretary general Washington Luís arrived. For my benefit youth leader Emanuel Espinal was brought in. Party president Miolán was called and soon appeared. After a talk we all went out on the balcony to wave to party supporters gathered in the streets below. Arrangements were quickly made for us later in the week to meet Bosch, Silfa, Castillo, Volman, and Horacio Ornes, another Kantor student in Costa Rica who had come home post-Trujillo to form his own party, the Vanguardia Revolucionaria Dominicana. He was the brother of Germán Ornes, the influential owner-publisher of the Dominican

Republic's biggest newspaper, <u>El Caribe</u>. Thus, within a couple of hours of my arrival in Santo Domingo, I already—thanks again to Kantor—had access to all the PRD's top leadership, to labor, peasant, and youth leaders, to the heads of several other political parties that bad spun off from the PRD, and to the head of the country's leading newspaper. What a wealth of contacts for my future Ph.D. dissertation!

The next week was a <u>whirlwind</u> of activity. The Dominican Republic had over twenty political parties and we visited almost all of them. Ramón Castillo and Nicolás Silfa, as part of the fractionalization underway, had both broken with Bosch to form their own small mini-parties; Castillo told us egotistically that all the applause when Bosch and the PRD returned to the country after Trujillo's death was really for him and that he would "easily" win the presidency in December. Horacio Ornes, whose party offices were on the Parque Independencia, had also split with the PRD because he, Ornes, in a <u>macho</u> thing, had not been named to a leadership post. The hot-headed Ornes had also once tried to overthrow Trujillo by launching a romantic but futile, Fidel-like revolutionary invasion of the country. With some of the other small parties, it was clear that they also had no chance for the presidency but had launched their campaigns as macho, ego things, and were trying to parlay their small regional or clientelistic support into a cabinet or other high position.

In visiting all these parties we found ourselves walking up and down El Conde and throughout the old city. Santo Domingo is full of wonderful history: not only the first cathedral but also the first monastery, the first hospital, the first convent, the first prison, the first fortress in the Americas—to say nothing of the house of Diego Colon, Columbus's son. Between appointments we would sometimes sit in the Parque Colon, sometimes the Parque Independencia, getting our shoes shined, talking to people, meeting strangers (and even prostitutes—could I do <u>that</u> back in Grand Rapids?), watching the Dominican world go by—all good ways to try to understand a culture other than your own. We drank and ate at little bars and popular restaurants as well as at the city's two premier restaurants: Vesuvios on George Washington Avenue, the <u>malecon</u>, overlooking the sea, and Lina's, very elegant, near Independence Park. As we strolled and talked and roamed around, we also began to figure out that there was a sociology and a systematic politics to the <u>turbas</u> and street demonstrations: that each bar and restaurant on El Conde was a hangout for different political groups, that many of the demonstrators were <u>hired</u> to demonstrate, that the <u>turbas</u> were regular, organized, orchestrated, and choreographed parts of the political process.

We went out to see Volman and his social-democratic school for young leaders. Volman seemed to have lots of young, tarty Dominican girlfriends; he invited me to go out night-clubbing with him and his friends one night, an unforgettable experience. Volman was mysterious, intriguing, playing all sides for his own advantage, completely untrustworthy from my point of view, and women swooned though he was not handsome. He was an ambiguous character that should have found a place in a John LeCarré novel; the DR seemed to be full of these types while we were there. The school, still funded with CIA money, was a growing concern, with about thirty students and a faculty that consisted of Bosch, Miolán, the Argentine Dardo Cúneo (an advisor to ex-president Arturo Frondizi), and the Cuban Alberto Arredondo. Kantor and I also met with the students, had lunch there, and came away—despite our misgivings about Volman—impressed with its efforts to train new leaders.

We had a long interview with Bosch one afternoon at the home of his niece Milagros, who in 2000 would be elected the country's first woman vice president. There was some tension between Kantor and Bosch which stemmed from their days in Costa Rica together. When Trujillo was killed, Kantor had urged Bosch (who was living in his house) to return immediately to Santo Domingo to take up the reins of leadership; but Bosch had demurred, sending his lieutenants (Castillo, Miolán, and Silfa) instead, arguing that they needed to establish a base first for his triumphal return, but earning the epithet of "chicken" behind his back because Kantor and others concluded the real reason for his not returning was fear for his life. As we sat on Milagros' veranda rocking in the famous mahogany Dominican rocking chairs, Bosch kept looking over his shoulders and told us he feared he was going to be assassinated at any minute. There were, in fact, armed guards outside that had me worried, but their rifles seemed to be pointed away from the house, not toward it. When we got back to Gainesville later that month, I wrote an article about the DR and my interview with Bosch for a campus magazine; it was my first published scholarly article.

Another morning we spent at the U.S. embassy. We interviewed labor attaché (actually a CIA agent) Fred Somerford, economic officer Harlan Bramble, and political officer David Shaw; Ambassador John Bartlow Martin, a prominent writer and Kennedy appointee, was out of the country at the time. Kantor knew a lot about Latin American labor movements and political parties—far more than these officials—and came away concluding that they and the embassy were badly informed. For example, both the economic and the political officer insisted to us that the business-oriented National Civic Union (UCN) would certainly win the December election and not the PRD, whereas Kantor and I, though in the country for only a few days, were already convinced of just the opposite result. In December, in fact, the PRD won by a 2-1 landslide—not even close! I recall Kantor telling me afterwards, a bit overstated but advice I have ever since thought entirely accurate, "Howard, if you want to know what's going on in a country, stay away from the American embassy."

Kantor was a colorful, flamboyant, controversial figure who often overstated the case; but he was also a careful researcher, thorough in his preparations, with wonderful connections, and a highly developed and astute political sense that came both from his background in Chicago and from long experience in Latin America. Before our trip to Santo Domingo, he had canvassed his friends and acquaintances for names and contacts in the DR—actually few in number because almost no one before us, certainly during the long Trujillo dictatorship, had done any serious research in the country. But we did have some names whom we now proceeded to call up, and then sat back waiting for Latin hospitality to manifest itself.

One of our invitations was to the home of a Dominican archeologist who was head of the archeological museum and a member of an oligarchic family. This was my first contact with a real, card-carrying oligarch, one of "the enemies" by my ideological compass. He lived in a beautiful tropical home (open-air, large verandas, magnificent tile work, mahogany woodwork) on Avenida 27 de Febrero in western Santo Domingo, overlooking the Caribbean. He was polite, gracious, very well educated, sophisticated, charming—a renaissance man. He received us in his home, entertained us with stories of the pre-Columbian inhabitants of Hispaniola, and showed us some of the archeological treasures from his own diggings. He could not have been more simpático. So much for stereotypes!

We met two other members of the oligarchy: Tomás Pastoriza and Luís Crouch. "Jimmy" Pastoriza was from the traditional Santiago (the DR's second largest city) oligarchy, the son of a former Dominican ambassador to the U.S. (so his English was better than that of most Americans), a businessman, banker, landowner, amateur historian (who made it his business to know all the foreign researchers in the country), and the politically shrewd eminence grise to a succession of Dominican governments. Crouch was an American and an engineer who had come to the DR as a youngster, married into one of the oligarchic families (in Santiago, they are all interrelated), raised his family as a Dominican, and became thoroughly integrated into Dominican society. Both men and their families were well educated, extremely hospitable, charming, and extremely well informed. Both had heard of my thesis on Trujillo, asked to read it, and offered numerous intelligent, insightful comments on it. They both became friends; and when I returned to the DR a year-and-a-half later to write my Ph.D. thesis, they were again extremely helpful and opened many doors to advance my research.

We paid a courtesy visit to Germán Ornes, owner-publisher of El Caribe. Ornes's newspaper had been confiscated by Trujillo who turned it into a propaganda piece, while Ornes went into exile and wrote a damning book about the dictatorship entitled Trujillo: Little Caesar of the Caribbean. He was rather cold to us at first, not at all simpático, but when he learned I had written my thesis on Trujillo and knew his book intimately, he warmed up considerably. Like Pastoriza and Crouch, he and his reporters were extremely helpful to me when I went back later to write my dissertation.

Nor did Kantor and I neglect the social life of Santo Domingo. One of Harry's undergraduate students at Florida was Bill ("Willie") Yates, whose father had been a pilot for Pan Am, had married a Dominican girl and settled in the DR, and who now flew for the Dominican airlines, CDA. So we also called up Willie who invited us over. While Kantor stayed with his folks, Willie took me out for a night of partying and carousing with his friends, including the young Marines who guarded the embassy and who (it was well known) threw the best parties in Santo Domingo. After what must have been a dozen party stops, Willie, I, a few Marines, and a carful of girls ended up at a nightclub that doubled as a house of prostitution. The Marines' way of attracting attention to our table was to take out their pistols and slap them down on the table with a loud thump. Boy, did that immediately determine the authority relations in the room; after that, our table got waited on fast. I have to confess that my own recollections of that night are a little hazy, clouded by an excess of good Dominican rum and beer (Presidente); I'm sure happy that none of my children engaged in the same youthful, wasted activities that I did!

Another invitation came from Dominican acquaintances who asked us to join them for a swim, tennis, and dinner at the Embajador Hotel, Santo Domingo's finest. I've forgotten the exact connection but at some point during the afternoon we were introduced to a mother (divorced)-daughter tennis team who asked us to join them for doubles. Harry, who had a wife back in Gainesville, was very attracted to the mother but didn't play tennis, so I played with the daughter who was also a knockout. I was a pretty good tennis player and played competitively in high school (at the #1 position) and college, but, much to my chagrin and embarrassment (and Kantor's delight), the girl not only beat me but beat me badly. My excuses were that I was playing with a borrowed racket and on clay, which I wasn't used to; but that afternoon I took a pretty good drubbing which Kantor ("losing to a girl!") never let me forget.

Into the Interior

By the end of the first week, Kantor and I had seen a lot, interviewed a large number of people, and gotten a good feel for Dominican politics. So we hatched up a plan to see the interior. We rented a car for a week, a small Renault Dauphine that to our later dismay we found out on mountain roads had insufficient power to make it up the hills. Kantor had the ingenious idea of bringing along two young political leaders from the PRD, Rafael Casimiro Castro and Carlos Vizcaíno. The plan was that they would show us the country and we would pay the expenses. It turned out to be one of the most incredible trips I've ever taken.

From Santo Domingo we headed west toward Haiti. As you go toward Haiti from virtually every direction in the Dominican Republic, the country gets (1) poorer, (2) darker, and (3) more African. Our first stops were in Haina, San Cristóbal, Baní, and Azua—all medium-sized cities on the country's south coast.

Wherever we stopped, Casimiro and Vizcaíno had a PRD contact. Casimiro, a school teacher, was the better educated of the two and an impassioned public speaker; at every crossroads he would give a speech and then he and local leaders would meet to set up a branch of the party. I was privy to all these meetings and negotiations. What an experience! I was present at the creation of the PRD institutional structure which would carry it to victory in 1962 and make it for the next forty years the best-organized party in the DR. How many people have ever had a hand literally in the creation of a party like this? Later, when we returned to Santo Domingo after a week of party organizing, Kantor and I were designated "Honorary Founders" of the PRD.

With all this political organizing, it took us a full day to reach our destination of Barahona. Barahona, on the south coast, is the biggest city and the "capital" of the Dominican southwest. Very hot and very dry, this area of the country is like a desert. It supports little agriculture, only some subsistence plots and a few animals. At various points it starts to look like nearby Haiti.

As we checked into Barahona's only decent hotel, my stomach was beginning to feel queasy, the product of some unknown parasite that had slipped past my defenses. I knew all the rules about not drinking the water or eating uncooked or unpeeled fruits and vegetables, but I did have some ice in my cola and that might have done it. Actually, we learned later that the amoeba count in the bottled coke was higher than that in the city water supply and, if truth be told, it was virtually impossible to live in the DR then without getting some form of dysentery.

The next day we set out for Pedernales, in the extreme southwest and right on the Haitian border. This is the route by which Haitian cane-cutters are often brought into the country illegally, frequently using army trucks; in later decades it became a major transhipment point for Colombian drugs shipped to Haiti, smuggled into the DR, and across to Puerto Rico for entry into the U.S. mainland. The road beyond Barahona was all gravel, deeply rutted and often washed out. Down the coast we went, through Oviedo, to Cabo Rojo, where Alcoa Aluminum had a giant open-pit mine, and eventually on to the sleepy fishing village of Pedernales. Alcoa was one of the largest foreign investors in the DR and we wanted to see "imperialism" in action. Again I was in for a surprise: Alcoa treated its workers well, fed them a good meal while at work, provided health care, and even built workers' housing. We had lunch with Alcoa administrators in their cafeteria, then went on to Pedernales where Casimiro gave another fiery speech; in the December election he would be elected Senator for Pedernales—maybe because he was the only politician ever to visit it! By the time we got back to our hotel in Barahona late that night (the Haitian border was closed and there is no other route out of Pedernales), after a whole day of bouncing up and down in that Dauphine, my stomach was in pretty bad shape.

The next morning we set off again, going west-northwest from Barahona, through Duvergé and on to Jimaní, again on the Haitian border. The road goes past Lake Enriquillo, the DR's biggest lake, but below sea level, a salt lake, and home to small but fierce caymans (crocodiles). The desert conditions continued dry, hot, no agriculture, no nada. Here and onward that day I saw the worst poverty I had ever seen in my life: malnourished children, no clothing, bloated bellies, malformed limbs, 100 percent illiteracy, no jobs, no hope, no possibilities. The housing was of sticks, mud, and thatch, so primitive that Kantor and I estimated 90 percent of it should be destroyed. Disease was everywhere. I sent a long letter to my parents describing the extreme poverty (zero per capita income; this was not a money-market economy), and think that I must have experienced some culture shock in the process.

But it only got worse. At Jimaní, since dictator François Duvalier in Haiti feared an exile invasion launched from the DR, the border was closed and we were unable to cross the bridge into the neighboring country. However, while standing on the bridge we were shot at from the Haitian side. I had never been shot at before and, even though the bullets missed me by a considerable margin, decided that being shot at was no fun. Rather than turn around, however, and go back the way we'd come, we elected to explore the border area, taking the "road" north to Elías Piña. This road, not even visibly included on my map, was far worse than the road to Pedernales—all rock, many washouts, no other cars or trucks on the entire route. We had to push the Renault up the first range of hills, the Baoruco Mountains. The poverty was worse than before, and whole families would come out of their shacks to stare. The way they gathered round, I had the impression they had never seen a car or a white, blond Yankee before. We limped into Elías Piña.

But along this route there was a surprise in store. As we climbed the mountains along the Haitian border, we would occasionally see kids, equally poor as their neighbors, similarly with bloated bellies, no clothes, and barefoot, but with blond hair, blue eyes, and tan skins. I had read about this in writing my MA thesis but now I was seeing it firsthand. For Trujillo, in order to "whiten" the predominantly black and mulatto Dominican population and thereby to distinguish it more sharply from black, African Haiti, especially in the border areas, had brought in several thousand refugees from Europe of the 1930s and 1940s, mainly Jews and Eastern Europeans fleeing persecution, and forced them to live in these remote areas. What I was now seeing was their children and grandchildren, often the products of liaisons with local Dominican women, and now ground down to the same level of poverty as their neighbors.

Returning east from Elías Piña, we visited San Juan de la Maguana, a provincial capital and home of a local <u>caudillo</u> ("man on horseback") and now presidential aspirant, Migual Angel Ramírez Alcántara, whom we interviewed. What a colorful character: flamboyant, charismatic, and a throwback to the early part of the twentieth century when regional men on horseback controlled the local customs houses, could round up their peasants to serve as cannon fodder, and marched on the national palace in hopes of gaining both power and the patronage that went with control of the treasury. Now in 1962, he hoped to parlay the regional base of his presidential candidacy into a cabinet slot. As visiting dignitaries, we were invited to his home, entertained over a long lunch, and finally had to excuse ourselves lest his oration last all day and night.

We returned to the main road again, back through Azua, to the turnoff that leads to San José de Ocoa and up into the mountains toward Constanza. It was already dark (and I was sick) when we reached San José, but our colleague Casimiro insisted on giving another speech there. Climbing to Constanza high in the Cordillera Central (the highest mountain range in the Caribbean), we had to again get out and push our powerless Renault up the hill. Finally around midnight we came over the crest of the mountain into Constanza.

We stayed at the Hotel Suiça, the best hotel in town. When I attempted a midnight swim, I discovered frogs, seaweed, and scum in the pool. Other than these and a few other inconveniences (no toilet paper, towels that sandpapered your skin), Constanza was a pretty city. A vacation city high in the mountains, elite Dominicans from Santo Domingo and Santiago spent the hottest weeks of the summer in the cool, clear air of Constanza. It was then also home to a sizable Japanese community, similarly brought in by Trujillo right after World War II to "whiten" the population, who produced most of the country's rice crop. Finally, when I later lived in Vienna, I learned from one of my friends there who had been a member of the Jewish Community of Sosúa (more on this below), to whom Trujillo had also given "refuge," that her father, believing as do many Austrians in the recuperating influence of mountain, Alpine air, had also brought his family to Constanza in the summers and had even stayed in the Hotel Suiça!

From Constanza we proceeded north to Jarabacoa, also in the mountains, on some of the steepest, most precarious, most winding (and no guard rails) roads I had ever seen. From there to Santiago, the "capital" of the Dominican north, known as the Cibão. Our compañero Casimero had a wife and family here, so he excused himself for a day while we moved around. In Santiago we met with the editor of the newspaper and were graciously received at the homes of our friendly oligarchs, Pastoriza and Crouch, whom we had earlier met in Santo Domingo. Not rich by American standards, they were nevertheless comfortably well off, enjoyed a quality life style, and had their hands in a large variety of activities: banking, government, business, cattle, and land. I don't mind admitting that I found these oligarchs fascinating, was attracted to their nice lifestyle, and tried to make discreet inquiries if they had any daughters my age.

From there we journeyed out on what's called the Linea Noroeste through the length of the Cibão Valley to Monte Cristi, the far northwest of the country where the Atlantic Ocean and the Haitian border (again) come together. The Cibo Valley is the agricultural heartland of the country but when we were there it was bone dry. Later, my friend Pastoriza and his Santiago friends got AID and the World Bank loans to build a dam on the Yaqui River to provide irrigation; only later did we learn that it was mainly Pastoriza's own land that got irrigated— only one of hundreds of instances that I know in which the Dominican elites were able to manipulate the international donor and lending agencies mainly for their own advantage.

Driving into Monte Cristi, we noticed people working the salt flats there which supplied most of the country's salt. Down the road was Dajabón, the DR's northern entrance to Haiti, but with the border closed we did not even attempt a crossing. Our hotel was comfortable but primitive: no air conditioning, mosquito nets, but with a good restaurant and rooms that faced the ocean and caught the sea breeze.

The next day we drove back to Santiago but did not stay there; instead we drove north to Puerto Plata on the Atlantic coast (Casimiro gave another speech) and from there along the waterfront to Sosúa. Kantor (Jewish but not observant, actually an atheist) and I met with the leaders of the Jewish community. Sosúa was a beautiful town fronting on a quarter-moon-shaped arcing beach where seemingly every home and store faced the ocean. But imagine the situation: most of these people were from urban areas in Austria and Germany; now they were forced to become farmers, an occupation for which they had no training or background (but their cheese and kosher sausages soon became known as the best in the DR). Most of them had never heard of the country to which they were heading until they sailed only a few weeks before; almost no one spoke Spanish or was at home in the Latin culture. In addition, they were fleeing the Nazi regime—only to find themselves under the similarly totalitarian and anti-Semitic Trujillo dictatorship. When they landed in the DR after narrowly escaping the holocaust, as one member of the community told me, they saw an "army" of persons (cane-cutters, as it turned out) armed with <u>machetes</u> whom they were sure were going to murder them just as Hitler had attempted to do. But at least these refugees <u>survived</u>, as compared with most of their family members. And by the time we arrived in 1962, the community, which once numbered 125 families, was down to about 25 families; almost all the young people had already left (there is little future in farming in Sosúa), and in the years ahead most of the remaining families would emigrate (mainly to the U.S.) as well.

From Sosúa we headed south once again, working our way back toward the capital. We passed through Moca, Salcedo, San Francisco de Macorís, Pimentel, and finally to Cotúi, with our colleague Casimiro speaking and organizing in every city. Momentum must have been building because by the time we arrived in Cotúi, a farming and sugarcane center, the crowd had built to several thousands. In honor of the foreign visitors, Kantor and myself, the mayor, a PRD sympathizer, ordered a goat to be roasted on a spit—a special Dominican delicacy. With toasts and multiple courses, the lunch went on for four hours. Late that night, our rental car finally made it back to Santo Domingo.

What an incredible trip. Could anyone have ever had a better introduction to a country than I had with Kantor? I'm sure I'd been in places, especially along the Haitian border, where no foreigner had ever been before—or maybe since. I had seen things, in the vacuum that followed the collapse of the Trujillo dictatorship, that no one had ever seen. And, accompanied by our PRD organizers, I had played a role in the organization of what then became the country's largest political party and one of the best organized in all of Latin America—well organized precisely because of the work at the base level and in local communities that our two colleagues had done. Those in the U.S. who work for NED, IRI, NDI, and other organizations who talk a lot about democracy but have no idea how to actually build political parties or develop democracy and civil society should take lessons from this experience.

Back in Santo Domingo

Returning to the capital, we now abandoned the Comercial and checked into the Hotel Jaragua. This was the old Jaragua built by Trujillo that ran east-west along the malecon, rather than the present structure, built on the same spot, running north-south. The Jaragua was more luxurious, had a pool (no frogs, no scum), and was temporary "home" to the legion of international businessmen now descending on Santo Domingo. Kantor and I decided that, after our long and trying trip and with my intestines still not in good shape, we needed a little luxury. We actually stayed in the motel-like annex (still standing) behind the hotel, which was a little cheaper.

I met several of these traveling businessmen and international operators in the hotel pool and dining room. One was a German political party official, in the DR to help create (and fund) a Christian-Democratic party modeled after the CDU in Germany. Another was a businessman from upstate New York trying to sell used voting machines to the Dominican government. His rationale was, "They're having elections, right, so they need voting machines." The bar at the Jaraqua, as at the even bigger El Embajador, seemed always to be full of furtive intelligence types talking in low whispers in the bar's dark corners.

Another person whom Kantor and I met and spent time with was John Emory, the CARE director for the DR. His task was to feed the poorest of the poor; he had previously served with CARE in the Gaza strip and filled us in on the miserable conditions in the refugee camps there. Several times we went with John on his rounds into Santo Domingo's teeming slums where not even the police would enter; he also told us horror stories of having to deal with the Dominican bureaucracy, port authorities, and the police in order to bring his food into the country—stories mainly having to do with bribery, kickbacks, payoffs, and sheer incompetence—all grist for my research. At one point he even offered me a job with CARE as an assistant country director in Latin America, which probably would have meant I'd move up to country director in two or three years. It was an interesting offer but Kantor advised—and I concurred— that I ought to finish my Ph.D. first. Then if I still wanted to work for CARE I could, but if I wanted to do other things I would have more options with the degree in hand.

Trying to wind down after the previous frenetic two weeks, relax, and get my stomach back in shape, this second stay in Santo Domingo was less active and more casual. We swam a lot for exercise and carefully watched our food intake. We reported back to PRD headquarters on our trip around the country (they had already heard about it in detail from Casimiro) and did some additional interviewing of party and labor leaders. Manny Espinal of the PRD's youth movement took me under his wing and showed me how the party was organizing young people. All of these contacts and entree would provide a tremendous boon when I returned to the country to write my doctoral dissertation.

The hotel faces south toward the Caribbean, and every day we would walk along the malecon (George Washington Avenue) to see the sights: the painters selling their works to the few tourists available, vendors selling iced coconuts in the hot tropical weather, young people strolling arm-in-arm, and pimps seeking to sell their sisters and girlfriends. At that time forty years ago the malecon was far less clogged with traffic than it is now; when we returned to Vesuvio's for a meal, we sat across the street from the restaurant on the waterfront side where the salt spray rose up from the jagged coral and the white-jacketed waiters carrying beer and food on silver trays on their fingertips had to navigate the traffic while making sure nothing fell.

We visited the grounds of the world's fair which Trujillo threw in 1955 and hired University of Florida mermaids to perform in an aquatic ballet, but then refused to pay them when few tourists showed up. Now these buildings were in the process of being converted into government offices. Unlike the centrally located Comercial, the Jaragua is about a mile from the city center, so every day we would stroll into town, or take a jitney, sit in the Independence or Columbus Parks, have our shoes shined (at 5 cents a shine, you can't afford to have dirty shoes in Santo Domingo, plus you get the chance to question the kids about their lives and families), and watch the world go by. Or we would go for a beer or an ice cream cone in one of the nearby parlors. As obvious foreigners, we were constantly approached by strangers while sitting in the parks: persons who wanted to convey some political message, those who wanted our help in getting to the U.S., cigarette and candy salesmen, and young prostitutes.

I remember one of the prostitutes whom we saw every day, Virginia, small and skinny who could not have been more than twelve or thirteen. As a proper and well-brought-up American, I was embarrassed by her direct approach, but Kantor insisted that she sit down and talk with us. We gave her a couple of <u>pesos</u> just for talking with us (I wonder if that had ever happened to her before) and another day, to my embarrassment, Kantor invited her to join us for lunch. The poor girl had never, I'm sure, been in a restaurant before and, as Kantor had surmised, was desperately hungry and wolfed down a huge meal even though she weighed only about half of what I did. In the process of all this, Kantor taught me that <u>every experience</u> and <u>every person</u> in all walks of life has something to say and contributes to your research and understanding of how cultures other than your own operate.

After three days of this more relaxed pace, and with my tummy not fully better but at least calmed down, we checked out of the Jaragua and flew to Haiti. Another intense experience.

Haitian Interlude

Port-au-Prince, Haiti, is only a short distance from Santo Domingo as the crow flies, about 150 miles, a half-hour flight. You take off from Punta Caucedo airport, fly straight west along the DR's southern coast, go inland near Barahona, fly up the Neiba Valley, over Lake Enriquillo and Jimaní (where we had been a week earlier), and down on the Haitian side into the capital.

The old airport in Port-au-Prince (a new one was built a few years later with U.S. funds, in return for Haiti's vote in the OAS supporting the 1965 U.S. military invasion of the Dominican Republic, and thus giving the U.S. the two-thirds majority it needed) was located close to the waterfront right near the center of the city. It was a small airport, suitable for props but not for jets, and had one unique, memorable feature. Probably because of inadequate fill or cheap cement, it had a large dip in the middle of the main runway. So as you landed or took off, there would be a huge bounce, like hitting an unexpected air pocket in midflight, when the wheels would actually leave the ground even though the plane was still on the runway. Our plan was to stay in Haiti for only a few days, not do much serious work there as we had in the DR, but only get a brief "feel" for the country since neither of us had ever been there before.

Haiti is <u>by far</u> the poorest country in the Western Hemisphere, with a (then) per capita income of about $175 a year—only half that of the DR. Once a wealthy, French, sugar-producing, slave-plantation colony, it had been devastated by a series of slave revolts beginning in 1795, by a history of cruel and inept rulers, and by deforestation which had made it an ecological disaster area unfit for anything more than subsistence agriculture. Whereas the Dominican Republic from the air is lush, green, tropical, and beautful, Haiti is brown, denuded, and ugly. The fact that Haiti was the world's first black republic, unloved, unwanted, and shunned at a time when most countries (including the U.S.) still practiced slavery, did not help its developmental possibilities.

I thought I had seen extreme poverty in the DR (and I had!) but that was as nothing compared with Haiti. Just getting into the airport, through customs, into a taxi and out onto the streets was a revelation. Here seemingly <u>everyone</u> was malnourished, had broken limbs, bloated bellies, and disease. Plus, Haiti had then twice the population of the DR on half the territory; it was terribly overcrowded, like India, and the push of constantly jostling bodies was overwhelming. Even the taxi could barely make it up the streets through the dense crowds.

Both are poor, underdeveloped countries, but there the similarities between the DR and Haiti end. One immediately senses that the sights, sounds, and even smells are completely different. The DR is an Hispanic country with a white elite, mainly mulatto, and with a large, black underclass. Haiti, in contrast, is French at the level of high culture and society, mainly black and African, and with a small mulatto elite. Whereas the DR is mainly Catholic and, therefore, Western Haiti has a thin veneer of Catholicism; but underneath the surface clings to African beliefs and customs. I have studied Latin America professionally and, therefore, the Dominican Republic is understandable to me, but I am not trained as an Africanist and, therefore, Haiti, located <u>geographically</u> in Latin America but not a Latin American country culturally, politically, socially, or psychologically, is more of a mystery to me. It should also be said that Dominicans <u>loathe</u> the Haitians as barbaric, uncivilized, primitive, black and "African" (which carries racial as well as cultural connotations in the DR), practitioners of voodoo and blood sacrifices, and an ongoing threat to the "purity" of blood of their more "advanced" Hispanic civilization.

At this time (1962), Haiti was presided over by its unscrupulous, tyrannous dictator, François Duvalier—Papa Doc. Duvalier had built a political following on the basis of his medical practice (though he lacked an MD), his practice of voodoo (popular with the masses but largely suppressed by earlier regimes), and by becoming a symbol and spokesman of Haitian <u>Negritude</u>. Duvalier, himself black, sought to speak for and elevate the huge black mass in Haitian society, as against the mulattoes who had long dominated social, economic, and political life. Duvalier was the first black president from the black underclass, and he played both class and racial politics to the hilt. His regime was also corrupt and bloody; his undoubted popular support was undergirded and reinforced by two of the only three national institutions in Haiti (the other is the Catholic Church): the Police (especially the feared Ton Ton Macoutes) and the Army. All this was best captured in Graham Greene's best-selling novel (and later movie) about Haiti, The Comedians.

Kantor and I had intended to stay at the hotel in central Port-au-Prince that Greene made famous, The Olafson. The Olafson was then owned by a wayward graduate student from our own University of Florida, Maurice De Young, who had gone to Haiti to write his thesis, married a Haitian, bought The Olafson, settled in Haiti and never (so far as I know) finished his degree. It was a quaint old place with a large veranda and lazy, languid ceiling fans; but much to our surprise, it was full when we arrived, and so we checked into a more modern hotel, with a pool, up on the mountain in Pétionville, overlooking Port-au-Prince, where the air was fresher and the sights, sounds, and smells of the downtown were, shall we say, not quite so pungent. I'm all for roughing it and seeing countries from the bottom up as we did in the DR, but when your guts are giving you constant problems, a few creature comforts are not all bad.

In Haiti (and in other dictatorial states), one does not just go out and hail a cab on the streets. Instead, one is assigned a car and driver at the airport and other points of entry, and that driver becomes your driver for the entire length of your stay. In our case (Americans, professors of political science, by definition "suspicious persons"), the driver (black, friendly, chubby-faced, with a white shirt and tie, driving a '57 Chevy Impala—the one with big fins) was obliged to report to the secret police each day on our activities and meetings.

We wanted to go up north to Gonaives and then to Cap Haitien, both to see the countryside and to visit The Citidel, the great fortress that the Haitian dictator Jean Jacques Dessalines had built to ward off a possible French reoccupation. But Duvalier, fearful that the U.S. was trying to assassinate him as it had earlier done to Trujillo, and might use the DR as a staging area for an invasion by Haitian exiles living there, had both closed the border (we had earlier experienced that in our DR travels in border areas) and forbidden any visitors from going beyond the confines of Port-au-Prince. Not knowing this at the time, we kept promising our driver more money to take us up into the country; but as we approached the city limits and a police checkpoint manned by the Ton Ton Macoutes that our driver knew was right around the corner, he turned almost pale with fear and refused to go even one block farther.

The result was that our Haiti visit was limited to the capital city, the mountaintop above, and the area around the (few) luxurious homes and shops of Pétionville where the few whites in Haiti and the mulatto elite lived. Nevertheless we saw and experienced a lot.

Not wanting to court trouble with the secret police, we told our driver that we were tourists and that we wanted to see the sights of the capital. So that's what we did, dropping down out of the heights of the mountaintop overlooking Port-au-Prince and into the hubbub (and stifling heat) of the central city. I found Haiti simply overwhelming: the poverty, the disease, the stench, the crowded conditions, the noise, the malformed bodies, the illiteracy, again the heat and humidity (right at sea level, no refreshing sea breeze as in Santo Domingo). As "tourists," we, of course, drove past the presidential palace, splendid in white stucco, but with endless lines of shouting petitioners hoping to corner some government official as he passed in or out. Within a block of the palace we saw a dead body on the sidewalk. What was striking was that it was just left there; people passed around or stepped over it; and no one made any effort to check it for life or to remove it.

From the palace, as "tourists," we went to the Port-au-Prince open-air market. The fruit and vegetables were nowhere near as good as in the Dominican Republic. I saw no meat, and the few scrawny chickens looked like they were meant not for eating but for ritual slaughter in some voodoo ceremony. I bought a couple of paintings, Haitian "primitives" at about $3.00 each, with bright colors and stylized figures. I also bought as presents for my parents two beautifully graceful, hand-carved, mahogany statues of Haitian peasants, with elongated figures and gradual, sweeping lines. Unfortunately the mahogany had bugs in it ("<u>bichos</u>"—no translation needed) and over the years turned to sawdust on my parents' fireplace mantle; I had not yet learned the trick, when you buy wooden objects abroad, of cooking the items in the oven for a time to destroy the bugs.

Kantor had some contacts in the mulatto business community in Haiti who invited us to lunch at one of their homes on the road to Pétionville, with a gorgeous view (from those heights you couldn't experience the noise, stench, and disease) of the city below. I'm sure our driver took due note of the address and the car license numbers of those who joined us. I was surprised, since Haiti under Duvalier was a police state, how frank the discussion was. But some of their criticism was colored by the fact these were men from the upper middle class, the elite, and mulatto community whose hatred of the black Duvalier was partly conditioned by class and racial resentments.

The businessmen told us not only of the economic difficulties of functioning in Haiti (the bribes required, the secret police, the armed musclemen who demanded a cut of their business, the chaotic and unresponsive bureaucracy, crooked customs officials, army officers requiring payoffs, the difficulties of getting import or export permits) but also about the brutality of the dictatorship. If I were they, I would not have spoken to us, complete strangers, so frankly. For all they knew, we could have been agents provocateurs, or turned them in to the regime, or spoken publicly about Haiti in ways that would have identified them as the source. We, of course, did none of those things and, from the businessmen's point-of-view, who in Haiti see few international visitors like us, I'm sure they assumed that we would carry their message to the U.S. Embassy and to Washington.

We obviously could not operate in Haiti as we did in the DR. We could not rent a car, tour the country, or go off on our own. We could not interview party, labor, or peasant leaders. Either there were none, or they were dead or in hiding or jail, or they had escaped into exile in Santo Domingo where we had had a meeting with their democratic-left leaders. Haiti under Duvalier was a repressive, smothering, bloody dictatorship where bad things happened if you stepped out of line. Worse for our purposes, at that time Duvalier, fearing an invasion or perhaps just wanting an excuse to clamp down more, had declared a state of emergency, closed the border, limited travel, and forbidden political activity. It was hard to function in that environment. I was not unhappy to leave. It was not just the political repression; my stomach and intestines suffered a relapse in Haiti as well.

En route home our plane stopped in Montego Bay, Jamaica, the beautiful resort development on the island's northwest coast. We were not able to disembark, but there I saw for the first time the modern, pencil-thin, four-engine jet aircraft (727s) that would soon become the staple of the U.S. fleet carriers. We traveled on to Miami, however, on our Pan Am prop.

Two more adventures, or misadventures, awaited us—mostly me. Bobbie Nichols met us at the airport. We had earlier arranged that we would drive up to her house in Fort Lauderdale, meet her parents (for the first time!), have dinner, and then drive back to Gainesville. On the way I told her I was not feeling well— by this time (and I'm ordinarily a very healthy guy, except now for all those Caribbean parasites) including a severe headache, fever, as well as the stomach/intestine problem. But this was a big deal for Bobbie's family: her mother had prepared a big meal and the folks were about to entertain both her professor and her boyfriend at the same time. I made it about half way through the meal and then spent the next half-hour in the bathroom. I hope her mother didn't think it was her food that made me sick. Everyone was very polite but it was not the best moment in our romance.

We arrived back in Gainesville after midnight, completely exhausted. It was the end of August. I had arranged to rent a new, nicer apartment for the upcoming year but the lease didn't start until September 1 and the landlord wouldn't let me have the key even a day early. Meanwhile Bobbie had left the key to her apartment with her roommate, whom we discovered had gone out of town with her boyfriend, taking the key with her. That meant neither of us had a place to come home to. Hearing these tales of "homelessness," Kantor volunteered to let us stay over at his house.

What a mentor! Kantor had just spent three-four weeks with me traipsing around the Caribbean, and sometimes having to play nursemaid, too. Now he was inviting his sick graduate student and the student's girlfriend to stay over at his house. That was certainly way beyond the call of duty. Fortunately, Mrs. Kantor, Vivian, also had an open, liberal, bemused, tolerant, welcoming attitude in these matters. Gruff and sometimes brusque in his outward behavior, Kantor had a heart of gold and always treated me well. Can anyone imagine going to these lengths for the sake of his graduate students? I doubt if I would do it for mine.

CHAPTER 2

MEXICO AND CENTRAL AMERICA—1963

After returning from the Dominican Republic and Haiti in late summer 1962, I spent the next academic year in residence at the University of Florida. I needed one more full year of course work after the first year to complete the requirements of the program and preparatory to taking Ph.D. comprehensive exams. I especially prepared myself in the fields of comparative politics, international relations, developing areas, and political theory, but also took some more courses in my specialty of Latin America as well as a year's work in the Portuguese language—part of the requirements of my NDFL fellowship. Bobbie Nichols and I drifted apart during the fall semester—not because of the fiasco of my getting sick to my stomach during a home-cooked meal at her parents' house—and I started dating a young woman from Spain (Galicia), María Rosa Uría Santos, who was a graduate student in the history department.

I visited the Dominican Republic and Puerto Rico in January 1964 (see Chapter 4), but it was a short visit to participate in a Peace Corps training program. I really wanted to concentrate on the work in my courses and get those and my "comps" (scheduled for the fall) over with, so I could go on quickly to the next stage, the research and writing of my doctoral dissertation. Actually, by the time I got to the dissertation, I had already completed three chapters of it in preliminary version in the form of lengthy research papers that I had written during my seminar work that year.

My recollection is that my NDFL grant included some travel funds. Plus, I was able to tap into the Latin America Center's Rockefeller funds for a second time. Besides, I was convinced that, if I were going to be a Latin America scholar and teach courses on the area, I needed to get into the field and see more countries, even if it meant spending my own money. I have <u>never</u> felt comfortable teaching about countries to which I had never been. So in the summer of 1963, between completing course work in the spring and comps later that fall, I lit out for Mexico and Central America.

Mexico

That spring, on a visit to Gainesville, my folks had presented me with a used Volkswagen "Bug." I loved that snazzy little car; it had a sliding canvas top so I could pretend it was a convertible and a stick shift so I could pretend I was a race car driver (earlier that spring Bobbie and I had spent a weekend at the Gran Prix races in Sebring, Florida; that had whetted my appetite for sports cars). In June I drove my "new" (used) car to New Orleans to catch a flight for Mexico City. What an operator I was in those days. And opportunistic, brazen, and fearless! Ah, youth! I stayed overnight in a New Orleans hotel and arranged to meet the young female desk clerk in the bar later that night. I poured out my tale of woe and must have appealed to her motherly instincts. I told her that I was all alone in New Orleans, didn't know anyone, was a poor struggling student, and that I needed a place to store my car for two months and to start it up and let it run for a while every few days. Lo and behold, she said she had an empty backyard and I was welcome to park it there; she would take good care of it. So the next morning I drove out early to her place, left a set of keys, and headed for the airport.

Mexico City is about two hours by air from New Orleans. I had arranged to meet up there with two friends from my undergraduate fraternity days at the University of Michigan, Barry Wood and Mike McGuire. Wood was six-feet-four-inches, an Abraham Lincoln look-alike, who used to enhance the effect by walking around the Ann Arbor campus in a stove-top hat and an old black coat. He was from a steel-mill town near Pittsburgh, an all-around good guy who required surgery his freshman year at the University of Michigan Medical Center to adjust slightly his off-center heart. We used to kid him that his heart was in the wrong place. McGuire was also a jovial guy, way overweight, a lackluster scholar who took seven years to complete his degree in naval architecture (he spent his afternoons vegetating in the fraternity TV room watching the cute teeny-boppers on "American Bandstand") and finished at the absolutely bottom of his class with a 2.0 grade-point average. Despite this inauspicious start, he landed a job designing warships for the U.S. Navy, a fact which did not inspire great confidence in the Navy. We used to kid him about designing cement ships that would surely sink; and whenever there was a Navy mishap in the news, we would cable Mike asking if it was one of his ships.

The next two weeks went by in a haze because of all the drinking and carousing we did. After all, this was a fraternity brothers' reunion; probably we were trying to recapture the carefree days of our undergraduate years. I vaguely remember visiting numerous Mexican bars and nightclubs, and that Corona beer—not yet exported to the U.S.—costs 8 cents a bottle. You can't afford to stay sober for that price. I learned to drink tequila—always buying the bottle with the worm in it!—by sprinkling salt on your wrist, downing a shot, licking the salt, and following it with a beer chaser. After a few drinks, Barry, Mike, and I would launch into some of our old fraternity drinking songs, most of them with dirty lyrics and some featuring Mexican whores—which didn't always endear us to other patrons. During one especially drink-filled night, we consumed prodigious quantities of beer and tequila in a revolving bar atop one of the city's main hotels—I think, but am not sure, on the Reforma, Mexico City's main street. Whether from the alcohol, the revolutions of the room, or likely both, I don't think I have ever been so sick.

One night we saw a fellow drunk staggering across the road in front of the nightclub we were exiting. A Mercedes full of four Mexican society women sped through the intersection and hit the drunk. Then, instead of getting out to see if he was OK, the women backed up over the drunk who was then still moving. Finally, they forwarded over him a third time to finish him off and then sped away. All this happening right in front of our eyes! Having already studied Mexican history and politics, I was pretty sure I knew, however appalling, what was going on here. Since the 1920s, Mexico had been an officially "revolutionary" society whose court system—short of bribes—favored the poor. My guess was that these rich society women had been instructed by their husbands that, if they ever hit anyone, rather than having to pay through the nose forever or be constantly hounded by the courts, they should finish the job. My friends still wanted to aid the poor (now surely dead) drunk but I, already knowledgeable (or perhaps cynical) about the ways of Latin America, cautioned them not to get involved.

The Mexican political system was at that time a one-party state under the hegemony of the Revolutionary Institutional Party (PRI), authoritarianly controlled from the top down by the president and what was called the "revolutionary family" (high government and party officials and former presidents). Like the Democrat Party in the old U.S. South, differences between the rival factions were worked out within the single-party system. The executive was dominant and the president virtually all-powerful; the congress and court system were subordinate to the executive and to the ruling party. Mexico was mildly authoritarian but not a complete dictatorship or a totalitarian regime. Civil liberties were sometimes violated but there was no systematic terror; the press seldom criticized the government but it was not wholly subservient. The system was, however, as in any country where one party had been in power so long, very corrupt; patronage, corruption, and grease oiled the machinery of government at all levels.

In my studies, I had been interested in the fact that the dominant party, the PRI, and Mexican society more generally, was sectorally or corporately organized, in ways that were quite different from U.S.-style liberal pluralism. Growing out of the Mexican Revolution of 1910-20, the party consisted of three sectors—a labor sector, a peasant sector, and a "popular" sector, which was a catch-all category for mainly middle-class and bureaucratic groups. The older corporate sectors, the Catholic Church and the landed oligarchy, had been largely destroyed in the Revolution. The Army had once been a part of this "family" of officially-sanctioned and government-controlled corporate bodies, but it had been eliminated as a corporate sector in the 1930s. These corporate bodies were vertically organized and controlled at the top by the Party; they formed part of an "organic" unified whole. In Trujillo's Dominican Republic I had noticed the same corporate-organic features and would later write about them in my book; here now in Mexico I had a second, though different, case of corporatism, a theme that I would later expand into a full-fledged theory of Latin American politics.

While Mexico was sectorally, corporately, and vertically organized, it was also divided by horizontal class divisions that were partially racially determined. The old landed oligarchy had been largely eliminated in the Revolution, but in its place was a wealthy, nouveau-riche class of uncertain social origin but with lots of money, like the society women who had run over the drunk. Below that was a growing middle class, often mestizo or mixtures of European and Indian, perhaps 15-20 percent of the population, that U.S. officials considered the great hope for stability and democracy in Mexico. And below that were darker mestizos and Indians, between 60 and 80 percent of the population, still not fully integrated socially, culturally, politically, or economically into Mexican national life. Mexico was thus stratified both socially and racially: as one went lower in the social pyramid, the population was both poorer and more Indian. How to assimilate and integrate this majority Indian population into national life constitutes the great theme and challenge of Mexico's five-hundred-year history.

Mexico, along with Africa, China, India, Egypt, Persia, Assyria, Palestine, and Greece, is one of the places where civilization began. Not Western civilization, so as I climbed Mexico's ancient pyramids, I did not have the same sense of this being part of <u>my</u> civilization as I did climbing the Acropolis to the Parthenon in Greece, but civilization nonetheless. For Mexico was home to two of the three, the Aztec and the Maya, great Indian civilizations (the other being the Incas in Peru) that predated Columbus's arrival in the Americas, as well as to hundreds of other, smaller groups, each with their own language and culture. At times Mexico has taken great pride in its unique Indian heritage; at other times the picture is a more ambivalent one that includes despair concerning its Indian elements and their non-Western character, and shame at the racial mixing that has left Mexico a <u>mestizo</u> society.

All these elements were on display as we toured Mexico City and traveled around the Mexican countryside. Mexico City is one of the great cities of the <u>world</u>, certainly of Latin America, and with some twenty million persons also one of the largest cities in the world. It was the capital of the ancient Aztec empire, and for the last five hundred years it has been the scene of the clash, conflict, and reconciliation (all three at once) of the European, Hispanic and the indigenous Indian cultures and civilizations. It is a big, often gaudy, sometimes bawdy, colorful, vibrant, noisy, terribly polluted, sometimes dangerous, always fascinating city, one of the most interesting cities in the world.

Mexico City is one I love to roam around in (though not in certain neighborhoods) because every street, every corner, almost literally every house and building brings a new vista, a new experience, something exciting and different. There are so many things to see and experience; it is a city best seen on foot, and yet the distances are so great that you also need a car to get around. But by now the traffic is so bad that, if friends in one part of the city invite guests from another part to dinner, the invitation is likely to be turned down because getting about by car is so difficult and time-consuming that it's not worth it.

We started our visit in the Zócalo or great main square, the Plaza Mayor, in the oldest part of the city. It is always alive with people—tourists, native Indians, official ceremonies and celebrations, weddings, flag raisings, protests, demonstrations. This is the historic center of the city as it was in Aztec times; there is nothing better than to have a beer or cafe, as Mike, Barry, and I did, on one of the restaurant balconies surrounding the square and watch the great procession that is Mexico go by.

On the north side of the Plaza is the cathedral, the oldest (1525) and largest in Latin America. It seems always to be crumbling and always under restoration; next to it Aztec ruins have been found, which means the area will probably permanently look dug up. The Zócalo is the center of Mexico, of both Indian and Hispanic civilizations.

The Palacio Nacional takes up the eastern side of the Zócalo, built over (to show the superiority of Spanish Christian civilization) the site of the palace of Aztec emperor Moctezuma. The staircase and walls are decorated with the murals of Diego Rivera showing Mexican history in a Marxist light. The Supreme Court building is also on the Zócalo and has murals by José Clemente Orozco. Three blocks away is the famous building of the Ministry of Education, with more Rivera masterpieces. Mike thought the Marxism was heavy-handed; Barry who came out of a labor-working-class family said, "Right on."

From the Zócalo we walked west along Francisco Madero Avenue, which turns into Avenida Juárez. The spectacular Fine Arts Palace is there where one night my buddies and I saw a rousing performance of the Mexican Ballet Folklórico. Around the corner is the big park of the Alameda Central, once the Aztec market and, later, the place of execution for the Spanish Inquisition. A block away is the mural museum of Rivera containing some of his most spectacular works glamorizing the masses and caricaturing foreign devils as well as the Mexican elite. Almost every house and building in this area had an incredible history behind it.

Our walking tour now took us down the Paseo de la Reforma, Mexico City's main avenue. Here are some of the city's best hotels (the Sheraton, where I stayed on a later trip) and embassies. This is the heart of the city, always noisy, active, and full of traffic. About two-thirds down the street is the American embassy where I had some interviews; a block farther is Mexico's Independence Monument. Just to the south of the Reforma is the Zona Rosa which at this time was the center of Mexico City's most fashionable stores, night clubs, and restaurants.

The Reforma eventually angles off to the west; if it continued straight, it would empty into the massive Chapultepec Park which houses some of Mexico's most spectacular monuments and museums. I spent a couple of days here and could easily have spent much more. In the Park one finds the Monument to the Child Heroes (who were killed defending Mexico from foreign invaders) and Chapultepec Castle, a military fortress with a view (through the pollution!) of the whole Valley of Mexico. Mike, Barry, and I clambered up and down the fortress; Mike, with his practical bent, took a dim view of children who could martyr themselves for some supposedly glorious cause. "We wouldn't do that in Battle Creek," he said. Here also in the Park are the National History Museum, the

Museum of Modern Art, and the National Anthropological Museum which opened my eyes to the full complexity and diversity of Mexico's Indian past.

Across the Reforma from Chapultepec Park is the Nikko Hotel, one of the new, modern, reinforced (against earthquakes) skyscraper hotels that was not there on my first visit but where I stayed on a subsequent trip. It has twenty-four stories, and I stayed on the twenty-third—weird because at that height you can see over the pollution and actually see the dramatic mountains and volcanoes rimming the city beyond, which are invisible from street level on most days. I also experienced an earthquake in the hotel—a weird and scary feeling because in my room I could actually see the hotel sway back and forth. I loved to roam in the Polanco district behind the hotel because, replacing the Zona Rosa, it has become a luxurious residential area with many fine shops, galleries, and restaurants—and yet not so busy and "touristy" as other areas.

After several days of touring Mexico City, my buddies and I headed by bus for Acapulco. The resort city on the Pacific coast had seen better days. It was run down and sleazy. The coastal scenery was still spectacular, but the people and buildings were decrepit. The construction was often shoddy and jerry-built, made of cheap materials, the contractors often cheating on the materials so that when earthquakes hit the damage was extensive. Mexican society in Acapulco had sold out for the Yankee dollar, lived completely separate lives from the ex-pats who inhabited it, and now watched bitterly as the tourists went on to other, more fashionable resorts like Mazatlán, Puerto Villarta, and Cancún. The ex-pats were mostly Americans, a few society types but mainly drop-outs, beatniks, and druggies who peddled hamburgers and beach gear on the streets to support their habits. It was sad to see these otherwise healthy Americans, who had so many more opportunities than the Mexicans, throw their lives away on drugs and wasted living.

We stayed in a nice resort hotel right on the beach; it was there that the most exciting event of our visit occurred. Mike and I were swimming in Acapulco Bay too close to a formation of boulders when a series of big waves washed us up against the rocks. Under the surface where they couldn't be seen, the boulders were covered with sea urchins with inch-long spines like a porcupine. I got washed up against them repeatedly by the breaking waves with the spines piercing my body. I thought the wounds were superficial, but when I emerged from the water my bathing suit was in tatters and blood was flowing from my legs, chest, and buttocks. I was a ghastly sight. On the beach people started screaming, assuming we had been attacked by sharks. The Mexican doctor, mainly amused by this spectacle, filled us full of antibiotics and started pulling the spines out with tweezers, but there were too many of them and too much blood, and eventually he gave up. It took <u>years</u> in some cases for all those remaining spines to work their way to the surface so I could pull them out; I wouldn't be surprised if some of them forty years later are still stuck in my hide.

After a couple of days of rest and recreation, I left my two fraternity brothers in Acapulco to begin the serious part of my trip. Back in Mexico City I visited PRI headquarters, met with the political section at the American Embassy (again poorly informed, I thought), and met with another Kantor friend, Victor Alba. Alba was a leading analyst of Latin American political and labor affairs, Spanish by birth and a Republican stalwart in the Civil War, a democrat but with vaguely Marxist, Trotskyite, and anarchist sympathies, exiled from Franco's Spain and living permanently in Mexico City where he had his own small think tank and magazine, <u>Panoramas</u>. He later published some of my writings on the Dominican Republic and invited me to contribute a book to a series on Latin America that he edited for Frederick A. Praeger, Publishers. Talking with Alba was a bit disconcerting because he had once been hit between the eyes by a rifle butt of one of Franco's thugs, and thereafter his eyes, instead of looking directly at you, pointed in two directions at once. Alba was enormously helpful in arranging interviews for me and inviting me to functions at his think tank in Mexico City.

Guatemala

I stayed in Mexico City for another week, and then, wanting to get on with the rest of my trip, bought a bus ticket for Guatemala. Naively, I thought that when I bought the ticket it would take me all the way to Guatemala City, but that proved not to be the case. Only rational Protestant, Calvinist societies would think in those terms. En route south, we passed through Mexico's poor and heavily Indian states of Oaxaca and Chiapas. We ate dinner at a hotel in the capital of Oaxaca; I remember the hotel lobby being full of Indians watching a John Wayne movie on television (probably the only television in town then) and cheering wildly, if incongruously, for John Wayne as he was shooting all the Indians. The bus got to the Guatemalan border in the middle of the night, but instead of proceeding on to Guatemala City, as my ticket indicated, it turned around and left us stranded at the border. After an hour's wait a Guatemalan bus appeared, a rickety old thing compared with my Mexican coach, with hard seats and wooden windows. We had barely started on our journey down the so-called Pan American Highway (all gravel, sharp curves, no guardrails) when the bus went off the road and hit a tree. Looking down, I could see the tree was all that was keeping us from a thousand-foot drop into the river gorge below. We got out of that bus in a hurry.

Guatemala was a whole series of adventures even before I got to the capital city. After the bus mishap, I saw no choice but to hitchhike—not recommended in a strange country with a violent history. I was picked up by two beefy ex-Marines driving a big Chrysler. They had sold their restaurant in Tucson, had a telephone contact, and were coming to Guatemala to fight "communism." Neither spoke Spanish or had ever been to Guatemala before. They were accompanied by two women, whom at one point the mercenaries started to hustle. I was not comfortable with this; my discomfort increased when we had a flat tire, they opened the trunk, and I saw it was loaded with guns and ammunition. That also explained the presence of the women, one of whom was the wife of the Guatemalan consul at the border, to whom they had promised a ride to the capital in return for not examining the trunk full of arms too closely. When we had a second flat on the so-called Pan American Highway and now with no spare, the driver's solution was to climb a hill and start firing his M-47 into the air to attract attention. This did not seem like a smart move to me, especially with all those guns illegally in the trunk, and at this stage I baled out of this particular ride.

My next ride was with a Guatemalan businessman, a nice young guy. By now it was daylight, and we sailed down through the Mayan Indian country of northern Guatemala: Huehuetenango, Quetzaltenango, and Chichicastenango. It was a colorful drive with gorgeous mountains, deep valleys, and real, live, kicking Indians carrying baskets on their heads and selling their wares in small roadside stands. These were often Westernized Indians who had learned some Spanish and were part of a money economy—ladinos they are called. My businessman driver had a boat at Lake Atitlán which he wanted to check on, so we took a detour off the main road to this beautiful lake whose surrounding volcanoes are reflected in the clear water. We had lunch there before driving on to Guatemala City.

I had gotten suggestions on where to stay in each capital from colleagues and faculty members in Gainesville; in Guatemala City they had recommended—naturally enough—the Pensión Florida. It was clean and centrally located but sparsely furnished with a bed, a writing table, and one bare light bulb. Meals were included with the price of the room; the total was under $10 a day. The only bathroom was down the hall and had to be shared with other guests. I now settled in for a ten-day stay.

The center of Guatemala City in those days was a lively, colorful place, a mix of the country's Hispanic and Mayan cultures. Since then, most of the banks, embassies, museums, commercial establishments, and best hotels have moved to the suburbs; but in 1963 Zona I was still where the action was. From the Pensión Florida I could walk to the center. At the city's heart was the Parque Central where many of the indigenous came to sell hand-made textiles. Also facing the plaza was the Palacio Nacional made of light green stone. Nearby, and in the classic pattern of Spanish city design, were the Police Headquarters, the Chamber of Deputies, the Post Office, and the National Library.

Following the lessons learned from my mentor Kantor in Santo Domingo, I used to sit in the Parque Central, watch the world go by, and talk with all and sundry, soaking up the culture. I had my shoes shined there every day by a small Indian kid and, of course, I "interviewed" him, too. It mystified me that he referred to his rural and Indian background in the past tense because, with my own North American stereotypes based on racial characteristics, he sure looked Indian to me. He would say, "When I was an Indian...." It took me a while to realize that, since he dressed in Western clothes (however ragged), wore a cross around his neck (Catholic), spoke Spanish, and functioned in a money-market (not barter) economy, he was no longer culturally "Indian." He had left his Indianness behind and was now mestizo or, the term used in Guatemala, ladino—a mixture of Indian and Hispanic but in a cultural more than a racial sense. In the DR I had seen this cultural sense of race in the mixture of African and European, now I was seeing it in Guatemala in the fusion of Indian and European.

Guatemala has a reputation as a classic "banana republic"; indeed for a long time that was its principal export. It was also the home of the United Fruit Company—"The Company"—the paradigm of an imperialistic firm that had been making and unmaking Guatemalan governments for decades. If Mexico had an "Indian problem," Guatemala had an even bigger one; fully 80 percent of its population, mainly Mayan, had never been integrated into national life. A traditional agricultural country of (1960) four-and-a-half million persons, Guatemala was riven by class, racial, and political conflict.

An effort had been made to modernize the country with the Revolution of 1944, which brought workers, peasants, students, Indians, the middle class, and young military officers together in a reformist coalition. The first president elected after the Revolution was Juan José Arévalo, an idealistic former school teacher who called himself a "spiritual socialist." No one—including Arévalo—knew quite what that meant, but it was sufficient to frighten the traditional elites who began to mobilize against the regime. Arévalo's successor, Jacobo Arbenz, swung the Revolution even further to the Left. The inclusion of several communists in his government frightened the U.S. Embassy and his bill to nationalize United Fruit lands scared The Company. In 1954 the CIA supported a coup by Guatemalan right-wing military officers to overthrow Arbenz; no one protested his ouster. His successor, chosen by the U.S., was Carlos Castillo Armas, a man who was so stupid he was assassinated by his own bodyguard.

When I entered the country in the summer of 1963, Guatemala was very tense. The president was Col. Enrique Peralta, a military man, not a great democrat, but quite moderate by Central American standards. Elections were scheduled; there were rumors that Arévalo had slipped back into the country from exile in Mexico and would be a candidate. The military was ordered to find and arrest him. Meanwhile, left-wing violence (Guatemala had both a real, organized communist party and a nascent, Castro-like revolutionary insurgency) was beginning to accelerate, and right-wing death squads sought to eliminate the left by midnight assassinations. When I was there, bombs and explosions were going off every night.

My contacts in Guatemala, from Kantor, were with the democratic left. Specifically, with Mario Méndez Montenegro, who was a graduate student in agriculture at the University of Florida. He was from an elite family: his father was currently a presidential candidate and his uncle, also named Mario, would be the last civilian president of Guatemala before the left-right civil war and intense repression of the 1970s. Though of the elite, the Méndez family was reformist, leaders of the Revolutionary Party which was the authentic heir of the 1944 Revolution. The Party was progressive, oriented toward social change, and democratic. It is of the same "family" of democratic-left parties as Bosch and the PRD in the Dominican Republic.

Young Mario, about my age, invited me to go out on the campaign trail with him, his father, and his uncle. I had visions of helping to organize a grass roots organization as we had done in the Dominican Republic. But the Méndez brothers, while intelligent and well meaning, lacked the charisma that Bosch or our other Dominican friend Casimiro had. They were not natural back-slappers, were uncomfortable with crowds (especially Indian crowds), and unable to give inspirational, rousing speeches. I concluded that their elite status, quiet and reserved demeanor, and sense of social distance from the masses—like George H. W. Bush—made them weak as politicians and candidates. Moreover, I discovered that their party lacked an organizational base; it was no PRD! One of Arévalo's mistakes as president had been that he had failed to create a strong party to carry on his reforms after his term ended; now I was seeing the results of that failure in a very weak party organization in Guatemala. Without a strong party base, it was almost impossible to get elected, let alone carry out a coherent reform program.

The Méndez Montenegros were very hospitable to me during my stay in Guatemala, inviting me to their home and to their social club. As fellow graduate students in Florida, young Mario and I got along well. But I was already concluding their political campaign was unlikely to succeed, and I wanted to see the rest of the country. My plan was to take the famous "banana" train that ran from Guatemala City down to United Fruit's headquarters on the Caribbean coast, Puerto Barrios. I wanted to see the epicenter of imperialism in Guatemala. But the day before I was scheduled to take it, left-wing guerillas blew up one of the railroad bridges, so I took a bus instead. It's funny that, with all this violence all around, coming not just politically from left and right but from personal feuds and vendettas as well, I never—perhaps foolishly—felt threatened, endangered, or in need of cancelling any of my travels. Probably it is the sense of immortality that young people have. The bus steadily drops from the highlands of Guatemala City to the hot, sticky, sea-level town of Puerto Barrios. It was a ramshackle town partly built on stilts extending out over the water. Arriving in the central area, only a few blocks long, I was reminded of a Graham Greene novel. The town, the buildings, the government, the people are all in a state of decay, moral and physical, and disintegrating all around. It was a port city with many of the characteristics of port cities: sailors, transients, prostitutes, quick money, illegal activities of various sorts. Except in Puerto Barrios, United Fruit had been curtailing its activities; there were, therefore, few sailors and transients and, hence, the prostitutes were also having a hard time.

I had learned in Santo Domingo that you can do things in foreign countries, especially if you're American, that you can't or wouldn't do at home. So the first evening I went into Puerto Barrios's biggest house of prostitution to buy the girls a drink and find out what was going on. Boy, did I hear an earful. Built by imperialism, this was a plush place with three bars, a dance floor, ping pong and pool tables, and a tennis court out front. How many houses of prostitution do you know that come equipped with a tennis court? But the house and the girls were having a hard time: there were rips in the felt of the pool tables, weeds in the tennis court, and only one other customer in the bar. The girls complained mightily that, with United Fruit pulling out, business was way down, the house would have to close, and they would no longer have a livelihood. I later elevated this experience into Wiarda's first law of imperialism: when United Fruit or other U.S. companies pull out, the nearby houses of prostitution go into decline, and that way you can tell that imperialism is in retreat.

I spent the next morning roaming around the town, which is small enough that it can be fully seen in an hour or two, and then went out to United Fruit headquarters where I had interviews scheduled. The company administrators I met with were remarkably candid as well as remarkably well informed about the national political situation. Shall we call that Wiarda's law of imperialism number two: Either because they've been there longer and think of their interests as permanent, or because for them the stakes are higher, American business representatives in Latin America are often far better informed concerning local political conditions than their U.S. Embassy counterparts. In the course of the conversation I learned that a bad disease had been devastating the banana trees and that was the reason United Fruit was pulling out, not as a result of any political pressure. I also learned that United Fruit, like Alcoa in the DR, treated its workers better than Guatemalan employers did, and even allowed unions to organize among its workforce, which ironically produced the largest and most militant, even communist, unions in all Guatemala.

Honduras

In looking at the map, I had seen that there were no roads connecting Puerto Barrios with my next country, Honduras. I had, therefore, resigned myself to repeating my earlier route by taking a bus all the way back to Guatemala City and then going on to Honduras from there. But I had heard about United Fruit's fleet of banana boats plying these coasts and so, mostly in jest, I inquired of my United Fruit interviewees if I could possibly catch a ride on the next banana boat down to Honduras. "Even better than that," said the chief administrator, "I'm flying down there tomorrow in my private plane. Why don't you come along?"

That's what I did, bumming a ride on a United Fruit Company plane flying to San Pedro Sula, Honduras. Had I, a young liberal, sold out to the United Fruit Company? To imperialism? This was not exactly a Lear jet; it turned out to be a single-engine prop piper cub. Nor were the surroundings plush: we took off from a gravel runway outside Puerto Barrios and landed on a similar gravel strip in San Pedro Sula.

In those days San Pedro Sula was a small town, not the booming agricultural/manufacturing/"platform" industrial city that it would later become. We landed at the airport; I took leave of my United Fruit host and looked for a taxi. There were none. So I was forced to walk with my big suitcase the entire distance from the airport to the bus station. I remember San Pedro Sula then as a sleepy town, with basically only one long main street, and the side streets still all dirt. There wasn't much to do or see and so I decided not to stay.

I caught an overnight "bus"—really a van, what in Central America is called a "busito" or "little bus"—to the capital city of Tegucigalpa. Hence, I didn't see much of the countryside—but then there aren't many towns or things to see on that route anyway. The road was empty and the countryside sparsely populated; I do remember bouncing along on stretches of unpaved road and sleeping only fitfully. Maybe it was just as well that it was dark and that I couldn't see because, as in Guatemala, the road was precarious, there were many hairpin curves, no guard rails, and steep gorges into which many a car had fallen. We arrived in the capital at daybreak and I went directly to the home of U.S. Embassy representative Tom Killoran.

Tom had been at the University of Florida the previous year and had been in a couple of my classes. He was at Florida under a program that brought mid-career foreign-service officers to the university for a year of advanced graduate training. Tom was older than I, in his late thirties, married and with a family. When he heard that I was planning a trip to Central America, he had graciously invited me to stay at his house in Tegucigalpa.

Teguc, as it's often called affectionately, is a relatively quiet and conservative city. It does not have either a spectacular history or spectacular architecture, but it does have its charms. The main square is Plaza Morazan (after its independence hero) but it is more commonly known as the Parque Central. The cathedral is located here as is the Palace. Close by are the Museum of the Republic and the National Gallery of Art. Some of my interviews were conducted in the Congress building near the Choluteca River which flows through the heart of the city.

Honduras was different from the other Central American countries: less violence, fewer extremes of left and right, more peaceful, traditional, and easy going. It was a mestizo country, with most of the population a mixture of Indian and white, hence fewer class and caste differences and less extremes between rich and poor. It did not have the problems that Mexico and Guatemala did of integrating large numbers of Indians into the national life. Honduras had Indians but few in numbers; it had much poverty but most of its people were, to a greater or lesser degree, assimilated into the national economic life. Another saving grace was that Honduras was less crowded than its neighbors: on the same territory as Guatemala, it had half the population. And its capital, Tegucigalpa, was really a "small town" of less than 150,000, considerably smaller than Santo Domingo or Guatemala City. It was a comparatively peaceful place; people sometimes complained that "nothing happened" (no revolutions, guerrilla violence, or coups) in Honduras.

In the summer of 1963 Honduras was governed by Ramón Villeda Morales, another one of Kantor's friends from the Latin American democratic left. He had been in office since 1958, the first democratically elected president in Honduran history. Like the Dominican Republic and Guatemala, Honduras had been governed in the 1930s and 1940s by a military dictatorship, that of Tiburcio Carías Andino. Although the regime was authoritarian, it had, like Trujillo in the DR and Jorge Ubico in Guatemala, brought considerable modernization to the country. But again as in these others, modernization had brought social change which included a larger middle class, organized workers, students, mobilized peasants, and younger military officers demanding democratization. Villeda had been elected by these new social forces; he responded by initiating new social security programs, a new labor code, agrarian reform, and a climate of freedom and civil liberties. His party was ideologically and programmatically linked to Bosch's PRD in the DR and to the PR of the Méndez Montenegros in Guatemala.

When I arrived in Honduras, an election campaign was already underway for the scheduled 1963 election. Honduras was basically a two-party system, even though the military had often been in power for long periods. The two parties were the National Party—conservative, traditionalist, dominated by large landowners, and often allied with the military—and the Liberal Party of Villeda which represented the new, democratic forces. Before the great wave of authoritarianism that would sweep over Latin America in the 1960s and 1970s, we all believed that parties were important agents of social change, that democracy showed possibilities of flowering in the region, and that elections were becoming the only legitimate route to power. Thanks to my host Killoran, I spent three or four happy days going around to the party headquarters, interviewing party leaders, and even meeting President Villeda on one occasion. He knew Kantor, Bosch, the Méndez Montenegros, and asked me to convey his best wishes back to my mentor.

Killoran also set me up with some interviews in the U.S. Embassy. Tom was himself a very sharp and savvy foreign service officer, and the people he introduced me to in the Embassy were similarly well informed and able. Perhaps I had just met some bad apples back in Santo Domingo, or perhaps it was because Killoran introduced me to the better people within the Embassy. Whatever the cause, I came away from Honduras with a much better impression of U.S. Embassy personnel than I had gotten in other countries. These were smart, savvy, well informed persons; over time I would learn how to distinguish between the many dummies and time-servers who inhabit U.S. embassies abroad, and the handfuls who are sharp, genuinely interested in the countries in which they served, and well informed.

El Salvador

I stayed with Killoran for a week and then set out for El Salvador. The road proceeds south from Tegucigalpa through mountainous territory until it rejoins the Pan-American highway. To get to El Salvador one goes west, crossing the border at the Goascorán River and then through the cities of San Miguel and San Vicente, skirting Lake Ilopango, to the capital, San Salvador.

I traveled by "busito," a "small bus" or van. What a way to see the countryside! There were a few long-distance passengers like me and several scheduled stops, but mostly the trip consisted of unscheduled stops, with pedestrians and walkers waving down the bus and negotiating a fare for short distances. Luggage, boxes, and crates were piled on top of the bus until it was way overloaded and top-heavy. Nor was it just people who got aboard but also persons carrying chickens, rabbits, even a goat to market. This is the Latin America not of the international airlines, cosmopolitan cities, and tourist centers but of real, rural, everyday life. A great cacophony of sights, sounds, and noise. Probably everyone who has traveled in the Latin American countryside has experienced the vibrant life of one of these busitos.

By afternoon we were in El Salvador, at lower elevations, and it was getting warmer. Naturally I lowered the window of the busito and began dangling my arm outside. To my great surprise, the driver actually stopped the bus, came back to my seat, and said, "Oh, señor, you should not hang your arm outside the window because those campesinos (peasants) with their machetes, if they see an arm hanging out, they are likely to go (here he made a swinging motion with his arm and a whoosh sound) and you will no longer have an arm." This was my first introduction to the violence, even the "culture of violence," that pervades and pervaded El Salvador even in this relatively peaceful, pre-civil war era of the 1960s. In the literature, some measures indicate that, of all the Latin American countries through the 1950s, Cuba and El Salvador were the most violent, and maybe that helps explain why both these countries would later be engulfed in revolution.

Entering the capital of San Salvador, the bus driver dropped me off (home delivery!) at the house of Mike Bozzelli, another foreign service officer who had likewise spent a year at the University of Florida. Like Killoran, Mike was bright and able; he had also graciously invited me to stay at his place while I was in El Salvador. He was a bachelor, not exactly a swinging bachelor but not inactive either. At one point he fixed me up with a Costa Rican friend of his who was the social affairs manager at the Intercontinental Hotel then the country's best and biggest—but that is another adventure to be told in a minute.

Also in El Salvador at this time was a fellow graduate student from Florida, Steve Rozman, who was writing his MA thesis there on the same basis (a Kantor student, financed with Rockefeller funds) that I had written my thesis on Trujillo. Steve was one year behind me in the program and more radical than I; he was determined to introduce me to the seamier, underside of Salvadoran politics, and to all his revolutionary friends in the student and union movement.

San Salvador was founded in 1525 by Gonzalo de Alvorado, brother of the conquistador Pedro de Alvorado who had conquered Guatemala for Spain. Since that time the city has been destroyed fourteen times by earthquakes. The Plaza Barrios is at the heart of the city. The National Palace dates to the early twentieth century and was built in the renaissance style. To the north is the cathedral—left unfinished for many years while Archbishop Romero (later assassinated) decided to use the building funds to help the poor. The National Theater has been beautifully restored. I roamed around all of downtown San Salvador but must confess I spent more of my time in interviews and political activities than in tourism. In those days the central city was safe but, when I was there in the '60s, had political demonstrations almost every day; now it is a high crime area and most of the life of the city has moved to the suburbs.

El Salvador is the smallest of the Central American countries but, with a population then of five million, the most crowded. As in Haiti, there is tremendous population pressure on the land: overcrowding, not enough arable land to carry out a large-scale agrarian reform program, and so overpopulated that many Salvadorans emigrate, either to the U.S. or to neighboring (and relatively empty) Honduras—an exodus that helped provoke a brief war between the two countries in 1969. Though overpopulated, El Salvador is also energetic, ambitious, and hard-working; it was the most industrialized country in the region and was known as the "Formosa" of Central America.

For nearly a century, El Salvador had been dominated by its "coffee oligarchy," the famous "fourteen families" whose fortunes were based on coffee exports. But now there was a new business elite, a growing middle class, restless and mobilized student and labor movements, and an aroused peasantry. Change was in the air but the country was divided over its future directions.

At the time I arrived, El Salvador was under the control of moderate military elements led by Julio Rivera. The military had stepped in following the rule of General Maximiliano Hernández Martínez, 1930-1948. Hernández was like

Trujillo in the DR, Jorge Ubico in Guatemala, and Carías in Honduras: an authoritarian leader who had presided over a period of growth and development producing social modernization, but leading to what? In the Salvadoran case it meant a relatively progressive, nationalistic, and benign authoritarianism—not democratic but not brutal either. Rivera as president had reformed El Salvador's labor and social security laws, introduced a modest agrarian reform, and sought to align the country with John F. Kennedy's Alliance for Progress. The oligarchs thought he was going way too far, while the students, unions, media, and emerging political parties wanted even greater freedoms and more, progressive reforms. It was a tense time in El Salvador in 1963, but in the 1970s the country would polarize even more into guerrilla upheaval, harsh repression, and civil war.

One day I went out with Rozman and his revolutionary friends from the university and the trade union movement. Most of them were still democrats, preferring an elected regime and complete freedoms as compared with the restrictions of the military government; but quite a number were also sympathetic to Fidel Castro's revolution in Cuba. Steve took me to the university—where other Americans were afraid to enter because of its radical politics, but I was myself a student, looked young for my age, and had a lively discussion with representatives of the various political factions. He also took me to trade union offices—these were often older and more serious people—who filled me in on the repression still practiced by the regime. For while Rivera was a moderate, he was fearful of unfettered liberalism and pluralism, and much preferred a corporatist, one-party state as in Mexico where the major interest groups were subordinate to the state and under its control and direction. During this "hot summer" in El Salvador these tensions were producing everyday street demonstrations on the one hand and repression, actual or threatened, on the other.

While Steve shepherded me around to the radical groups, my host Mike introduced me to the moderates. These included the new opposition political parties (Christian Democrats, Social Democrats) that had been allowed to organize because of pressure from U.S. Ambassador Murat Williams, as well as the regime's official party, National Reconciliation. Mike also brought me to the Embassy for interviews there and set me up with interviews with representatives from the business community. I saw a lot of El Salvador in a short period of time.

One of the great (or not so great!) stories of El Salvador during this period concerns a white-elephant hotel built with Alliance for Progress funds. It sits atop a mountain with great views, including of a live volcano below, but no way to get water pumped up that high. So it sat empty, except for Salvadoran military officers who would take their girlfriends (and the water) up there by helicopter. While the officers and their girlfriends drank and partied on the veranda, military helicopters would fly by dangling a peasant from a rope. As they passed over the live volcano, the rope would be cut and down would go the peasant into the molten lava, for the entertainment of all. Doubtless the officers believed, as did the conquistadores before, that since peasants were less than human and doubtless lacked souls, they didn't feel the pain. It tells you a lot about El Salvador and why revolution and civil war would soon break out. If you can kill peasants this way, you can also rape and murder Maryknoll nuns as in an infamous event of 1979.

One day I took Mike's friend, the Costa Rican girl, up to Lake Cojutepeque for a swim. She was very pretty, from the prominent, newspaper-owning Castro Beeche family in Costa Rica. The lake is spectacular: absolutely pure mountain water, clear as transparency, and with the surrounding volcanic mountains reflected in its tranquil (later it became a guerrilla stronghold) surface. We swam and dove for a time, then retired to a small restaurant on the lakeshore for lunch. It was all very romantic and she was quite charming.

As we were beginning lunch, I heard the roar of motorcycles outside. Who should walk in but President Rivera himself, with his entourage. He had been up in the next city, Santa Ana, dedicating a bridge and had stopped by for lunch on the way back to San Salvador. Immediately the girl I was with got up, gave a kiss to the President, and was in turn embraced by him. President Rivera invited us to join him and his party at their table.

It was a delightful lunch, with spirited, animated conversation in the Latin style. The President also picked up the tab, which greatly endeared him to me. Now, I may be naive (still only twenty-three) but not that naive. Judging from the body and eye motions and the flirtatious conversation over lunch, I began to conclude that the girl was not only my date-for-the-day but probably the President's girlfriend as well. It is not good to compete for the attentions of the same girl with the President of the republic! And already knowing something, at least academically, both about Latin machismo and El Salvador's culture of violence, I began to worry. The President was extremely gracious and solicitous of me as well as the girl over lunch and gave me a warm abrazo as he departed. But I was starting to wonder if this was the Godfather-style kiss on the cheek before the stiletto in the back?

Perhaps I should not have thought any more of it, and most likely nothing would have happened. But immediately upon returning to San Salvador I called Mike at the Embassy. He took it very seriously and consulted with colleagues and even the U.S. ambassador. The consensus was unanimous: El Salvador was a very violent country; we should not take any chances; and I should leave the country immediately. So that very evening, not even waiting for the next morning, Mike put me on an overnight bus to my next destination, Nicaragua. I never saw the girl again.

Nicaragua

Back down the Pan American Highway. Once again through the towns of San Vicente and San Miguel. Across southern Honduras but, instead of taking the spur up to Tegucigalpa, we continued east and south on the Pan American Highway. Another bumpy ride in a busito, many stops for passengers, and more chickens and goats. It was dark outside and the countryside in Latin America is not well lighted as it is with all those kilowatts in the U.S. But no matter, I had been on this part of the trip before. For the only way to go by road from El Salvador to Nicaragua is to cross the south of Honduras.

By this time I had been on the road in Mexico and Central America for about six weeks. My stomach and intestines were starting to act up again—not as badly as in the DR but still leaving me weak, a bit wan, and drained of energy. Anyone who has suffered the same ills in the Third World will know what I mean. The busito and its fumes and the bumpy overnight ride were not helping matters any. I began to think that it would be nice to be back in my comfortable, air conditioned apartment in Gainesville with its purified non-amoeba water supply and food that I didn't always need to be careful of.

The busito bumped across the Nicaragua border in the middle of the night. We alighted to check in with the consulate at the border. There I noticed on the wall not a picture of René Schick, the then President, but of the Somozas, Anastasio, Luís, and Anastasio, Jr., the ruling family of Nicaragua for the past thirty years. Since I was a smart-alecky graduate student who already knew the answer, I asked the consul why he had a picture of the Somozas on the wall and not the current president. What I got back was not an answer but a look of such absolute disdain that implied, only a gringo like you could ask that stupid a question. Welcome to Somozaland.

Down the Pan American Highway we went, through the large spaces of near-empty northern Nicaragua. Through the towns of Somoto, Condaga, Estelé, San Isidro, Sébaco, Cuidad Darío (after Nicaragua's most famous poet), and San Benuto. I don't remember much of that area: it was still dark and I must have been dozing off. Much of it is mountainous, hilly, and bumpy—on the so-called Pan American Highway (now a phrase of irony after so many rough rides). In the early a.m. we arrived in the capital of Managua—still a nice, pleasant city in those days, before the twin devastations of both the 1972 earthquake which flattened much of the city (and is still not completely rebuilt) and the Somoza-Sandinista civil war of the 1970s which destroyed still more.

Tired, drained from the overnight trip, and with my tummy rattling again, I checked into a pensión that had been recommended to me back in Gainesville. I really needed some sleep before I could go out on my day's explorations of the city, but as I lay on the bed I heard strange, scratching sounds in the room. Searching around, I found one of those large, scaly, two-foot long Central American iguanas under my bed. Obviously I couldn't sleep with that critter in my room. Complaining at the front desk, the young manager broke into howls of laughter at the inability of this young gringo to cope with such a minor problem. At first he refused to do anything; later he came with a broom to shoo the critter out. Even in an inexpensive pensión, I figured, a few creature comforts—not having to share my room with this giant iguana—were necessary.

Managua is my least-favorite capital in Central America, and it has steadily gone downhill since my first visit. It was artificially created as a capital as a compromise between the cities of León and Granada and, therefore, lacks the history of these other centers. Built over the confluence of no fewer than fourteen subsurface seismic fault lines, it is regularly shaken and was several times destroyed by earthquakes. Fire and revolution have destroyed more of the city, which is too poor to rebuild itself. Vast areas of the city, devastated by the earthquakes, have not been rebuilt and look like a wasteland. It has no hills to give it character but does at least have Lake Managua. The Presidential Palace on the Parque Central is garishly painted; the old cathedral on the opposite corner is nondescript; and the architecture of the new cathedral has been described as "post-nuclear." It's not a place where many tourists would want to spend time.

Nicaragua in those days was peaceful. The Sandinista insurrection had not yet broken out. There were no bombings, no violence. Everything seemed calm. But it was the peace of the dead. An explosion would come soon.

Nicaragua is the largest of the Central American countries, about 25 percent larger than both Guatemala and Honduras. But it is also the least populated with, at that time, less than two million population. The capital of Managua, then with 270,000 people, was half as big as Guatemala City but twice as large as Tegucigalpa. It is a predominantly agricultural country with large areas of near-empty territory. Eighty percent of the population was rural in the early 1960s; that was also about the illiteracy rate.

Managua is quite a nondescript town with few distinguishing features. It is hot and low-lying—unlike most Latin American capitals which the Spaniards had the good sense to build in the highlands. Managua is located on a scorching plain between the country's two famous lakes, Lake Nicaragua and Lake Managua. Actually there was little to commend Managua as a capital; and the only reason it became the capital was that the two bodies of elites in Nicaragua's only two other sizable cities, the Conservatives in Granada and the Liberals in León, were so often in contention, including over which would be the capital, that they fought numerous civil wars and could never agree on anything. Hence, Managua, in between the other two, became the capital as a compromise solution.

Even though I never spent a lot of time in Nicaragua, I thought that I instinctively understood it. This is because it bore a striking resemblance to the Dominican Republic. Both were predominantly rural, agricultural, traditional, "sleepy" countries—but with the beginning of greater social pluralism, modernization, and the mobilization of lower-class elements. Both were at about the same levels of social and economic underdevelopment, with similar rates of poverty and illiteracy. Both had been long-term preoccupations of the United States: the DR because of its command of the Caribbean sea lanes (and now the fear of a Cuba-like revolution), Nicaragua because of its potential for a trans-isthmian canal (and also now Cuba).

Most importantly, the Trujillo regime which I had studied extensively and the Somoza family dictatorship were remarkably similar. Both had come to power in the early 1930s and had been in power for thirty years. Both Trujillo and the elder Somoza (Tacho) had been officers in the U.S.-trained constabularies which the Americans had created during their recent occupations of the two countries, had used the constabulary to seize power, and thus were widely seen by their own peoples as products of the U.S. forces. Both had vastly enriched themselves, their families, and numerous hangers-on during their long rules; but both also brought gradual social, economic, and institutional (roads, public works, etc.) change to their countries. Both used strong, authoritarian, verging-on-totalitarian techniques to stay in power, although Trujillo's rule was bloodier and he was more of a megalomaniac. Thus, although I didn't know the details of the Somoza regime so thoroughly as I knew Trujillo's, I felt that I intuitively <u>understood</u> the regime because of these many similarities.

Because of the dictatorship, there was really no democratic-left inside Nicaragua at this time, so my mentor Kantor could not provide very many contacts. Many of the democratic leaders and their families had long since left the country, settling in next-door (and democratic) Costa Rica, the U.S. or Mexico. Nor, unlike all the other countries I had visited except Haiti, was there an election campaign underway or planned, no political party activity, no political activity of any kind. This, after all, was not an open society but a full-fledged dictatorship; later, in Alfredo Stroessner's Paraguay, Antonio Salazar's Portugal, and Franco's Spain, I would have to learn how to do research in the still-dangerous context of an authoritarian regime.

President Schick was well-meaning, a moderate, trying to do a good job, and, like my "friend" Rivera in El Salvador, attempting in the early 1960s to align (and reaping the aid benefits therefrom) his regime with Kennedy's Alliance for Progress. But, as my experience with the presidential pictures in the consulate at the border had shown, Schick was a puppet president, completely under the control of the Somozas, and no one took him seriously. This proved to be disastrous for Nicaragua. Had the moderates in the country been able to stay in power, it might have avoided the disastrous civil war that followed in the 1970s. Instead the <u>Somoza family</u> returned to power, first elder son Luís who was not effective and died at a relatively young age, and then Anastasio, Jr. (Tachito) who brutalized the country, stole everything in sight, and forced the polarization of society that led to civil war, the Sandinista takeover, and Nicaragua's slide into economic ruin that came close to matching that of perennially backward Haiti.

My only good contacts in Managua at that time were, again, two students from the University of Florida, but they were undergraduates and not too sharp politically. Nevertheless, I threw myself into the embrace of the only "hosts" I had, sticking to the adage that the best way to see a country is to let the natives show it to you. They took me out nightclubbing a couple of times and drove me around Managua. We did take a short trip with a number of their girlfriends to Lake Nicaragua where, with much laughter, they urged me into the water—even though, curiously, no one else was swimming. Only later did I learn that Lake Nicaragua was famous for having the only fresh-water sharks in the world—there and in the San Juan River which divides Nicaragua from Costa Rica and where, had not some elaborate money payoffs to U.S. congressmen taken place, the trans-isthmian canal <u>should</u> have been built instead of in neighboring Panama. And even today China, Japan, the U.S., and other countries keep open the possibility of a new, alternative canal using the Nicaragua route.

Costa Rica

There was little political activity in Nicaragua; I was getting homesick after several weeks in dingy pensións and with their equally dingy food; and my tummy was once again in bad shape. It was not that I was careless with what I ate or drank; I think it was probably inevitable in those days that, if you spent more than a week or two in the Third World, you were bound to come down with some form of amoebas, intestinal disease, diarrhea, or dysentery. The option was not to avoid these ills altogether but to keep them within manageable bounds so you could still function.

By the time I left Nicaragua I was not certain that I could function much longer. I was tired, pale, without my usual energy, and my belt was two notches looser than before. But my airline ticket home said Costa Rica was my point of embarkation; I had wonderful contacts there; and I was determined to finish the trip. So I bought a ticket for San José, the capital, and settled in for another long busito ride.

The road goes southeast from Managua, down along the isthmus of Central America, skirting Lake Nicaragua (and its sharks) for about fifty miles. Peña Blanca is the Costa Rican border town, next comes La Cruz, Liberfa, Las Canas, Barranca, San Ramón, Grecia, and Alajuela. It's a long trip by busito but, wonder of wonders, the Costa Rican part of the Pan American Highway (no longer "so-called") is paved.

I noticed another striking difference from Nicaragua as soon as we crossed the border. Whereas Nicaragua seems all brown and dusty, Costa Rica is green, lush, and tropical. The difference is almost as stark as that between Haiti and the DR. The green beauty of Costa Rica becomes even more striking as you come out of the foothills and enter the lush Central Valley. This valley, about thirty miles long and ten wide, surrounded by mountains and still-active volcanoes, is the heart of Costa Rica: 80 percent of its population, all of its government and banks, almost all of its business and commerce, most of its industry and agriculture, and almost all of its social life. This tight, integrated valley (about the size of what would later become our beloved home in the Pioneer Valley of Massachusetts) helps explain why Costa Rica is considerably more developed than its neighbors and more democratic.

For Costa Rica is happily unlike its Central American neighbors and one of the nicest, most democratic countries in the world. Unlike Mexico or Guatemala, it has few unintegrated Indians and few other racial tensions. Its people are more prosperous and mainly middle class. Literacy is close to 100 percent, higher than the U.S. Life expectancy is as high as most European countries; and one does not see disease, malnutrition, and bloated bellies in Costa Rica. Again unlike its neighbors, Costa Rica has been mainly democratic since the nineteenth century; its democratic traditions strengthened by a brief civil war in 1948 launched against an attempt to steal the election of that year.

Costa Rica does not have a ruling landed oligarchy, a strong Catholic Church holding back change, and it abolished its army as part of the 1948 revolution. It has advanced social programs, universal health care, and free education. Its citizens are hard-working, middle-class family farmers and small businessmen, not <u>conquistadores</u> looking for quick riches, many servants, and immense feudal estates as elsewhere in Latin America. But its experience and development are unique and cannot be repeated elsewhere. Some twenty years later when I was asked to testify before Congress on the then-Central American crisis, the Senators and Representatives would always ask me why the main trouble spots, Guatemala, El Salvador, and Nicaragua, couldn't be more like Costa Rica. I had to tell them, sorry, it doesn't work that way; you can't transplant one country's culture, history, sociology, economics, and politics to another.

Costa Rica in those days had only a million-and-a-half people. Its neat capital of San José had only three hundred thousand. With nineteen thousand square miles, Costa Rica was one-half to one-third the size of neighboring Nicaragua, Honduras, and Guatemala; but two-and-a-half times the size of El Salvador. Its name is translated as "Rich Coast"; but, in fact, that is an ironic name because the country lacked the gold, silver, and Indians that the conquistadores craved and, because of that, was not of much interest to the Spanish crown. The lack of riches proved to be a blessing in disguise because, in the absence of either a get-rich-quick possibility or mentality, the Costa Ricans actually had to <u>work</u> for what they have.

On the day I arrived in the Central Valley, it was only 4:00 in the afternoon and yet the sky was strangely purplish dark. An army of street sweepers was out pushing brooms at a strange, white powder that covered everything to depths of a half inch. But it clearly wasn't snow, not here in the tropics. I couldn't figure out what it possibly was until someone on the bus mentioned Iguacú. Then it dawned on me. Iguacú was the volcano at the end of the Central Valley. It had just erupted the day before, and what I was seeing was the layer of volcanic ash it had rained down on the valley. Sadly, it had not only covered San José with volcanic dust but was also poisoning fields, cattle, agriculture, and water supplies as well.

San José and the Meseta Central are quite delightful places to visit—maybe to stay permanently, as there are now quite a number of U.S. retirement communities here. The climate on the Meseta is comfortable; the vegetation is green; the agriculture produces year-round fruits and vegetables; and the views of the surrounding mountains and volcanoes are spectacular. It's basically a free, democratic, middle-class, honest, efficient, largely crime-free country—by all the rankings the most consistently democratic country in Latin America over the last half-century.

San José does not have the cultural richness of a major metropolis like Mexico City, Rio de Janeiro, or Buenos Aires, but it is lively, clean, and interesting. One of the highlights is the National Theater with its European-style marble staircases and frequent performances by international groups. The Plaza de la Cultura is good for people-watching; below it is the Gold Museum with its treasures going back hundreds of years. The National Museum has wonderful archeological displays—the best in Central America. The modest cathedral seems to fit Costa Rica's character as the least Catholic country in Central America, while the National Palace is worth a visit to see the only congress in the region that truly functions as an independent legislative body. I liked the National Library because it has a good collection and is actually used by this literate and book-reading population. The Union Club is the principal social center in the country—it piqued my interest not least because the family of the girl of my short-lived romance in El Salvador holds a membership. San José also has a good zoo and botanical gardens, impressively well kept up. In fact, that is what is so nice—and unique—about Costa Rica: almost alone among Latin American countries, its public (as well as private) spaces, streets, and parks are clean, maintained, well-kept-up, and actually meant to serve the public.

Once again because of Kantor, I had wonderful political contacts in Costa Rica. Harry had lived in San José in the 1950s and had written a book about political parties and elections there. Then, he had lived there again in 1960-61 when he had taught at the school for young party and labor leaders financed by the CIA. Most important, he was a close friend of José "Don Pepe" Figueres, the hero of the 1948 revolution, a two-term president of Costa Rica, and one of the founding fathers of the Latin American democratic left. Many of my Dominican friends—Juan Bosch, Angel Miolán, Manny Espinal, José Francisco Peña Gomez, and the ever-present Sacha Volman—had been teachers or students at the school. Figueres's party, the National Liberation Party (PLN) was also like the PRD in the DR: social reformist, democratic, and the best organized party in the country.

The Kantor family (Harry and Vivian) was very close to the Figueres family, including—José, Jr. (who was also elected president) and Muni (a future president?), who also became friends of mine. The Kantors could not have children, so they adopted two Costa Rican children. But Costa Rican law required adoptive parents to be Catholic; because they were Jewish, the Kantors were not allowed to take the children out of the country. They had to obtain a special presidential decree (decreto) from Figueras himself before they were able to take the children back to Gainesville.

I had a marvelous time in Costa Rica. After Nicaragua, it was nice to be back in a democratic country again. I was able to meet Figueres, his family, and most of the top leadership of the PLN, including another future president, Daniel Oduber. I visited the university, met much of the student leadership, and even gave a lecture there—on U.S. policy toward Latin America. I went out to the agricultural/technical university at Herédia where many of the agrarian reform plans for Latin America were being formulated by U.S., Costa Rican, and Latin American planners. I also visited the offices of the more conservative political parties, including that controlled by the Castro Beeche family. Doubtless in my subconscious (or maybe more than that!) I was hoping, if only vicariously, to run into the Costa Rican girl I had gone swimming with in El Salvador but had had to abandon precipitously when it appeared President Rivera and I (there was no doubt who would win that competition) were vying for the same woman.

I have returned to Costa Rica (as to the other Central American countries) many times since then. On those trips (see Chapter 21) I saw much more of the Costa Rican countryside, went to the beach at Puntarenas on the Pacific side as well as to black, English-speaking Puerto Limón on the Caribbean side. I also visited the impressive national preservation parks that Costa Rica has created and, on one spectacular trip, went up to the rain forest on the Caribbean northeast coast where I saw the largest collection of strange, tropical birds, animals, and, it was reliably reported, the late Richard Nixon and William (Bill) Casey (!!!), I had ever seen.

But all good things, even Costa Rica, have to come to an end. It was the end of August; my classes in Gainesville started up again in a few days; and I had Ph.D. comprehensive exams to take later in the fall. Plus, and it's now a too-oft-repeated lament, my stomach and intestines were still not in good shape.

Taking a plane out of the San José airport is quite an experience. Because of the surrounding mountains and volcanoes, it's a very tight, steep takeoff. The plane makes a run toward one end of the valley but then, because of the volcano ahead, banks sharply and races toward the other end of the valley. Only then do you have enough height to clear the mountains. If you're lucky, the pilot will dip the wings so that you can see down into the glowing mouth of a live volcano.

The Pan Am flight (a four-engine prop) that served Central America in those days was just like the one serving the Caribbean: a milk run. It hit every stop before getting back to New Orleans, all short hops. So we went from San José to Managua, Nicaragua; next to Tegucigalpa, Honduras, where the main runway ran downhill seemingly into the center of the city; I was sure we were going to hit the cathedral. From Teguc we went to San Salvador, and from there to Guatemala City. This way I could say I had been in every Central American capital city <u>twice</u> on that trip. An added bonus was flying low over the mangrove swamps of Belize where I could see the sun's reflection of the plane on the water below and concluded that the whole country must be one great swamp. We also landed at the Belize airport, so that way I could put one more notch on my belt of countries visited, even though the only part of the country I saw was the airport—and the swamps, of course.

We arrived in New Orleans in the early evening. I took a trolley out to the home (just off Canal Street) of the woman where I had left the car in the back yard. She wasn't at home and the keys I'd left her were not in the car. The last thing I wanted to do at that stage (very tired, still sick) was wait around, let alone stay overnight, and fortunately I'd kept an extra set of keys in my luggage. My faithful Beetle started right away and, after leaving a thank-you note for the girl, I headed back to Gainesville. I wouldn't be at all surprised if someone told me I had fallen asleep several times that night while driving. Again that restless, impatient, impetuous, seemingly invulnerable youth. Once more I'm happy my children never did reckless, stupid things as I did—or did they also do these things but never told me? I arrived back in Gainesville in the early morning hours.

NOTE

1. Howard J. Wiarda, <u>Dictatorship and Development: The Methods of Control in Trujillo's Dominican Republic</u> (Gainesville: University of Florida Press, 1968).

CHAPTER 3

PEACE CORPS TRAINING PROGRAMS IN PUERTO RICO AND OTHER PLACES

Back in Gainesville in the full of 1963, I prepared to take the political science, Ph.D., comprehensive exams, or "comps." Comprehensive exams were exams covering all your major fields; they were the biggest and most important exams I would ever take. They were offered after you had completed all course and seminar work and had spent a summer or semester doing little but reading and studying. But before you did the research and writing of your doctoral dissertation. Once you passed your comps you were ABD—All But Dissertation—near the end of your graduate career.

At Florida in those days you had to take written comps in five fields (now the norm is two or two-and-a-half) and then, in addition, be subjected to a follow-up oral exam. My fields were: comparative politics, international relations, political theory, American politics, and area studies—Latin America. Each one of the five written exams was five to six hours long, offered on alternative days—Monday, Wednesday, Friday, Monday again, Wednesday again. The oral was on the second Friday. That way you had a day to catch your breath before each exam. It was a grueling two-week ordeal. I had read every book on every syllabus and reading list, had extensive notes, and thought I knew it cold. At the end of this exam period, I probably knew more (I won't say I was smarter) than I had ever known in my life—or ever would again. I passed easily and with distinction, although I must confess I don't remember a thing about the final oral. Never mind. Regardless, now I was ready to work full time on the dissertation.

Big things were meanwhile happening in "my country," the Dominican Republic. In December 1962, Juan Bosch had been elected in an overwhelming two-to-one landslide. But nine months after his inauguration, and just weeks before I took comps, his government was overthrown in a coup d'état. Bosch was exiled to Puerto Rico and a three-man civilian-military junta representing the country's more conservative and traditional interests retook power. So instead of my Ph.D. thesis being about a successful transition from authoritarianism (Trujillo) to democracy, it had to be refocused as a study of the problems of democratic transitions.

Sometime in the fall of 1963, after I'd finished my comps but before I was ready to go off for the dissertation field research, the newly created Peace Corps ran one of its training programs for the young volunteers at the University of Florida campus. My personal notes on this period are quite incomplete so I do not have complete records of dates and locations. But I do know I was invited by the University's Latin America Center, probably at Kantor's suggestion, to lecture on society and politics to a group being trained to go to the DR. Thus began a happy, four- or five-year relationship with the Peace Corps that almost resulted in my taking a permanent job with the new agency. My recollections are that I participated in about seven or eight training programs, and I do have the social background studies—at least four of them, my first serious social science research and writing—that I compiled as part of my Peace Corps work. These include the fall 1963 training program in Gainesville; another in January 1964 in Puerto Rico; a third, also in Puerto Rico, in March 1964; a fourth at Kansas State University in July 1964; and several again in Puerto Rico, in 1965 and 1966. These brief, one- or two-week trips brought me mainly to Puerto Rico for the training programs and several times back to the Dominican Republic since it was en route to Puerto Rico. It was an enjoyable association and, since they paid me (but not well), a remunerative one as well at a time when I sure could use the money.

Puerto Rico

Before the Peace Corps brought me there, I had not been in Puerto Rico before. To get there, when I was still living in Florida, I could fly the familiar route: Miami, Jamaica, Haiti, Dominican Republic, Puerto Rico, or some combination of these, often staying over for a few days in one or another of the countries. When we later moved to Amherst, since there was then still no direct service to the DR, I would fly New York, Puerto Rico, Dominican Republic, and return. In effect, the Peace Corps excursions to Puerto Rico enabled me to finance numerous side trips to and around the Caribbean. Between 1962 and 1966 I must have made a dozen-to-fifteen visits to the Caribbean.

The first time I went to Puerto Rico I stayed on the Condado Beach at the Condado Hotel—at Peace Corps expense. It was a gorgeous place near the international airport and facing north toward the Atlantic Ocean. Because I was going to interview Jean Bosch, now deposed and living in San Juan, and would use that material as part of my lectures to the volunteers, the Peace Corps also approved my renting a car for a week. Especially when it was done with someone else's money, the life of what I would later call an "international scholar" could be pretty cushy.

The first night there I went off to visit Old San Juan. San Juan is one of the oldest cities in the Americas, dating to 1521. The island of Puerto Rico, as well as Cuba, was first explored by Columbus and conquered by Spain from its first main base in Santo Domingo on the neighboring island ("my" island) of Hispaniola. The first settlement on the island was established by Juan Ponce de León, whom American readers will recognize as the founder of St. Augustine in Florida and the frustrated seeker of the fountain of youth. From my thesis work, I already knew the history thoroughly.

Old San Juan, the most ancient part of the city, was built on a two-mile spit of land, a peninsula, that juts out westerly from the main part of the city and that separates the Atlantic from San Juan Bay. Old San Juan commands the entrance to one of the finest natural harbors in the Caribbean, which is why the Spaniards established their first settlement there. When I was there, the U.S. Navy had taken over a big hunk of waterfront on the southern side of the peninsula and Navy ships were a major presence in the Bay.

The Old City is partially surrounded by walls that date from the 1630s. Much of Old San Juan—some four hundred buildings—has been beautifully restored to the Spanish architecture of the sixteenth and seventeenth centuries: heavy, dark, wooden, usually mahogany, exposed beams, and white stucco walls. There are graceful, wrought-iron balconies with beautiful tropical flowers hanging down—this in what I think of as the cold, gray, snowy month of January. The streets are narrow and many are paved with a blue-gray stone that the Spanish used for ballast in their ships. Old San Juan is chockablock with beautiful shops, gorgeous homes, tree-lined squares, imposing monuments—and millions of pigeons.

At the tip of the peninsula on a rocky promontory facing the ocean is the Fuerte San Felipe del Morro, a massive fortress of six levels meant to guard against foreign interlopers and pirates entering the harbor. Here I scrambled out of my rental car to explore for a time the fort's labyrinth of dungeons, towers, turrets, and tunnels, noting that the huge complex now accommodates a nine-hole golf course. Down the street is La Fortaleza, another fortress overlooking the Bay which is the residence of the governor of Puerto Rico and is the oldest executive mansion in the U.S. As I drove around more of Old San Juan, I also saw the ancient city hall or <u>alcaldia,</u> the cathedral, the Plaza of Columbus, and the Fort of San Cristobal which guarded the city against land attacks. The. Plaza de Armas is beautiful and is the main square of the old city; the Paseo de la Princesa runs along the port and has been spruced up with trees, flowers, benches, and street lamps. As the name implies, it is the place where many Puerto Ricans come to stroll in the evening; I spent a couple of hours there sipping beer in an outdoor cafe and soaking up the <u>ambiente</u> (atmosphere). It was obvious that Puerto Rico was far wealthier than the Dominican Republic and the Central American countries, and it had done a beautiful, tasteful job of restoration. I was beginning to really like Puerto Rico.

Puerto Rico was a Spanish colony for four hundred years and an American one for the last hundred, since the Spanish-American War of 1898 when defeated Spain ceded the island (along with The Philippines) to the U.S. Puerto Rico is not a state of the U.S. (although its people have U.S. citizenship) and is not an independent country either, but exists as a "commonwealth"—a flexible, changing, often renegotiated relationship that exists somewhere between statehood and independence. This ambiguous relationship leaves many Puerto Ricans who favor either of the other two options dissatisfied; commonwealth status is a compromise solution that has proved manageable and workable because neither the statehood nor the independence options are able to command majority support. Meanwhile, the rest of Latin America looks down on Puerto Rico, a sentiment the Puerto Ricans also feel deeply, because it has not achieved independence and has, purportedly, "sold out for the Yankee dollar," become "Coca-Colaized." Poor Puerto Rico: not fully accepted by the U.S. and rejected by Latin America as well.

But it is the very fused, mixed, overlapping nature of Puerto Rico's two cultures that attracted me to the island. For after four centuries of Spain, Puerto Rico is a thoroughly Hispanic culture; I knew that culture well, spoke the language, and felt at home in it. At the same time, because of the American influence, almost everyone at least in San Juan speaks English as well as Spanish; the island has shared in America's prosperity; and at many levels Puerto Rico has American-style rationality, entrepreneurship, and efficiency. That is not a bad combination, an attractive combination I would later occasionally find in other areas of my travels as well.

For example, in my Peace Corps work, I would become acquainted with numerous African-American ex-volunteers who had settled, and found jobs and a life in Puerto Rico. They felt comfortable there because as ex-volunteers they knew Spanish and felt at home in Latin culture; they liked American efficiency (and also higher salaries), and, as black Americans, they felt more at ease in Puerto Rico's fluid and culturally based (depending on education, dress, way of speaking, job or position more than color per se) racial context than they did in the often still segregated and more rigidly defined and color-conscious U.S. I understood and sympathized with their position; I also felt comfortable in a mix of the two cultures.

I interviewed Bosch in his hillside house in Aguas Buenas, overlooking San Juan, the Bay, and the Atlantic Ocean beyond. It was a house owned by Luís Muñoz Marin, then the governor of Puerto Rico and one of the architects of its commonwealth status. Since Bosch and Muñoz were charter members of the Latin American democratic-left, Muñoz felt some obligation to provide refuge and a house for the ousted Dominican leader, though later I came to understand that Muñoz had concluded, as I had, that the rigid, mercurial, inflexible Bosch was at least partially responsible for his own ouster.

Isolated in the house in Aguas Buenas, Bosch was already a bitter man. He mainly blamed the Dominican Church, the oligarchy, and the Army for his ouster, but he also blamed the U.S. for not coming more strongly to his defense and the defense of democracy, the two being synonymous in his mind. There were only two or three low-ranking members of his party around, one of whom I had met in Santo Domingo; already other PRD leaders still in the DR were disillusioned with Bosch and plotting to wrest control of the party leadership from him. It was obvious to me, meanwhile, from several things that Bosch said, that he intended to hang onto the party leadership and that he was already plotting to make a comeback and to return to the Dominican Republic as the (still) constitutional president. That was precisely what would happen when the DR exploded in revolution in April 1965.

While in Puerto Rico, I also made contact with the important Institute of Caribbean Studies at the University of Puerto Rico and, because of my liking for the island, even began to formulate a plan (at least in my own mind) to secure a position there. The Institute in those days was the premier institution for Caribbean Studies; it also published Caribbean Studies which was the journal in the field. I met leading Latin American scholar Richard M. Morse there for the first time and also such major Caribbean scholars as Harry Hoetink, Thomas Matthews, Robert Anderson, Henry Wells, and the García Passalaquas, Dora and

Juan Manuel. It was a stellar team into which I sought to ingratiate myself; but while I remained close to many of the individuals listed, I also learned over time that the Institute was a hornet's nest of rivalries and backstabbing having to do with both individual personalities and with the larger issue of the future status of Puerto Rico. In retrospect, I'm glad my efforts didn't pay off in a job offer because, once that kind of office politics and nastiness get imbedded in a program, they are very hard to get rid of.

To the Peace Corps Camp

After several days of roaming around San Juan, I decided I had better go to work doing what the Peace Corps was paying me to do: training their volunteers. So I hopped in my little rental car and headed west out of San Juan along the north coast of Puerto Rico. The road (Route 22) passes the towns of Dorado, Vega Baja, and Manatí, as well as along some spectacular oceanfront views. Once outside of San Juan, the international flavor of the island becomes much less pronounced and English is much less spoken. It became much more Puerto Rican.

About sixty miles west of San Juan, my directions were to turn south on Route 10 and head up into the mountainous center of the island toward Utuado. Once off the main coastal road, the international character of the island ends abruptly and its "Puerto Ricanness" becomes even more pronounced. The roads are narrow and windy; there are no guard rails; people, chickens, and cows are everywhere, including on the roads. In short, the interior of Puerto Rico looks very much like what I had already seen in the Dominican Republic and Central America.

Up and up into the mountains, the central spine of Puerto Rico, the road winds. One fork leads off to Utuado, the only city in the area; the other climbs still higher into the mountains. It is lush and green up here, the look of a tropical jungle or rain forest. There are no tourists up here, but there is a radar station, part of a long string of radar stations throughout the Caribbean archipelago that the U.S. built and maintained for security purposes.

After about two-and-a-half hours (and a couple of wrong turns), I arrive at the camp. It doesn't look like much. The camp is an old Works Progress Administration (WPA) project camp built by Franklin Roosevelt's administration in the 1930s, designed to provide employment during the Great Depression. It had lain idle and neglected for decades. Now it had been inherited by the Peace Corps who were fixing it up as a training base for the volunteers. The logic was that the volunteers would learn and adapt to the language and culture better and faster if they were actually in a Latin American environment far removed from

English speakers. As I arrived the sound of hammering was in the air; construction was still underway.

The complex had the look of a summer scout or YMCA camp that you might have attended as a kid. It was hilly and rugged all around. There was one small central administration building with no air conditioning, air conditioning being thought a luxury that Peace Corps Volunteers (PCVs) and even their administrators could do without. It didn't fit the image of volunteer self-sacrifice for the sake of helping poor countries.

There were several covered but open-air classrooms when I arrived where Spanish was being taught, mainly by native speakers, to small groups of volunteers. Around the area were ten or twelve living "cabins"—mainly tents holding ten or twelve volunteers each—built on wooden platforms above the ground. There was a large mess hall where meals were served cafeteria or "dorm" style, and wooden picnic tables to eat from. A flat, open area about the size of a volleyball court was used for calisthenics and pickup soccer, basketball, and volleyball games. That was about it. It was pretty primitive. As we said, like summer camp. It could handle two training groups of about forty volunteers each at one time.

The Peace Corps had just been created a year earlier by the Kennedy Administration. By coincidence, I had been, as an undergraduate, one of those present at the Michigan Union in Ann Arbor when, during the 1960 campaign, Kennedy had stopped by there long after midnight and briefly announced his plans for the Peace Corps. Like many other young people at that time, I had been caught up in the dynamism, idealism, and energy of that campaign—even though my late November thirty birthday meant I couldn't vote in that election. I thought the Peace Corps was a great way to build democracy and foster development at grass roots levels and show off the best of American young people and their idealism. The idea had certainly caught on with my generation.

But Congress worried that too much emphasis on "idealism" would result in a bunch of hippies and beatniks being sent off to the Third World, getting into trouble, and doing damage to U.S. interests and our image abroad. To guard against that (which would also result in its budget being slashed), the Peace Corps looked for down-to-earth, "all-American" volunteers, no less idealistic but with practical skills in agriculture, construction, nursing, engineering, fisheries, and other useful occupations. Other volunteers specialized in the catchall category of "community. development" (teaching basic organization literacy in often-disorganized Third World countries); failing that, one could always teach English to the local people.

Future senator Chris Dodd went through one of the earliest training programs for Dominican Republic volunteers, but my records cannot confirm if he was in one of my classes or not. In later years he, as a member of the Senate Foreign Relations Committee and chair of its inter-American subcommittee, and I would both clash and cooperate on a number of policy issues relating to Central America, but we shared a passion for the Peace Corps. Dodd's Peace Corps background, as well as that of the late Paul Tsongas and other ex-PCVs who later worked at high levels in government, importantly shaped his views about foreign policy. For once you've lived in some grassroots hut in the boondocks, primitive, poor, and without amenities, and suffered dysentery and other intestinal diseases, your worm's-eye (often literally) view of U.S. policy will be fundamentally different from that of the affluent embassy officials in the capital city. There is no doubt that Dodd's often contrarian foreign policy views were importantly shaped by his earlier Peace Corps experience.

I loved it up there in the Peace Corps training camps of Puerto Rico, which were so successful that the Peace Corps soon had two of them going, Camp Crozier and Camp Radley. For one thing, I still shared some of the same Kennedyesque, youthful idealism as the volunteers. For another, my experience in the DR and Central America had convinced me that grassroots development of the sort the Peace Corps advocated got better results than did grandiose projects emanating from the capital city. For a third, I loved the fresh, clean air, the lush, green, tropical vegetation, and the spectacular mountain views of that area of Puerto Rico. Finally, I was at twenty-three or twenty-four (when I first went to the camps), about the same age as the volunteers, and thus could closely identify with their dreams and ambitions. Actually, it was more complex than that: while I was the same age as they, I was more advanced than they in educational background and already more experienced in Latin America; and as their teacher they looked up to me as a role model—always a nice position to be in.

Almost alone among the outside teachers brought in, I would get up with the volunteers at the crack of dawn (when the Puerto Rican cocks crowed), do early morning calisthenics with them, and also go on their early morning runs, which were often grueling on those steep, interior mountain roads. I would eat with the volunteers in the mess hall, meet with them personally and individually, and try to give them honest answers about what they could expect when they "shipped out" to the DR. They appreciated that I did all these things with them, operated at their level and was not condescending, and gave them honest, if not always easy and comfortable, (especially about the U.S. role) answers. At night, by then exhausted from a terribly long day, we would go out for a beer and occasionally, on weekends, dancing together. I had great rapport with the students; and because the Peace Corps administrators liked what I did, they kept inviting me back.

After calisthenics, the early morning run, and breakfast, the volunteers would have three or four hours <u>daily</u> of language classes. Language training was considered the most important part of the curriculum, which is why they did that early while the students were still fresh. After lunch and a brief "<u>siesta</u>," it was my turn to hold forth on "area studies" and "country studies," which consisted in my case of the history, sociology, and politics of the DR. These consisted of two, two-hour sessions with a short break in between. In each session I would lecture for an hour and then have Q-and-A for an hour. That meant ten sessions of two hours each in one week. Two sessions of two hours each in the hot, afternoon, Puerto Rican sun (no air conditioning, remember) was grueling. At the end of the day I was drained, pale, exhausted. Teaching is hard work and tiring; you're "on stage" all the time. A quick shower (also outdoors!) and dinner revived my flagging spirits. After dinner the volunteers would have another program, an informative film or maybe a session on disease and health care; about 8:30 as it got dark we would go up to Tomasito's for a beer.

That is a story in itself—and a lesson in how the Peace Corps could be an instrument of ruin as well as good. For a long time Tomasito (no one knew his last name) had run a small <u>colmado</u> (a little shack where he sold an occasional cigarette, candy, or can of soup) on the hill above the camp. Then the Peace Corps came in and the volunteers began going up there at night for a beer. Tomasito began to grow wealthy, by neighborhood standards, and also greedy and ambitious. One night his house burned down—as I recall, with his mother-in-law in it—set by Tomasito himself, it was said, in order to collect the insurance and build a bigger house. He also started drinking up his profits and would be quite drunk by the time the volunteers arrived in the evening. Eventually the volunteers started frequenting another bar farther down the road which had a juke box and a dance floor. They also built a community center for the town there. Abandoned by the Peace Corps, eventually Tomasito, now a ruined drunk, regressed back to his earlier existence as a small-time seller of occasional cigarettes and candy.

While the camps in Puerto Rico became the main locus of Peace Corps training programs, they were not the only places where training was done. The Peace Corps continued to utilize U.S. university centers as well, such as Florida, Kansas State, Arizona State, and the University of California at San Diego, which had empty classrooms and dormitories in the summer and were happy to rent their facilities to the Peace Corps. I recall teaching in two programs in Kansas State University, in Manhattan ("the little apple"), Kansas, where the summer temperature must have been 110 degrees in the shade, where the artesian-well-fed local swimming pool was a godsend at the end of the day, and where the pillow in our (again non-AC) dormitory room at the end of the day was still warmer than our body temperature—a weird feeling if you're not used to it.

On another occasion, when the Peace Corps was training a group of volunteers for urban community development, it rented facilities in Mayaguez, Puerto Rico, at the university there, on the far western end of the island. That way the training had the advantages of an urban setting, but still in the context of a Latin culture and a Spanish-speaking location. On this occasion we teachers were put up in the comparative luxury of a downtown hotel, the Mélia, while the volunteers were housed in a university dormitory. But we still did our daily calisthenics and distance run around the city, attracting gaping stares because in the 1960s in traditional Puerto Rico (or anywhere else in Latin America), only thieves would ever be seen running anywhere, not "people of substance." The trip to Mayaguez also enabled us to see more of Puerto Rico because on the trip out there I took the northern coastal route and on the way back went the southern coastal route, through Ponce, around the eastern side, and eventually back to San Juan, thus completing the circle of the entire island.

Every time I participated in one of these Peace Corps training programs, I used the opportunity of access to the official files to do a study of the social background of the volunteers. This was some of the first serious social science studies that I had ever done.[1] The studies were published in the Peace Corps newsletter of the Dominican Republic, called Polymagma. Later on, when I applied for my first academic jobs, I'm sure these publications listed on my curriculum vitae helped get me the job since, to my academic colleagues, the name of the publication sounded serious and prestigious. Little did they know that Polymagma is actually the name of the medicine that the Peace Corps recommends for diarrhea.

The studies I did, however, were serious studies and revealed interesting things about the volunteers. Most of the training groups numbered about forty volunteers. Of these, I discovered, everyone had gone to college; 90 percent were graduates; several had advanced degrees. Almost all of them had language training before joining the Peace Corps; about half had lived or traveled extensively abroad. Three-quarters of the trainees in these early programs were men; 90 percent were between twenty and twenty-five. Almost all, besides being talented and able, had special skills that would be useful in a developing country, as lathe operators, carpenters, truck drivers, specialists in farm equipment repair, surveying, tree surgery, fisheries, nursing, market research, cement work, accounting, forestry. Eager to learn and to help abroad, these were among the best students I have ever worked with—always intensely interested in the course material (not true of all my later college students) because this would literally be life-and-death for them for the next few years.

The makeup of the groups changed over the years. More women joined the program. At some points teaching skills were valued; at others, practical work experience. The age of the volunteers also fluctuated: at some periods the Peace Corps favored older, more mature members with extensive work experience; at others, it recruited eager, enthusiastic, young people directly out of college.

The Dominican case was especially complicated because, while I was doing these training programs, the country experienced a bloody revolution that resulted in a U.S. military intervention.[2] A large percentage of the volunteers thought the U.S. intervention was mistaken, self-defeating, and wrong; that was my own publicly stated position as well. Some of the volunteers demonstrated against the intervention, and the issue became very political and very controversial. Then, after the revolution, the Peace Corps had to rebuild its contingent in the DR because many volunteers had resigned or been shipped out to remove them from any possible danger. These events made our training program in Puerto Rico even more intense.

The director of the Peace Corps camps in Puerto Rico when I was there was Richard Hopkins, who later switched over to pursue a career at AID. Increasingly, as the Peace Corps matured, it hired former volunteers as administrative staff. Many of these were still quite young but had the advantage of language and culture skills that people from the outside didn't have. Hopkins and the other administrators often went out with the teachers and volunteers for a beer at Tomasito's at the end of the day.

We also worked closely with the country directors. For the Dominican Republic in my days there that meant Andy Hernández, Robert Sattin, and B. J. Warren. I liked and was close to all of them. We coordinated plans, guest speakers, and syllabi. It was useful to me to know what they thought it best to cover in the training program and, at the same time, they often profited from sitting in on my classes. We often went back and forth between Puerto Rico and the DR—only a half-hour flight.

These Peace Corps contacts proved tremendously useful to me in 1964-65 when I went back to the DR to do research for my doctoral dissertation. For one thing, country director Sattin, probably illegally, allowed me to use Peace Corps jeeps when I needed to go into the countryside to do research, but we covered this by saying I was meeting with the volunteers. For a second, having worked with and trained a succession of six or seven groups, most of whom were now deployed in-country, I had a rich network of contacts all over the country. It meant that wherever I went in the DR, in whatever little rural town, there was usually a Peace Corps volunteer there who knew me, where I could stay, and from whom I could find out about the local power structure. Third, there was one time while working in the DR that I was given a mistaken and potentially life-threatening inoculation, and as a Peace Corps "employee" I was able immediately to see the knowledgeable, young Peace Corps doctor who probably saved my life.

The director of the Peace Corps in these early years was Sargent Shriver, JFK's brother-in-law. He was an impressive, roll-up-the-sleeves-and-get-busy, hands-on administrator. He liked to get out of Washington and visit the training camps in Puerto Rico. I met him there and he, Hopkins, and I went out for a beer at night—at Tomasito's, of course. Shriver had apparently heard of my work in energetically and enthusiastically training the volunteers and on the spot offered me a job as assistant country director. This was my second major job offer, the first being with CARE. I think I was twenty-three or at most twenty-four at the time. An assistant country director job at twenty-three or twenty-four almost certainly would have meant a full country director job at twenty-five or twenty-six. Wow! Talk about a fast track! But the Peace Corps was a new and innovative agency, non- and even anti-bureaucratic, and you could rise fast in those days.

However, I decided to turn Shriver and the Peace Corps down. At that moment I was ABD, wanted to complete my dissertation and get the Ph.D., and had a Fulbright-Hays award to spend a year in the DR to do the dissertation research. I've never regretted the decision made, but it sure was flattering to be asked.

NOTES

1. I have been able to find three of the articles I wrote about the Peace Corps volunteers, though there may have been more. These were published as "The Background of Peace Corps Volunteers: DR XIII Trains in Puerto Rico," Polymagma, II (April 8, 1965), 4-6; "After the Dominican Revolution: Rebuilding the Peace Corps Contingent," Polymagma II (May 1965), 1ff; "The Peace Corps and the Dominican Revolution: The Perspective of the Trainees," Polymagma, II (August 1965), 1-2.

2. My opus magnus on this period is Dictatorship. Development. and Disintegration: Politics and Social Change in the Dominican Republic (Ann Arbor, MI: Xerox University Microfilms Monograph Series, for the Center for Latin American Studies, University of Massachusetts, 1975), 3 vols.

CHAPTER 4

THE DOMINICAN REPUBLIC AND THE DOMINICAN REVOLUTION—1964–65*

In the fall of 1963 I had finished my Ph.D. comprehensive examinations and begun work on my doctoral dissertation. My M.A. thesis had dealt with the methods of control in the dictator Trujillo's Dominican Republic; now for the Ph.D. dissertation I proposed to study the transition to democracy and the emergence of a more pluralist group structure in the post-Trujillo period. Mine was to be a study of the transition from authoritarianism to pluralism and how civil society and new groups and social movements emerge from the shadow of dictatorship. There would be chapters on the armed forces, the church, the oligarchy, political parties, labor unions, the media, peasant groups, and, not least, the U.S. Embassy. For, in contrast to next-door Cuba, the White House had determined to make the Dominican Republic an example of democratic development and thus a model of President Kennedy's recently approved Alliance for Progress.

My plan was to exhaust the materials in the rich University of Florida library before going on to do the field research under my Fulbright-Hays grant in the Dominican Republic. The work involved about four months of archival research as well as pouring through daily microfilms of the major Dominican newspapers. In this research Dr. Irene Zimmerman, Ms. Susan Hodgkins, and Mr. Ray Jones of the University library's reference staff were enormously helpful. Zimmerman was then, along with Nettie Lee Benson of the University of Texas, one of only

---

* An earlier, more institutionally or university-focused version of this chapter appeared in Howard J. Wiarda, <u>Universities. Think Tanks. and War Colleges</u> (Philadelphia: X Libris for the Washington Center for International Politics, 1999).

75

two librarians with a Ph.D. in the entire country specializing on Latin America; Hodgkins got her degree under Zimmerman at Florida and then went on to head the Latin America collection at the University of Wisconsin. All this archival research, especially the microfilm reading machine, wreaked havoc with my eyes; with new glasses it was revealing to recognize again that trees consisted of individual leaves rather than just a large green mass.

During this same period, my love life had taken a more serious turn. While at Florida I had dated several women from the Latin American Studies Program as well as others from other departments, meanwhile continuing to see some old flames from Michigan over holidays when I returned home. The community of graduate students at Florida, as at other universities, is a fairly small and close-knit (mainly commiserating over heavy course and exam requirements) group with the result that everyone knows everyone else and everyone else's business. It is somewhat like Latin America in this regard: strongly interpersonal. In this context it is impossible to keep secrets for very long. The problem was infinitely compounded since two of the women I was dating shared the same apartment.

There are wonderful places around Gainesville to take a date: Saint Augustine (the oldest city in the U.S.), Daytona Beach, Cross Creek (where Marjorie Kennan Rawlings wrote The Yearling), Ocala for the horse farms and springs, Sebring for the Gran Prix races, and my favorite, Cedar Key, on the Gulf of Mexico side, which had a wonderful old, New Orleans-style hotel where the state legislators from Tallahassee took their girlfriends and which served an absolutely marvelous heart-of-palm salad along with always-fresh seafood. Our other favorite social hangout in Gainesville was around the swimming pool of the University Inn just south of town (across the street from my apartment): the manager there, who was a close friend and fellow grad student, saw the advantages for enticing customers of having a core of young people (no undergraduates!) lounging in his pool area. I brought books along and spent many days by that pool studying for comprehensives; I also enjoyed the company of Lisa Lovlie and Jacqui Goldman, graduate students in the Psychology Department, who were platonic buddies of mine around the pool and, occasionally, after hours.

In the spring of 1963 I had been dating Maria Rosa Uría Santos, a history graduate student from La Coruña, Spain. She was bright, attractive, petite, shy, Catholic, conservative, and, I thought, a little naive. But as a conservative Spaniard from dictator Franco's home town, she thought my political idealism in favor of Latin American democracy and development was naive. We went out frequently, enjoyed each other's company, and I took it upon myself to introduce this very Catholic and traditionalist Spanish girl to the joys and rigors of American bars, football games, parties, and dating. But while I dated Maria Rosa, I had also become intrigued with her roommate.

Iêda de Barros Siqueira was widely thought by our fellow graduate students to be (along with future Senator John East) the smartest person in the Political Science Department. She had been born in Belo Horizonte, Minas Gerais, Brazil, into a Protestant (Methodist) family; her father was a school principal and her mother had come from a well-to-do family that was part of the panelinha (patronage network) of President Juscelino Kubitshek. In Minas she had received one of the highest scores in the state on the medical school entrance exam but had given up her medical school position when she won a nationwide competition for a Department of State exchange fellowship to study in the United States. As an undergraduate in the U.S., she had compiled a near-perfect, almost all-A grade point average—except for one course in phys ed which she loathed and refused to attend. Wishing to be self-supporting, she had chosen to attend the University of Florida because it was the only graduate school that offered her a complete free ride: assistantship, tuition waiver, books, everything.

I had not gotten to know Iêda at all well the first two years in graduate school. First, she was a year ahead of me; second, she was majoring in Political Science while I had initially enrolled in Latin American studies and History; and third, even after I switched to Political Science, she had concentrated in American Politics and Public Administration while I was in the Comparative Politics and International Relations fields. We never had a course or seminar together. She was cute and perky, but I was especially intrigued by her being thought of as the smartest graduate student in Political Science. Since I also, with no sense of modesty, aspired to that lofty position, I had to find out more about this person and what made her tick. Plus in our occasional early meetings she was always cool, aloof, very professional, and obviously unimpressed by my attempts to be charming. So Iêda became a challenge, a project, more attractive precisely because she was so coolly aloof, distant, and, seemingly, unattainable. One day I gathered my courage and asked her out; to my surprise, she accepted.

A key problem was that Iêda and Maria Rosa were sharing an apartment, and I was at the time still dating Maria Rosa. There is a wonderfully comic Jerry Seinfeld show with which I later identified, entitled "The Switch," where this complicated dating procedure is hashed out. Jerry too wanted to change girlfriends, a move complicated by the fact the two women involved were roommates. So he and sidekick George Costanza talk it over, try every angle, explore every technique, and finally conclude that The Switch "can't be done!"

There is <u>no</u> smooth way that a dating switch can occur from one roommate to the other without lots of ill feelings, recriminations, bad relations, and conflict both between the roommates and between one <u>or both</u> of them and the person trying to pull off The Switch. This show was so close to my situation then as to be uncanny.

I do not know and do not want to know all that transpired between the two women; I do know that, as I continued to see Iêda, there was a falling-out between them, nasty words were exchanged, and Iêda eventually moved to a separate apartment. I continued to see her regularly; we spent a lot of time together. Meanwhile the person that I thought to be so cool and aloof turned out on closer acquaintance to be warm, friendly, nice, kind, and very personable. Eventually, I met her only family in the U.S.: a brother who was a neurosurgeon in Chicago and his wife; I brought her to Grand Rapids to meet my folks. Meantime, Iêda had managed to expand her fields to include Comparative Politics; she passed her comprehensives with flying colors and went off to Venezuela to write her Ph.D. dissertation. Being separated like this was no fun and so we determined to do something about it. During an interval between trips (Venezuela for her; Puerto Rico and the Dominican Republic for me on one of my excursions for the Peace Corps) we were married in a small, private ceremony.

We spent our honeymoon in New Smyrna Beach, a (then) lovely little town on the Atlantic Ocean just south of Daytona. It was a wonderful spot, clean, not yet built up, few tourists, right on the beach, marvelous seafood, and with an unspoiled nature preserve along the coast that stretched almost as far south as Cape Canaveral. We spent several weeks there with both of us working on our dissertations; we were young and in love and, at least on my part, unconcerned about our uncertain future even though neither of us had much money. Afrer the honeymoon we moved from New Smyrna to Coral Gables in Miami while we (naively) awaited a work visa from the Dominican government (under the Fulbright award, that's what I thought was required) so I could do the research for my dissertation. While there we explored Miami, Fort Lauderdale, Palm Beach, and the Everglades. The Dominican consul assured me every day that the visa would come "mañana," but it never came. It turned out that applying for a work visa was very complicated—especially since my "work" consisted of research on the Dominican Republic itself. Eventually tiring of the wait and despairing that the visa would ever come through, we booked airline passage anyway on the basis of a ninety-day tourist visa, assuming it could easily be renewed for a longer time once we were there. We then left for "the DR" (as everyone called it); the time was early 1964.

In the DR

The Dominican Republic in 1964 had few facilities available for international visitors or for scholars who wished to stay there on a year-long basis. No flats, no rental agencies, no used furniture, no tag sales, no nada. Upon arrival, we checked into a downtown hotel, the Comercial where I had stayed on my earlier visit with Kantor but which we could not afford for more than a couple of days. Next stop was a dingy pensión, the Europa, which would have been OK temporarily when I was a single, junketeering graduate student; but now I had a wife and responsibilities and I could not let Iêda stay in this place, which was pretty grimy and where the soup got thinner and thinner on a daily basis. Immediately we began combing the want-ads of the main newspaper El Caribe for vacant apartment announcements but there were very few listed and none of them was furnished. Plus, the Dominican Republic is a traditional, personalistic, family and clan-based society; things there do not often work on the basis of impersonal ads in the newspapers.

Finally, afrer a week of searching which largely consisted of spinning our wheels, we got lucky. We located an apartment on Jose Reyes #24, right in the center of old Santo Domingo, two blocks from the ocean, in the historic colonial section. It was the former maid's quarters on the top floor of the house of one of the Dominican Republic's elite families. The houses of aristocratic families in that neighborhood were generally three stories tall. The first floor consisted of a family calling room and, if the family member was a professional as this one was, an office and reception area. The second floor contained the family living area and bedrooms. But the third floor, up a spectacular but precarious spiral steel stairway, was the maid's quarters. Few Dominican families could afford live-in maids anymore so this upper floor had been converted into an apartment.

The apartment had a living room, a bath, a bedroom, and a kitchen. It was sparsely furnished, but we bought some things and culled others from our landlady who lived downstairs. Its best features were two open patios in back designed to give the (former) maid ample room to wash and dry clothes, and a large patio in front which overlooked the old city as well as the entrance to the Santo Domingo harbor. Iêda and I would sit out on our front patio at the end of the day, have a drink of the local rum (less than $1.00 per bottle) mixed with lemon and quinine, and watch the ships come into port. Frequently there was a political demonstration at the end of the day along the main street of El Conde which we could also observe from the safety of our patio. Because it was on the third floor and open, we always had a breeze, which was not only refreshing in the warm climate but also kept the mosquitoes away. Only once did this prove disadvantageous: in the late summer a tropical hurricane passed just south of the island and we spent a sleepless night listening to the howling wind and trying to keep the doors and windows (no screens or glass; all open-air) from crashing in.

The owner of the house was Doña Ernestina Mejía-Ricart. Her husband, Gustavo Adolfo, had been a prominent university professor, a lawyer, and a politician and government official; but Doña Ernestina had recently been widowed, had invited her husband's sister to share the house with her, and had decided to rent the third floor. Doña Ernestina was also a university graduate, a lawyer, and had been president of the Dominican Federation of Women; she was well educated, politically connected, and very gracious and nice. They had three children who no longer lived at home and were all prominent: Marcio, a university professor, businessman of uncertain means, and leftist leader of an undefined Marxist persuasion; Tirso, a university professor of psychology and much more pleasant and politically more moderate (a PRD member) than his older brother; and Magda, a former beauty queen who married a Puerto Rican businessman and later became head of the Dominican Feminist Association. I'm sure the two brothers believed I was a CIA agent but they were also, in the Dominican tradition, unfailingly polite, cordial, and very useful in getting me access to sources for interviews. Marcio took us swimming with his family out at Boca Chica, while Tirso introduced me to all the University student leaders. The mother, Doña Ernestina, was a gem, treating us like her own children, taking us under her wings, cashing checks for us (she wanted the dollars to visit her daughter in Puerto Rico), and doing numerous things to make our life in a foreign country easier and more comfortable. She admired America, thought Americans were honest and trustworthy, and came to consider us as members of her family.

We quickly settled into a research routine. In the mornings Iêda and I would take a público, or jitney, out Independence Avenue (then a two-way street) to the corner where the Hotel Hispaniola was located. There we would disembark and walk four blocks to the Archivo General de la Nación. The Archivo had a superb Trujillo collection because the old dictator made sure all materials published in the Dominican Republic during his reign were deposited there. Its holdings on the post-Trujillo era were more irregular, but it had political party, military, and trade union publications unavailable anywhere else that were very useful to my research. The Archivo also had Venezuela materials useful for Iêda's dissertation. The Archivo was headed by Virgilio Alfau Duran and Julio J. Julia, its subdirector. Both were historians (there was no political science then in the

Dominican Republic) and very helpful in locating material for us. Indeed, they were flattered by the fact we were interested in their obscure country (and the only persons using the Archivo) and went out of the way to be helpful. The Archivo was open from 8:30 to 1:30 and we were usually there when the doors opened; at midmorning, Iêda and I would go outside to have a coffee and delicious <u>pastel</u> (snack) that was sold on the streets.

At 1:30 we would head back to our apartment for a light lunch. Iêda would often take a nap after lunch while I used the <u>siesta</u> period to write up my notes in detail. At 4:00, when the heat of the day subsided and the siesta was over, I would visit party offices, labor unions, peasant organizations, etc., for interviews. The interviews were open-ended, meant to solicit information and to supplement the often incomplete materials from the archival research. Most party, labor, and other officials whom I wished to interview worked at other jobs during the day so the only time I could see them in their party and political roles was late in the afternoon or early evening. Frequently Iêda and I would end the afternoon with a dish of ice cream (coconut, mango-flavors then unavailable in the U.S.) in one of the coffee houses along <u>El Conde</u>, each one of which had a different political orientation and from which almost daily political demonstrations, strikes, and parades were launched.

My research on the Dominican Republic was aided by several groups and individuals who helped give me access that few foreigners would ever enjoy. First, there was the Harry Kantor-Juan Bosch-PRD connection from our earlier visit in 1962 which gave me instant access to the leadership of the largest party in the country and to other parties as well. Second, while in Gainesville, I had been the host for a touring group of Dominican journalists that the United States Information Agency had brought to the U.S.; now back in the DR these journalists—including Virgilio Alcántara, Rafael Herrera, Rhadames Gómez, and others who later became prominent editors—were enormously helpful when I looked them up in filling me in on how things worked in their country and even brought me along as they covered the armed forces, the president, and other institutions. Third, Tomás Pastoriza and Luís Crouch, who had hosted us on my earlier visit with Kantor, provided access to the elite business community. Fourth, the Peace Corps volunteers whom I had helped train in Puerto Rico were now in-country; that meant that in virtually every small town in the DR I had a point of access, a place to stay, and a great source of information. Fifth, Malcolm McLean, the USIA director, was very helpful in setting up interviews through his vast rolodex and in putting the books of his Lincoln Library and even some secretarial services at our disposal. I found the rest of the U.S. Embassy both less well informed and less helpful—until they found out that we had access and information that they lacked. But following Kantor's advice, I was leery of getting too close to the Embassy.

There were a lot of strange, interesting characters in Santo Domingo in those days, and we met most of them. The only "supermarket" in the country then, "Wimpy's," was owned by Lorenzo Barry, an American (former pilot) with a Dominican wife; he had been part of the U.S. sponsored plot to assassinate dictator Trujillo. So while Iêda shopped for canned soup and other American "luxuries," I cornered Barry to interview him about the Trujillo plot and his CIA connections. Another character was our old "friend" Sasha Volman, the Romanian-born, U.S. citizen who worked for the PRD as well as the CIA. Volman was still director of the school to train peasant, party, and union leaders; he was also the liaison between Bosch, the PRD, and the U.S. government. Volman fancied himself a ladies' man and took me out to nightclubs a couple of times. We met John Westbrook who was doing research on agrarian reform, and Wolf Grabbendorf, a German party official and social-democrat (Friedrich Ebert Foundation) who was trying to increase German influence in the country.

For nearly a week I ushered around Evron Kirkpatrick, then executive director of the American Political Science Association, and his colleague George Demetriou, who headed the Institute for the Comparative Study of Political Systems. Kirk and Demetriou were interested in meeting political party leaders and government officials, and they asked me to help arrange interviews for them. The Dominican Republic had twenty-odd parties at that time and I was sure my visitors would be bored meeting them all, but I underestimated Kirk who liked nothing better than to talk politics and elections. I have never seen a man who was happier swapping political stories and "lore" than Kirk; he spent at least three days doing nothing but talking politics with party leaders. He and Demetriou also wanted to publish a small, edited volume (part of a series) on Dominican political parties and election statistics, and they asked me to collaborate in preparing the volume. This was my first consultantship and I remember discussing with Iêda if she thought $25.00 a <u>day</u> was too much to charge for this service. Later on we discovered the Institute received funding from the CIA. Kirk later recruited me and became a colleague at the Washington-based American Enterprise Institute (AEI), a leading think tank.

Various congressmen came junketeering through Santo Domingo and I was sometimes asked by the U.S. Embassy to brief them and usher them around. A particular pain was Congressman Daniel Flood of the House Armed Services Committee who thought there were "commies" under every piece of coral and who made outrageous requests to the Embassy for entertainment and personal services. The funniest episode involved then-Congressman Thomas P. ("Tip") O'Neill who got involved in a scandal over campaign funds with a Korean businessman, Tong Sun Park (dubbed "Koreagate") and his bosomy American girlfriend. When the House panel investigating the scandal tried to get Park and the bosomy girlfriend to testify, they "disappeared" for a couple of weeks to a beach resort in the Dominican Republic. But the girlfriend, not too bright, gave the game away by agreeing to pose cheesecake-style for Dominican tabloids, and her revealing pictures were plastered all over Dominican newsstands.

Iêda and I were poor but very happy during our time in the Dominican Republic. For us the DR was an extended honeymoon, what is commonly called a Victorian honeymoon, a chance to discover and learn about each other. Our hosts, the Dominican people, were very kind, helpful, and generous. At the local open-air <u>mercado</u> where Iêda went to shop and I carried the grocery bags, vendors always gave us extra meat, free lemons, and extra vegetables because they knew we had little money but we were viewed as <u>simpático</u>. People went out of their way to be helpful to us. We took tours to virtually every corner of the country, often traveling by Peace Corps jeep (probably illegal) and public car. We visited a variety of places that Kantor and I had not gotten to on our earlier trip, including La Romana and Higuey in the east, Samaná Bay, more of the north coast, and a return trip out to the Haitian border. People were flattered that we were interested in their country and their stories, they had never been interviewed before, and they simply poured out their tales of woe as well as of hope—all of which provided more background lore and information for my dissertation. Meanwhile, Iêda had continued to work on her Venezuela dissertation. The DR was a research experience never to be forgotten—or repeated.

While living in the Dominican Republic during this period, we received an offer from Kansas State University in Manhattan to help train new groups of Peace Corps volunteers heading for the DR and for Guatemala. The pay was good and sorely needed, the Peace Corps would pay our transportation, and it was a good opportunity to renew our ninety-day tourist visas. So we flew to Miami, retrieved the car we had stored there, and headed for Kansas. En route, however, a truck clipped our bumper and we rolled over, doing great damage to the car but leaving us unhurt but severely shaken. It was the seatbelts that saved our lives. The driver of the truck never slowed down, never stopped to see if we were OK. After doing a complete rollover, the car landed on its wheels with the engine still running. It looked a mess, the body totaled, but it was still serviceable.

That night we limped into Tuscaloosa, Alabama. Living in Santo Domingo, we had received little U.S. news and were completely unaware of the civil rights protests and the violence—except for the occasional pictures published in Dominican papers of police dogs snapping at civil rights demonstrators—now stirring in the summer of 1964 throughout the South, especially Alabama. Tuscaloosa would provide our first hints as to how much American society was changing.

By sheer coincidence, the day before we arrived actor Jack Palance had just integrated the only movie theater in Tuscaloosa, the BAMA. The city was very tense and there we were—not knowing any of this—with a wrecked car, Michigan license plates, a Yankee accent, and a foreign-born wife. I'm sure we were considered carpetbaggers, interlopers, and worse. No one would wait on us in the restaurant and the motel would not accept our check (no one had credit cards in those days). So we were stranded in a hostile and, I thought, dangerous city and could not leave until I had personally gone to a local bank and paid for a long-distance call to my bank in Gainesville to assure the bank that I had sufficient funds to cover the check. We were then able to pay our motel bill and we left town immediately. We were frightened and never so glad to leave a place—although in later years I returned frequently to Tuscaloosa to lecture at the University of Alabama and to visit our son who was a student there for a time. Tuscaloosa has changed a lot since this early and unhappy visit.

The rest of the trip was uneventful—except for the heat in Kansas in the summer. The Peace Corps Volunteers were nice kids and both of us enjoyed working with them as well as with Andres Hernández, the Peace Corps director. Our big treat at the end of the day was a swim in the municipal pool in Manhattan which was fed by cool, refreshing water from artesian wells. We stayed in unair-conditioned student dorms; even at bedtime, the pillow was still hotter than one's body temperature, which is a weird feeling. After two weeks in Kansas we headed back to Santo Domingo, happy to be back in what we now considered our "home": our little apartment up in the third floor maid's quarters.

After living in the DR for several months, going to the Archivo every day, and gathering reams of information, I decided in the late fall that I had enough materials to begin the actual writing of the dissertation. That way, if I found gaps in the information, I could quickly return to my sources to fill them in. So instead of riding daily out to the Archivo, I now began staying in the apartment and writing. I already had all my notes organized into chapter folders and several chapters in first-draft form based on seminar papers I had written back in Gainesville; now I did a detailed written outline for each chapter and put all the notecards and materials into the order in which I wished to use them. That way, with everything organized, the writing would flow easily; and, as a former journalist, I was already trained to write fast and easily. I sat at that writing table ten to twelve hours per day for the next twelve weeks; sometimes I would produce twenty pages a day but the usual output was twelve to fifteen. I averaged one chapter per week in a prodigious explosion of writing. I had to sit on the chair with my legs under my body on the chair because otherwise the mosquitoes under the table would attack them—a position I still sometimes find myself in for writing purposes even today. In midmorning and midafternoon Iêda would bring me a cookie and a glass of iced V-8—very expensive because it was imported but a refreshing lifesaver and pick-me-up during these intense days. At night we would still go out for coffee, ice cream, or for additional interviews. By the time we left the DR in 1965, I would have a complete first draft of the dissertation.

Quite a number of academic visitors came through Santo Domingo in those days and we met most of them. Malcolm McLean introduced me to Abraham Lowenthal from Harvard who had good connections in the U.S. Embassy and the Dominican business community; Abe and I would be friends, occasional colleagues and collaborators, and sometimes rivals in various capacities for the next thirty years. Robert Packenham from Yale was also our guest for drinks one night: he was on his way to Brazil to do a doctoral dissertation, but he spoke no Portuguese and still had no idea what he would write about. Meeting for the first time these supposedly high achievement types from Harvard and Yale led Iêda and me to conclude that at Florida we had received far better training certainly in Latin America and perhaps in Political Science than they had at their prestige institutions.

There were numerous U.S. Embassy functions and junketeering Washington high mucky-mucks, most of whom were forgettable. One memorable event occurred the night of the 1964 U.S. elections when the Embassy invited several scores of Dominicans to the Dominican-American Cultural Institute to observe "democracy in action"—actually most of the Dominicans there were already plotting against their own government and much preferred nonelectoral routes to power. Several American congressmen also came through, visiting the sunny Caribbean in midwinter but always announcing they were on "fact-finding missions." Many of the visitors we met were technical consultants brought in by AID, experts in particular fields, knowing nothing about the DR, but often determined to impose their U.S.-modeled solutions on the hapless Dominicans, whether they were appropriate and relevant there or not. It is out of these experiences that some of my early writings on ethnocentrism would come.[1]

Some of the Embassy types we had spotted as CIA operatives. For example, the Embassy had two political sections, one of which was CIA; the labor attaché, Fred Sommerford, who helped ruin the Dominican labor movement and was later killed while sitting in his car under mysterious but never-explained circumstances, was also CIA; and Volman seemed to be present everywhere. Among both civilian and military officials attached to the Embassy, I found, in general with only a couple of exceptions (like McLean, and even he would later prove disappointing), an appalling lack of knowledge about the Dominican Republic, widespread inability to function in Spanish, very little interest in or empathy for the country where they were stationed, and a pervasive inability to see things other than through U.S. perceptions.

The Dominican political situation had begun to heat up again in the fall of 1964, and we found ourselves both observers of and eventually participants in that process. Recall, Trujillo had been assassinated in 1961; a series of interim governments followed; elections were held in December 1962; and Juan Bosch and the Dominican Revolutionary Party had won an overwhelming, two-to-one victory. But Bosch had been overthrown in September 1963 after only seven months in office by a combination of business, church, and military groups; I was just in the process of documenting all of this in my dissertation. Hence, by the time Iêda and I got there in early 1964, the Dominican Republic was governed by a three-man junta, headed by Donald ("Donnie") Reid Cabral, a former used-car salesman, although the real power behind the throne was the military. I met and interviewed Reid on two occasions.

The political system after the coup ousting Bosch was becoming more repressive, authoritarian, and corrupt. Bosch had been exiled to Puerto Rico where I had interviewed him while on one of my stints for the Peace Corps a few months earlier. The democratic political parties, labor unions, and peasant groups that had once seemed so promising and were the focus of my dissertation were now being suppressed through the use of strong-arm techniques. The PRD and its affiliated labor and peasant arms which constituted the major threat to the status quo—not the small left-wing groups—were particular targets of the repression. Donald Reid, not corrupt himself but weak and unable to control the corrupt military and police, was seeking to perpetuate his rule by holding elections from which the PRD would be excluded. The U.S. Embassy which had earlier grown disillusioned with Bosch was quietly backing Reid and his plans for continuismo.

I wrote a sharp report back to my mentor Kantor about all this. I documented the repression and corruption. The report, which was required as part of my Fulbright-Hayes grant, focused particularly on the armed forces who were bringing in military air transports full of goods duty-free (in contrast to other importers who had to pay high tariffs) through their PXs which they were then selling on the black market. The police had gone so far as to <u>incorporate</u> their contraband (including big-ticket items like appliances and automobiles) activities, as the National Police Company, Incorporated. I dramatically entitled my report "Trujilloism without Trujillo." Kantor liked the report and, without asking my permission, sent it to the <u>New Republic</u> which published it.[2] It was then translated into Spanish and published throughout Latin America. Eventually it was republished in the Dominican press and caused a considerable stir. I began to worry that the police might come looking for me and so made copies of all my research notes. As I wrote chapters of my dissertation, I also made copies of those, sending one by ordinary mail to my father in the U.S. and prevailing upon McLean to send another copy out through the diplomatic pouch. <u>All</u> of these copies arrived safely and I never had any trouble from the Dominican police, but for a time we ran scared.

I did receive trouble from an unexpected source, the U.S. Embassy. After my "Trujilloism without Trujillo" article appeared, I got a call from the ambassador's office: would I meet with the ambassador the next day. The U.S. ambassador then, succeeding John Bartlow Martin, was W. Tapley Bennett, a courtly Georgian and a career officer who would later request U.S. military intervention in the DR. Bennett wasted little time on amenities. He attempted to persuade me that Reid was a good man, worthy of U.S. support. I replied that might be true but that the Embassy could not expect to establish a stable government by getting too close to an unelected, undemocratic regime widely viewed as illegitimate by excluding the largest group in the country, the PRD, from the political process.

Then came the bombshell: "Aren't you here on a U.S. government fellowship?" the ambassador asked. Yes, I was there on a Fulbright-Hayes grant. The obvious implication of the ambassador's not-very-subtle question was that, unless I shut up, my fellowship would be withdrawn and I would have to leave the country. He did ask explicitly that I refrain from writing anything further for publication until I left the Dominican Republic. Had I known then what I know now or been a more experienced and established scholar I would have gotten on my high horse and denounced the ambassador for this attempt at censorship and suppressing free speech. But I was a lowly graduate student then and in no position to argue, plus losing the fellowship since we had no other source of income would have been a financial disaster for Iêda and me. Twenty years later, in Washington, probably long after he had forgotten me or this incident, I would again become a social acquaintance of Tap Bennett and see him frequently at receptions, the Council on Foreign Relations, and think tank gatherings. But I have never forgotten this incident nor his actions during the Dominican Revolution.

In the fall and winter of 1964, while Reid was campaigning to perpetuate his rule, the PRD was also quietly rebuilding its grass roots support. This was a tricky matter because the PRD main leadership was still in exile, many of the Party's activities were proscribed, and its labor and peasant groups were still experiencing repression. But precisely because of the now-widespread repression and corruption, the PRD, which prided itself on its honesty and commitment to democracy, was more popular than ever. It was popular no longer just among the lower classes but now among professionals, intellectuals, and even businessmen. Many of these business leaders had earlier opposed Bosch; now, faced with severe competition from military contraband, they were concluding that maybe the scrupulously honest Bosch and the PRD were not so bad after all.

The PRD hence held a series of <u>agapes</u> (receptions) for its professional, intellectual, and business supporters. This was pretty sophisticated stuff for a mass-based party in a small, poor country. They were held in Santo Domingo's biggest and most expensive hotels and social clubs. The food was catered and delicious. It was very elegantly presented and served. Everyone who was anyone in Dominican society was there. It was a massive demonstration of PRD support among, as they called it, the "thinking classes." As a known friend of the Party and as the only outside scholar working in the Dominican Republic at that time, I was invited. A couple of representatives from the political section of the Embassy were also present—the only other Americans—who tried to pump me for information about the PRD. Having recently had my session with Bennett, I saw no reason to cooperate with the Embassy. But I did make clear to the Embassy reps what the PRD was trying to do: to demonstrate to the Dominican media, intellectuals, businessmen, the U.S. Embassy, and foreign observers (me!) that the PRD was a powerful force in Dominican affairs, that it could not be ignored in any consideration of the Dominican future, and that it would have to be included or contended with in any upcoming political scenario. This was a nice example, in Charles W. Anderson's classic statement, of how Latin American politics work, of the "demonstration of a power capability."[3]

In the winter and early spring of 1965, as I was finishing the first draft of my dissertation, there was not just the PRD campaign but several other plots, plans, and conspiracies were being contemplated in the Dominican Republic. Numerous political balls were in the air. On the one side, there was Reid, maneuvering to stay in power and to hold elections that he would win because the other leading candidates had been excluded. On the other was the PRD, hoping to restore constitutional government most likely by restoring Juan Bosch to the presidency but with some factions favoring constitutionalism without Bosch. A third major player and conspiracy involved former president (and Trujillo puppet) Joaquín Balaguer, in exile in New York but plotting his return, who had his own faction in the military to aid his comeback. Fourth was Elías Wessin y Wessin, the Air Force commander who had led the military's overthrow of Bosch and had his own agenda and ambitions. These various plans were not a case of military versus civilian; rather, each civilian faction, including the PRD, had its own faction within the military (and other sectors) with whom it overlapped. So it was one political group or patronage network versus other political groups/patronage networks, each of which had both civilian and military members and all of which were jockeying to pick up key supporters and to increase their strength.

It was my strong impression that the U.S. Embassy, supporting the Reid faction, was only vaguely aware of these other plots and of the complex maneuvering and coalition-building that was going on by the various factions. I only became fully aware of them through my Dominican journalism friends. They would take me out at night to reconnoiter the homes and hangouts of the various leading actors involved in the complex plotting. By jotting down the license numbers of the cars parked in front of the several leaders' homes, we could tell who was meeting with whom, who was involved in which factions, and who might be shifting loyalties. Sometimes after a politically tense day we would go out to the highway to see if General Wesson's tanks might be rolling in from the San Isidro Air Force base in a coup attempt. This is a far cry from party politics and elections U.S.-style. But such personal relations among the elites, patronage networks, demonstrations of violence, and constantly fluctuating factional and clan politics are at the heart of the Dominican political system.

While all this political maneuvering was fascinating, an equally fantastic event was occurring in our family: the birth late in the year of our daughter Kristy Lynn in the Dominican Republic. But even that event, as with everything Dominican in those days, had political connotations. First, our gynecologist, Asela Morell, had been as a young university student one of the founders of the Dominican Social Christian or Christian-Democratic Party; this was while Trujillo was still in power, and for her efforts she had been jailed and personally tortured by

Angelita Trujillo, the dictator's daughter. Then our pediatrician, Ligia Fernández Reid, was the widow of one of the conspirators who had assassinated Trujillo; as the secret police had closed in on Roberto Reid, rather than face torture by Trujillo's goons, he had committed suicide. She was also the sister-in-law of the president. Even Kristy's birth, in the Clínica Gómez Patiño on Avenida Independencia, was a celebrated event with its own political reverberations: the staff brought in rum and coke (instead of a tranquilizer) to put Iêda to sleep after the delivery and provided another one or two for me; they also brought in a cot so I could stay overnight. It's hard to imagine a U.S. hospital doing any of these things. The birth of a <u>Dominicana</u> also made us "half Dominican," our friends told us, cemented our relations into Dominican society, and forever endeared us to the Dominicans.

While Iêda was recuperating, it became my job for a few weeks—even while continuing to work on the dissertation—to cook, clean, and wash diapers. There were no Pampers, Huggies, or disposable diapers in Santo Domingo in those days; all the cloth diapers had to be washed by hand—my job! We bought a metal bucket and filled it with a mix of water and clorox (imported and expensive!); once a day I would scrub, rinse, and set all the diapers out to dry. But the water pressure at that time of year was usually insufficient to raise the water up to our third floor apartment, so I had to carry it up from our landlady's apartment below in old beer (<u>Presidente</u>) bottles. One day, wearing old shower tongs and carrying six bottles at once, I slipped on my landlady's newly scrubbed and still wet tile floor going around a corner too fast. As the beer bottles and I went crashing down, one of the broken bottles pierced my hand, the neck of the bottle going all the way through and protruding out the other side. Blood was gushing everywhere. Iêda helped me get to the public hospital only three or four blocks away where, still dripping blood, we sat in the emergency waiting room for hours. Finally, the doctor neatly removed the glass, sewed up my hand (I still have the scar), and gave me an anti-infection shot made of horse serum. I recovered in fine shape, but later I learned from the Peace Corps doctor that, if you're not used to that particular horse serum (I wasn't), the reaction that might set in could easily kill you. I continued to remind my daughter of this story whenever, as children do, she would ask what I had done for her lately.

This was a very exciting and at the same time highly uncertain period politically in the Dominican Republic. Unfortunately, in the midst of the complex political maneuvering, though we were sad to leave, my fellowship period in the country came to a close. We had lived there for nearly a year and enjoyed our stay immensely. But I now had a first draft of my dissertation in hand. I had learned a lot and felt I had come to know the Dominican Republic and how it operates as well as any foreigner can really know. We had great friends and marvelous access. But my Fulbright-Hayes award was nearly expired; it was time to move on.

So in the spring of 1965 we said our good-byes and boarded a plane for Miami. It was only a few weeks before the Dominican Republic would explode in revolution and civil war, and the country would be occupied militarily by U.S. forces. The Dominican Revolution and the U.S. intervention would be the first great mistake of Lyndon Johnson's presidency; it led to a severe credibility gap; and it provided a foretaste of the dissent and foreign policy crisis over Vietnam. As we boarded that plane in Santo Domingo with my dissertation under my arm, we did not fully realize that we were carrying the most complete and up-to-date analysis of the Dominican Republic then available, and that suddenly our data would be in great demand—with enormous personal and political consequences.

Florida Atlantic University

During our last months in Santo Domingo, we had been in contact with one of our former mentors at the University of Florida, Prof. John De Grove. De Grove had that year moved from Gainesville to Boca Raton to head the Political Science Department at the newly created Florida Atlantic University. He had inquired if I might be interested in teaching a Comparative Politics course during the spring/summer term at his university. There was no commitment for the future; it was only a short-term appointment. But it was perfect for us since it would enable me to stay in Florida and commute easily to Gainesville while I polished the dissertation and put it in final form. Plus it offered a very handsome salary that would tide us over until a full-time and tenure-track teaching job could be found, hopefully, for the fall.

My parents met us at the airport in Miami. They had bought us an old gas-and oil guzzling Chevrolet Belair, hitched it to their car, and pulled it all the way from Michigan to Miami so that we would have transportation after our year abroad. That's what parents do who really care about their children! They greeted us especially warmly not only because they hadn't seen us for over a year but because we were carrying in our arms, in addition to my dissertation, our baby daughter born in Santo Domingo only a few weeks earlier. We drove up the coast about thirty miles to Boca Raton and my folks stayed with us and cared for the baby for a few days while we located an apartment. The apartment was a one-bedroom, located on 40th Street north of Boca, just off Route 1. It was far fancier and furnished more luxuriously than our Santo Domingo apartment, but it lacked the view, the fresh breezes, and the "character" of that other place. I bought plywood and wooden legs and rigged up a good-sized writing desk (which we still have) in our bedroom.

Unfortunately, those few days in Boca Raton were the last time we saw my mother: she developed inoperable pancreatic cancer soon after that visit and died very suddenly. We had rushed to Grand Rapids, but she had passed away before we got there; we received the devastating news as we landed at the airport. She was a wonderful person, generous, kind, and politically shrewd; it was she who had lined up my summer factory and road crew jobs that paid my way through undergraduate school at the University of Michigan and launched me on my way to Florida. I am still saddened not just by her early death but by the fact she never had a chance to really get to know her wonderful daughter-in-law and grandchildren.

Boca Raton is located on the Florida Atlantic Coast about midway between Miami and Palm Beach. In those days it was still a "sleepy" small town with wide open spaces. When we played golf on its courses which bordered the Everglades, we were told never to chase a ball into the rough and, least of all, over the earthworks that separated land from swamp. In fact, as we played a round, we could hear the croaking of alligators just off the fairways.

Boca had one small shopping center in the middle of town. It also had the pink, stucco, art-deco Boca Raton Club where Sammy Snead was the pro. The wealthier homes were between the ocean and the Intracoastal, and also around the mouth of the protruding inlet that gave the town its name: Boca Raton ("Mouth of the Rat"). Our mentor, friend, and now colleague, John De Grove, had bought a house on the Intracoastal and we had the opportunity to do the same: for about $100,000 we could have gotten a beautiful home that today would be worth millions. But that was an astronomical amount of money for us in those days; plus we were scheduled to be there just temporarily.

Boca also had a religious conference center as well as world-famous polo grounds. We learned that Ramfis Trujillo, son of the assassinated dictator I had studied and a real SOB in his own right, played there; and other members of the Trujillo family, such as Flor de Oro and her first husband Porfirio Rubirosa, frequented Boca. So did the wealthier exiles and hangers-on of the ousted Batista regime in Cuba. Boca was a lovely place but some of its inhabitants belonged in an Irving Wallace novel. In fact, Wallace's <u>The Prize</u> is rather transparently based on the life of Rubirosa and the Dominican Republic.

Florida Atlantic University was a brand-new university that had just been opened by the state. Its impressive and shiny new buildings were located on a tract of land directly west from the center of town that had been an Air Force bomber base during World War II. The base had been abandoned after the war but the grass-filled runways were still visible. Now the expansive tarmac was being used for student and faculty parking.

The state of Florida's conceptions in founding the new university were basically two. First, it was to be an upper division university only. Miami already had the private University of Miami as well as the country's largest junior college, Miami-Dade. Palm Beach also had a junior college. So the idea was that Florida Atlantic, located midway between these two, would offer courses at the junior-senior level only. Palm Beach and Miami-Dade junior colleges were to constitute a feeder system which would channel its best students into the upper division program at Florida Atlantic. Only FAU would offer bachelor degrees and eventually some graduate degrees.

The second innovation at FAU was that it was supposed to be experimental and high-tech. Located not far from Cape Canaveral, it was billed as "the space-age university." It was to be "experimental" in this technical and scientific sense, not in the sense that, slightly later, Vietnam era colleges like Hampshire were "experimental" in an "Age of Aquarius" way. For example, my lectures were supposed to be filmed for future reuse and there was fancy camera equipment in the lecture hall; but for reasons that were always obscure the equipment failed to work properly or the "parts were missing." The lectern was similarly high-tech with a variety of switches and dials connected to buttons in the individual seats. The device was explained to me as a way I could give a pop-quiz to students: by asking a question and having them push the buttons at their seats, I could get an instant reading on the dials of my lectern of what percentage knew the right answer. I suppose this was a handy device to check if the students were awake or not, but since it did not give me a reading on <u>individual</u> scores, I used it once and then abandoned it.

Florida Atlantic had recruited a first-rate faculty to begin its academic year, mainly by raiding the University of Florida faculty and by hiring top-notch young people who had just completed or were still finishing (like me) their Ph.D. theses. Robert Huckshorn, a first-rate political scientist and a gem of a person, had been hired as the dean of arts and sciences; he also taught a course in the Political Science Department. John De Grove, a specialist in American national and state politics, who had been on both my and Iêda's Ph.D. comprehensive exam committees, was chair of the Department. Doug Gadlin, from the University of North Carolina, had been hired as the specialist on political parties and interest groups. And Jack Snyder had been hired to teach International Relations.

I taught Comparative Politics. It was the first time I had ever taught a full course. I used the Eckstein and Apter text, <u>Comparative Politics: A Reader</u>, and also relied on my notes from Arnold Heidenheimer's stimulating seminars. Rather than the usual tack of going country-by-country (Britain, France, Germany, and the Soviet Union were the usual countries covered in introductory Comparative Politics courses in those days), my course was organized conceptually and functionally. The best students got it and liked it, but average students did not. They wanted a concrete <u>country</u> to understand and hang their hats on, not all that "theory stuff." But in those days I knew the theory far better than I knew the countries named above. I enjoyed teaching the course my way and learned a lot in the process, but I also learned the limits of what one can and cannot effectively teach to undergraduates.

The Department treated me very nicely and my teaching load consisted of just this one course. Things were going swimmingly and we had settled into Boca and were enjoying the area. Iêda found her favorite mangoes at a little fruit stand in neighboring Delray Beach. On a regular salary for the first time, we were frequent visitors at the restaurants in Fort Lauderdale, Delray Beach, and other nearby towns. We would take our small daughter along in her car tray and she would promptly go to sleep, enabling us and the other diners to enjoy our meals; sometimes we splurged and hired a baby sitter. Every other weekend I would go to Gainesville with a newly completed or repolished dissertation chapter; Kantor would spend his <u>Saturdays</u> going through it sentence by sentence—another service of his that was way beyond the call of duty. But his advice was sound and I pass it on to my own students. "Howard," he would say, "you want to write a dissertation that's so good and interesting that people will want to publish it immediately."

On the weekends when I didn't go to Gainesville, Iêda, Kristy, and I would go on family excursions. We enjoyed Coral Gables and the Everglades. But our favorite haunt was just north of Palm Beach, around Jupiter Island and Hobe Sound. This was a beautiful area, with pristine beaches and almost no traffic. There were splendid houses whose architecture I (as the son of a home builder) admired. We would pack a picnic lunch, take Kristy in her car tray, and find some lovely spot on the beach.

We enjoyed an active social and intellectual life. The De Groves and Huckshorns invited us to their homes. Several young scholars in the History Department became close personal friends and tried to entice me into radical social and historical interpretation. On the other extreme of the political spectrum, we met and were invited several times for dinner to the home of Sylvia and Nathaniel Weyl. Weyl had been a Communist in the 1930s, had known Trotsky in Mexico as well as the Mexican Marxist muralists Orozco and Siqueiros, and told us he had known the Stalinists who had assassinated Trotsky in Mexico. He seemed to know everyone in left-wing politics and had wonderful stories to tell of Lillian Hellman, Theodore Draper, and many others. But in the 1950s a disillusioned Weyl, like Whitaker Chambers and many others, had moved way to the right: his most recent book was an anti-communist diatribe called Red Star over Cuba. Weyl also had what I thought were strange theories about eugenics and the inheritance of intelligence (or the lack thereof) by different ethnic groups.

In the midst of this nice, even idyllic, existence, a "bomb" dropped. On the night of April 24, 1965, a Saturday, we heard on the radio that a revolution had broken out in the Dominican Republic. The revolution was launched and led by the PRD and was aimed at restoring Juan Bosch and constitutional government. The revolution included both civilian and younger, honest, military elements who were loyal to the PRD. Other, smaller groups joined the revolution for their own purposes; the revolution also set loose a variety of dissident forces (pro-Balaguer, pro-Wessin, etc.) that reflected the complex factions that had been jockeying for power just before we had left. However, the PRD was the main force in the revolution and maintained its leadership position. By Monday, two days after the outbreak of the revolt, the PRD forces appeared to be gaining the upper hand over the forces of authoritarianism and repression.

But the U.S. Embassy in Santo Domingo had other ideas. It feared a "second Cuba"—that is, another Marxist-Leninist state in the Caribbean allied to the Soviet Union. The Embassy knew, given the weakness of the Dominican leftist groups, that was an unlikely possibility; but it was unwilling to take a chance. Faced with the choice between an uncertain democrat (Bosch) and an authoritarian but "anti-communist" military, it chose the "lesser evil" of the authoritarian military. Later interviews convinced me that the main reason the Embassy took this stand was not because it reflected accurately the real situation in the DR but because of career considerations on the part of the foreign service officers. Knowing what had happened to those State Department officials who had failed to see the Marxism-Leninism of the earlier Chinese and Cuban revolutionaries and who had been professionally disgraced or drummed out of the foreign service for their oversight, the FSOs in Santo Domingo were determined not to make the same mistake. So even if the chances of a Marxist triumph in the Dominican Republic were only 1 or 2 percent, the Embassy could not take that chance. Better to err on the safe "anti-communist" side than to risk a definite career-ender by saying the revolution was non-communist.

That same Monday when the PRD-led forces appeared to be gaining the upper hand, the "critic" cables began going out from the Embassy. "Little foxes are nibbling at the grapes," said my old nemesis Tapley Bennett, in what was presumed to be a reference to communists but what was really a stupid and meaningless comment. Meanwhile in Washington, the conservative assistant secretary of state for inter-American affairs, Thomas Mann, who knew nothing about the Dominican Republic, was prepared to accept the patently false assumption that this was a communist conspiracy. Nor did Dean Rusk, George Ball, W. W. Rostow, or Robert McNamara, the president's foreign policy team, have any independent knowledge about the country; they had to rely solely on Bennett's and Mann's recommendations. President Johnson himself, having witnessed as vice president Cuba's unfolding communism, the disastrous Bay of Pigs, and the Cuban missile crisis of 1962, was similarly disinclined either to question the judgments of lower officials or to wait to see who was who in the revolution or in which direction it would go. As the PRD forces appeared to be winning, Johnson, in the name of "anti-communism," authorized U.S. military forces to go ashore, separate the contending factions, side with the repressive military against the constitutionalists, and prevent the PRD from winning.

I have written about the Dominican Revolution at length elsewhere[4] and need not repeat all but the outlines here; but I have never written about my personal role in this, what ensued, and the role of my university in these events. On April 28, four days after the revolution began, U.S. military forces began landing in the Dominican Republic to contain and defeat the revolution. The build-up continued until we had 24,000 troops there. Those troops were directed to side with the repressive and corrupt Dominican military and they began to tighten and squeeze the noose around the Bosch-led constitutionalists. Over 2,000 Dominicans were killed. Many of them were my friends or people I had just interviewed. I couldn't believe what my own country was doing in crushing a democratic revolution. It was all a gigantic and extremely costly mistake.

The CIA sought to justify the intervention by publishing lists of first fifty-one and then eighty-four "communists" supposedly participating in the revolution. But the journalists investigating the claim showed that most of them were dead, in jail at the time of the Revolution, or out of the country. Former U.S. Ambassador John Bartlow Martin, an Adlai Stevenson liberal who certainly knew better, wrote a silly piece (which also took the form of a report to the president) acknowledging the PRD's dominance of the constitutionalist movement but arguing that in the process of the "bloodbath" (there had been none, except the one our forces instigated), communists would inevitably take over. However, I had just studied the communist groups in the DR and interviewed their leaders: they were small, disorganized, not very competent, and usually consisted of two professors of sociology at the University of Santo Domingo, a handful of their students, and their girlfriends. Certainly there was no mass support for a Communist revolution in the Dominican Republic, nothing comparable to Castro's 26th of July Movement or Cuba's experienced and well-led Communist Party, no possibility whatsoever for a <u>Fidelista</u> takeover.

Years later I was able to interview some of the men around Lyndon Johnson at the time (Ball, Rostow) as well as the reporters (Tad Szulc, Phil Geyelin) who covered these events. All agreed that in hindsight there was little basis to the Communist charge—a fact that Johnson himself recognized within the first two weeks of the occupation and tried to make amends for by shifting the personnel involved, changing course, and offering massive assistance to reconstruct the country. Johnson was mainly motivated by Kennedy's political dictum that no American president could be reelected if he permitted a "second Cuba" in the Caribbean. He also wanted to send (recall, this is in the spring of 1965) an elliptical message to North Vietnam (!) by way of Santo Domingo: that Communists should not muck around with American allies or they will suffer the full retaliation of the American military. Obviously the North Vietnamese did not get let alone heed the message; meanwhile, Johnson and the U.S. Embassy had wreaked enormous havoc on a poor, small, defenseless country whose only "sin" was wanting to restore the democracy that, ironically, the U.S. had earlier helped bring into being.

During these early days of the Revolution and U.S. intervention, I sat glued to my radio listening to the news in disbelief. I have to confess that my first and selfish thought was that the uprising would mean I'd have to rewrite parts of my just-finished dissertation. But the dissertation stood up well against these fast-moving events, confirming the thesis that Dominican democratic institutions, brand new and sometimes imposed by the U.S., were exceedingly fragile and prone to fragmentation and breakdown.

But my concern for the validity of my dissertation quickly turned to outrage as the U.S. troops went in and I listened to the lies, dissembling, and fabrication offered by U.S. officials. Even my "friend" Malcolm McLean, now the public affairs officer in Santo Domingo, to say nothing of Bennett, Martin, Johnson, and the brothers Rostow (Walt and Gene), lied through their teeth regarding

Dominican events and the U.S. role. I even have a long, personal letter from Eugene Rostow (then Undersecretary of State), in response to some newspaper accounts he had seen of my critical comments, claiming that because constitutionalist military leader Francisco Caamaño had once been photographed in a clenched-fist salute, it "proved" he was a communist. All this was very disillusioning to the young (twenty-five) and still idealistic man from Calvinist Grand Rapids who grew up expecting public officials to speak the truth. The experience confirmed what I had smilingly learned in the classroom but that now began to sink in literally under circumstances of hard reality: that the definition of a diplomat (even American diplomats) is a person who is sent abroad to lie for his country.

No one in the U.S. government seemed to know anything about the Dominican Republic. Not only were U.S. officials making misleading, mistaken, or outright false statements to the public and the media, but U.S. policy had gone in disastrous directions not only as regards the Dominican Republic but with enormous negative reverberations in Latin America, the Third World, and among our European allies. Here was another case of stupid, heavy-handed, self-defeating U.S. military intervention in the Caribbean reminiscent of the gunboat diplomacy of the early years of the twentieth century. I was enormously frustrated because here I was sitting on all this data and information about the DR—with all modesty, probably knowing more about the country than anyone else in the world at that precise moment—and not knowing how to communicate it to public officials. This was still the mid-1960s before the era of CNN and televised talk shows; I was still young and naive; I knew no one in the media; and I had no political connections.

Knowing that I had all this information, my friends in the FAU History Department put me in touch with Jim Giltmier, a reporter for the Miami Herald. I gave the Herald a complete interview laying out all the facts as I knew them. But there was one dramatic sentence in the interview, what we now call a "newsbite," that received all the attention. "Texas-style," I said, "Lyndon Johnson decided to shoot first and ask questions later." That became, of course, the lead paragraph in the story and a banner, front-page headline in the Herald. Quickly thereafter the local and Miami radio and television stations were calling for an interview. The story went out over the wire services. Even the New York Times picked it up where I was portrayed as the one knowledgeable—and dissenting—voice on the Dominican intervention. This was still the first week of the revolution and intervention, before the national reporters got ashore and before other dissenting voices were heard.

The <u>Herald</u> interview became a major event, mainly because I seemed to be the only person who knew the factual situation and all the players, and we were soon besieged by requests for more interviews. In Andy Warhol's terms, this was to be my "fifteen minutes of fame." The national media called up and I was frequently quoted. I received numerous university speaking invitations. Senator J. William Fulbright's Committee on Foreign Relations asked me to testify. Political Science Chairman Manning Dauer in Gainesville put me in touch with his former student, and now congressman, Sam Gibbons and his staff. The Special Operations Research Office, a CIA front, as part of a large and ill-fated research undertaking called Project Camelot which was aimed at studying the role of the military in Third World countries, called and requested the data and interviews from my chapter on the Dominican military; SORO also invited me to Washington for a conference. The Defense Department also called asking for a copy of my chapter, based on interviews with the top command, on the Dominican military. Theodore Draper, an acerbic critic of U.S. policy both in the Dominican Republic and Vietnam, summoned me to his suite at the Pierre Hotel in New York where he offered to turn over all his files to me if I would write <u>the</u> book on the Dominican Revolution. The collaboration with Draper would have made my career, but I wanted to write my own book on the Dominican Republic and also thought Draper a bit strange and that his criticism of U.S. policy was somewhat off the mark, so I turned him down. In retrospect, that may have been a career mistake, but I don't regret the decision.

However, there was a dark side to all this attention and notoriety as well. Within two days of my headlines in the <u>Miami Herald</u>, a group of Florida legislators called for me to be fired from my teaching job at Florida Atlantic, which was after all a state university. They complained that I was "following the pro-Moscow or pro-Chinese line"—apparently they weren't sure which—and asked for a University investigation into my qualifications for saying what I did. My wife and I also received strange, occasionally threatening, and sometimes terrifying calls at all hours of the day and sometimes in the middle of the night. The Ku Klux Klan (remember this is still the Old South in the mid-1960s) burned a cross to protest my criticism of U.S. policy, but not, fortunately, on our front lawn. At this stage I still had not yet received the Ph.D. degree, I had a wife and small baby, and I had no job yet assured for the fall. I don't mind admitting that I was frightened and intimidated by these attacks. As a result, I softened my criticism of U.S. policy and began turning down media interview requests. Had I been more secure in my position, not had a young family, or been more knowledgeable about the ways of politics and the media, I probably would not have bowed to the pressure.

But I also wish to emphasize how well my University, Florida Atlantic, came through on my behalf. It stood up under the legislative and political onslaught and came out squarely for free speech—even for untenured and temporary professors. Friends and colleagues rallied to my defense. The chairman and the dean did exactly what they should have done. Both John De Grove and Bob Huckshorn asked me to come in so that they could help build a case in my defense. It was obvious that they had received calls from the president of the University, Kenneth Williams, whom I as a lowly lecturer had never met. Under pressure from the legislature and like all college presidents worried about the budget, he wanted to know who I was and what qualifications I had for saying what I did. Huckshorn and De Grove therefore asked me to prepare a few paragraphs that they could pass on to the president stating that I had recently completed a doctoral dissertation on the Dominican Republic, that I knew the country intimately, and that I was eminently qualified to speak out on the subject. They then passed these paragraphs on to the University president who used them verbatim in his own response letter to the legislators. But what if I had not been so well qualified on the subject; would free speech still have held up?

Others weighed in as well. Manning Dauer and Harry Kantor up in Gainesville both wrote letters on my behalf. Dauer also contacted his former student, Congressman Gibbons, who in turn got in touch with the state legislators and told them to lay off and stop the pressure. Other colleagues, friends, and even complete strangers came to my defense with letters and phone calls. The issue soon died down. The U.S. government subsequently followed a more sensible and moderate course in the Dominican Republic—in part, I like to think, because of my and others' criticisms. At the University the issue also faded away, and so did the cross burnings and midnight phone calls. Weeks later I ran into University President Williams in the elevator, just the two of us. I had still not met him personally and so I introduced myself and thanked him for supporting me. He was cordial, but it was plain that my statements to the press had caused him a considerable amount of grief and cost him much-needed political and financial support in the legislature. He mumbled something about free speech and then the elevator got to the bottom. We parted and I never saw him again. At Florida Atlantic I had been given a wonderful opportunity to teach and finish my dissertation, but at the same time I sure learned a lot in a short time about the media, national political affairs, and academic politics.

NOTES

1. Howard J. Wiarda, <u>Ethnocentrism in Foreigrn Policy: Can We Understand the Third World?</u> (Washington, D.C.: American Enterprise Institute for Public Policy Research, 1985).

2. Howard J. Wiarda, "Trujilloism without Trujillo," <u>The New Republic, CLI</u> (September 19, 1964) 5-6; the Spanish language edition was published in <u>Panoramas</u> [Mexico], 15 (May-June 1965).

3. Charles W. Anderson, <u>Politics and Economic Chancre in Latin America:</u> The <u>Governing of Restless Nations</u> (Princeton, NJ: D. Van Nostrand, 1967).

4. Howard J. Wiarda, <u>The Dominican Republic: Nation in Transition</u> (New York: Praeger, Publishers, 1967); in far greater detail, see my <u>Dictatorship, Development, and Disintegration: Politics and Social Chancre in the Dominican Republic</u> (Ann Arbor, MI: Monograph Series, Xerox University Microfilms, 1975).

CHAPTER 5

AROUND THE HORN: SOUTH AMERICA—1966

In the spring of 1965 we had returned from the Dominican Republic with the first draft of my dissertation, quite literally (because of fear the Dominican police might confiscate it), under my arm. We had spent the late spring and early summer teaching at Florida Atlantic University, while rewriting and polishing the dissertation. In August of that year I received my Ph.D., still only twenty five years old.

While at Florida Atlantic I began searching for a permanent academic position for that fall. Three things were working in my favor. First, in the mid-1960s, because of the Cuban revolution, the Dominican intervention, and rising academic and foreign policy interest in Latin America, there was a large demand for specialists in Latin American politics. Second, at that time it was widely recognized that the University of Florida had the best program in Latin American studies in the country, so other universities contacted Florida when they were looking to hire newly-minted Ph.Ds. Third, I came out of the DR with my dissertation in hand about a month before my friend, colleague, and rival (for jobs) Larry Graham came out of Brazil with his dissertation in hand. So that spring I had the first pick of many good job possibilities.

My first academic job offer came even before I had started the dissertation, at the University of North Carolina—Charlotte; but while the department there and the city of Charlotte were just beginning to boom, I thought it was too small scale, and not the main campus, for my tastes. While in the DR, I had been offered a position at the American University in Cairo, but the pay was in Egyptian pounds and we were not sure we wanted to settle in Cairo. Back in the U.S., I received an offer from Miami University of Ohio, but it was primarily a teaching institution, the teaching load was four courses each semester, and I thought of myself as more research oriented. The University of Wisconsin—

Oshkosh also made an offer and kept raising the salary by a thousand dollars a year (big money in those days) every time I turned it down, but Iêda and I figured (with no disrespect), once in Oshkosh, always in Oshkosh. Tulane University and the University of Colorado also contacted me but for reasons I cannot remember, I never followed up on these.

The decision came down to a choice between the University of Texas and the University of Massachusetts. Iêda preferred Texas because of its big Latin America program, wonderful Latin America library collection, and the sizable community of Brazilians there. But Texas had offered me the job over the phone, which I thought a little suspicious, and so I suggested they invite me out there for a visit. They insisted I teach Texas politics (a required course that I had no knowledge of or interest in—except I assumed it was probably a lot like Latin American politics), said I might be able to teach a Latin America course the second year, plus the chairman, Malcolm MacDonald, was nasty about it besides. The first day I was there, the old guys in the department (MacDonald, Wallace Mendelsohn, E.E. Schattschneider) took me out to lunch and told me how awful the young people in the department were; the second day the young guys took me out and told me how bad the senior professors were. I thought, if you can't hide this nastiness and back stabbing from a visitor for at least twenty-four hours, I don't want any part of this place. For as a young scholar you need to be free to teach your courses and do your research without constantly having to look over your shoulders to see who's about to stab you next. So I turned Texas down. Larry Graham a month later accepted the job but has been unhappy at Texas ever since. Once that degree of nastiness becomes embedded in a department it becomes self-perpetuating and almost impossible to eliminate.

In contrast, the University of Massachusetts was warm, friendly, like a womb. The colleagues were friendly, enjoyed each other's company, were competitive yet cordial, and became over the years my best friends.

In Amherst I taught Introduction to Comparative Politics but also taught that first year (which then became a permanent offering) a two-semester sequence on Latin American politics. Like Kantor at Florida had done in his course, I did an introduction to Latin America and the politics of the South American countries the first semester, and Central America and the Caribbean with a greater attention to U.S. policy (since that's where we intervened more often) the second semester. I already knew and was quite confident in teaching about Central America and the Caribbean (see chapters above) but at that moment I had never been to South America. So I submitted a project to the University's Faculty Research Council outlining these teaching needs and also incorporating a comparative research project. The proposal was approved, I received a Faculty Research Grant (I believe for the then princely sum of $1,200.00), and in June, 1996, Iêda, our two year-old daughter Kristy, and I set off for an eight-week tour of South America. I envisioned this as like my earlier Central America tour, a get-acquainted visit, with about a week in each country.

The Dominican Republic

Our first stop, flying New York to Santo Domingo, was the Dominican Republic—not exactly South America. But that had been my major country of specialization so far and I wanted to keep up. Plus I was already at that stage working on turning both my MA and Ph.D. theses into books and wanted to incorporate the most current materials. By this time, in mid-1966, the Dominican Revolution of the previous year had largely run its course, the U.S. military occupation was beginning to wind down (as the civilian or what we would now call "nation-building" phase wound up), and new elections had just been held in which former Trujillo puppet but now viewed as a symbol of stability Joaquín Balaguer won over Juan Bosch, the symbol of the revolution but now seen as a divisive figure.

I thought the Dominican Republic was in bad shape—in part because of the American intervention—and said so in print.[1] It was deeply divided, fragmented, fissured, and polarized. The fledgling labor, peasant, and political party organizations that I had studied in my dissertation had been disrupted, broken up, and repressed. The economy had slid down hill into strongly negative numbers and much of the national infrastructure had been destroyed. The political culture was angry, bitter, hostile—no longer the warm, friendly country of our dissertation year. The natural course of Dominican development had been interrupted and severely set back by the revolution and intervention; some things—faith in America, confidence in their own future—would never be the same again. I was profoundly saddened by the destruction I saw all around me, not just physical destruction but damage to the nation's soul as well.

U.S. policy was wrong-headed as usual and I got into a public row over that too. For the Balaguer regime was already seen as corrupt, repressive, an attempted throwback to an earlier status quo ante that had by now in the DR forever disappeared. I argued that the massive economic development program that the U.S. had designated for the DR, in part as atonement for the intervention and the destruction the U.S. had wreaked on the country, would be wasted without having a genuinely democratic government in place that was genuinely dedicated to development, not patronage and cronyism.

This was part of a larger critique of U.S. foreign aid and development policy that I was fashioning and which would become a main theme in my writings. In contrast to the dominant paradigm of prominent sociologist S.M. Lipset and leading economist W.W. Rostow (then Lyndon Johnson's national security adviser and the intellectual architect of the U.S. foreign aid program) who argued that economic development and social modernization would lead inevitably and universally to a stronger middle class and hence to democracy, I argued: (1) this approach was ethnocentric and did not take individual cultures, histories, and sociologies into account; and (2) that the causation was backward, that first you needed a decent government in place committed not to self-aggrandizement but to development, democracy, and pluralism, and only then would real economic development take place. I published an early article on the theme which then prompted a response from U.S. AID officials and a rejoinder from me.[2] Since U.S. AID has not learned a thing in the intervening thirty-five years, it is an argument that continues to this day.

Venezuela

From Santo Domingo we flew (two hours) to Venezuela. I had not been in Venezuela before but this was Iêda's third research trip to the country. Earlier she had done a reconnoitering trip there with her professor Alfredo Pareja Diazconseco as I had with Kantor to the DR, then in 1963-64 she had been there for an extended period doing the basic archival and library research for her doctoral dissertation. Now she needed to supplement these materials with further interviewing and to finish the writing of the thesis, which was already more than half done. Her thesis, parallel to mine, focused on the emergence of new social and political groups and political parties in a country that was considerably more advanced and rapidly developing than was the DR, but was still in the early stages of emerging from dictatorship.

The difference this time was that now we had a little daughter who was a year and a half old. So my role on this first visit to Venezuela was to serve as babysitter while Iêda did her interviewing. Nevertheless, with Kristy on my back in her comfy backseat, I saw an awful lot of Caracas in a short period of time.

The first surprise came at the airport, La Guaira. It is located right at sea level and very near the equator, so it is hot and steamy. But Caracas the capital, some twenty-five miles away, is up in the mountains at 3,000 feet and at an average temperature of 75, is one of the most agreeable cities on earth. The central valley where Caracas is located and where 80% of the population, business, banking, industry, etc. is centered runs east and west so that the pollution is also swept out of the valley by the prevailing westerlies and, for a big city, the air is clear and fresh.

A four-lane divided highway runs steeply from La Guaira up to the capital, interspersed with several tunnels and in places surrounded by the urban slums that precariously balance on the mountains surrounding Caracas and which in bad times rain people down on the main thoroughfares to loot, rob, or stage political demonstrations. On the road here I received my first indoctrination into Venezuelan politics. For even though Venezuela was now a democracy, first under Rómulo Betancourt and at the time of our visit President Raúl Leoni, everything that was worth anything, according to the <u>taxista</u>, had been built by the earlier dictator, Marcos Pérez Jiménez. That included the superhighway we were on, numerous public buildings, the expressway (<u>autopista</u>) through central Caracas, the university complex, and much more. Of course the fact that this and other taxistas had all received their cars as gifts of Pérez Jiménez probably had something to do with his political views.

Lacking gold, silver, or very many native Indians, Venezuela had not been one of the main centers of the Spanish empire in America. It was disorganized and chaotic through much of the nineteenth century. But it did have this black, oily, gooey stuff that seeped from the ground in places. In earlier times, it had been mixed with native herbs and alcohol, bottled, and sold in Europe as an aphrodisiac! It was not until the 1920s that Venezuela, under dictator Juan Vicente Gómez, began to exploit its vast petroleum resources and sell the oil abroad. Thereafter the country had boomed economically, vast social changes (new labor, middle, and entrepreneurial classes) had occurred, and since 1958 democracy had flowered. The goal was to "sew the petroleum," to use the petroleum, unlike the oil exporting states of the Middle East, to diversify the economy, develop the country's vast resources (iron ore, rich agriculture, precious metals), and build a democratic, socially just society. At the time we were there it all seemed to be working, and that is precisely what Iêda's thesis was all about.

Kristy and I had little time to investigate all this but we sure did see a lot of Caracas. One day we went down to the Plaza Venezuela, crossed over to see the Central University, roamed next door into the Jardín Botánico, and ended up in Caobos Park where I could let Kristy play and run a little. The university was fun for me because it was highly politicized, with each faction associated with one of the main political parties. At that time Venezuela was a center of the conflict between those who wanted to achieve social justice through democracy and those who preferred a Cuba-like revolutionary route to socialism. The university had autonomy, which means the police were not allowed to enter its grounds, and the students took advantage of this immunity to bring arms and ammunition onto the campus, located on the main east-west route through Caracas, and to fire at policemen, soldiers, and even civilians who happened to be passing by.

Another day Kristy and I explored El Centro and the Plaza Bolívar, which incorporates the cathedral, the Presidential Palace ("Miraflores"), the capitol, and a rich variety of museums. Kristy was still so young that she was only along for the ride and the parks, but as a political scientist, whenever I'm in a new country, I always like to get a visible sense of the centers of power, where they are, and their relationships to each other. Also in the Center is the birthplace of "the liberator," Simon Bolívar, the "George Washington" of Latin America and one of my favorite people. For not only did Bolívar lead the movements for independence from Spain in Latin America but he also was an international traveler (Europe, the U.S.), an intellectual (inspired by Rousseau and the Enlightenment), and above all a realist. He favored independence but he also recognized that Latin America lacked the training, the political culture, the institutional infrastructure and civil society for successful democracy and self-rule. So he ingeniously wrote constitutions for several of the Latin American nations that incorporated democracy and republicanism as goals for the nations to achieve, meanwhile, in order realistically to hold the country together, enshrining centralization, strong executives, strong emergency laws, and the military as the "guardians" of the constitution. This seemed to me a reasonable compromise; and in still under-institutionalized Latin America with weak civil society and fragmented political cultures, it still seems to me a good compromise, as distinct from the unrealistically pure forms of democracy and human rights that the U.S. and the international community keep insisting on.

Venezuela in the mid-1960s looked awfully good to Iêda and me. It was a far more generously endowed and developed country than was the DR or Central America. It had vast wealth and a large middle class. Its main political parties, labor and business groups, and farmers' and peasants' associations were far more institutionalized than those I had studied in the DR. The government and its ministries really functioned, often effectively, in delivering goods and services. Most impressive to us, again in contrast to the DR, was that Venezuela had, probably because of the Pérez Jiménez dictatorship when many of them were forced abroad to travel and study, a huge pool of educated, experienced técnicos, managers, administrators, government and party officials who could actually run a country and do so effectively.

A key element in Venezuela's success at this time was the Punto Fijo, a pact signed between the major political parties and civil society groups which seemed to offer possibilities for stability, continuity, consensus, and a peaceful democratic alternation in power between the contending forces. But the Punto Fijo was also monopolistic, a closed and corporatist arrangement that at the same time offered the possibilities for corruption and clientelism on a mammoth scale. At the time that we were there the agreement seemed to be working well and democracy and the political system were flourishing; little did we expect that in the 1990s this system would become massively corrupt, patronage dominated, and dysfunctional, leading to a near-breakdown of the democratic system, the coming of populist-authoritarian Hugo Chávez to power, and conflict verging on national disintegration and civil war.

Paraguay

From Caracas we flew to Brazil: first Belém, then Rio de Janeiro, up to Belo Horizonte, back to Rio, then on to São Paulo. But since Iêda is Brazilian, we have family there, we spent more time there than in any other country, and since I almost decided to become a full-time Brazilianist, that experience deserves a full chapter of its own. Hence we reserve that story for Chapter 6; meanwhile let us continue our South American tour where the next stop was Paraguay.

I love Paraguay! It may be the greenest, most beautiful, wildest country I have every seen. It's people are extremely friendly, hospitable, unpretentious (with good reason, if you come from Paraguay), and simpático—like the DR. It has this incredible history: exploited initially by Spain, rumored to be the site of the famed golden city "El Dorado," said also to be the location of a matriarchal tribe of fighting (or "Amazon") women. After no gold was found, it was of little value to the Spanish crown; during the colonial period it was made into a preserve and protectorate of the Jesuit order, who ran it and its native Guaraní Indian population for two hundred years as a feudal estate and gigantic catechism class keeping out all foreign influence and "heresies."

In the nineteenth century, after independence, its isolation was maintained by a succession of three long-lived dictatorships who sought to preserve its idyllic, pristine purity. The last of these, Francisco Solano López, involved Paraguay in a disastrous foreign war against an alliance of much bigger and more powerful nations—Argentina, Brazil, and Uruguay—that resulted in the elimination of 80% of Paraguay's male population. In the 1930s Paraguay fought another war with Bolivia, over the empty and wild Chaco, under which oil had recently been discovered. In the war, Paraguay was supported by one of the big global oil companies (Shell) and Bolivia had the other (Standard). In 1954 began the long, record-breaking (in length of tenure, until Fidel Castro surpassed him) regime of

General Alfredo Stroessner, a scion of one of the many German families in Paraguay. At Florida I wrote my first, full-length, detailed, publishable monograph on Paraguay and the Stroessner regime—another reason I liked the country so much, because I knew it so well.

We arrived in Paraguay in the twelfth year of General Stroessner's rule. His regime was similar to that of Trujillo in the DR and Somoza in Nicaragua, both of which I had studied extensively along with that of Stroessner. It was an authoritarian regime, a police state, a staunch defender of order and anti-communism. At the time of our visit, fully one-third of the population was in exile—mainly "downriver" (the Paraná and Rio de la Plata) in Argentina and Uruguay. While in Paraguay, we were followed the entire time; but the agents must have learned their tactics from James Bond movies: when we stopped and looked back over our shoulders, we would catch glances of furtive little men quickly jumping back into storefronts and lighting a cigarette so as to appear unobtrusive.

Asunción, the capital, population then of 350,000, has pleasant, tree-lined streets, many colonial plazas, and belle epoche architecture in its residential and downtown areas. It remains a nineteenth or early twentieth century city, friendly and unpolluted. On the drive in from the airport, we passed the magnificent mansions lining Avenida Mariscal López, named after one of the country's nineteenth century dictators and war heroes. We also noted the Paraguayan cavalry, still mounted on horses and not, as in the U.S., on helicopter gunships. In the heart of the city the cathedral and Government Palace are worth visiting. When we toured the Palace, I noticed several high-speed riverboats anchored out back; when I pressed the guide privately on this, he told me that the speed boats were there in case the president and high government officials faced a coup and had to be spirited across the river to Argentina in a hurry.

Paraguay is probably the most traditional, least developed, most conservative, most Catholic country in South America. Its friendliness is the friendliness of an isolated traditional society; its order and tranquility are similarly the order both of tradition and of the stifling Stroessner dictatorship. It is the order of the grave. I found that as long as one avoided politics, one could live very comfortably and pleasantly in Paraguay; but if one were politically active, that was very dangerous. The Stroessner regime carefully encouraged the conservatism of its people since that helped maintain the status quo and kept the dictatorship in power; it was the change-oriented groups—labor, peasant, middle class opposition parties—that mainly felt the brunt of the dictatorship.

Paraguay is so traditional, undeveloped, and conservative that I always begin my South American Politics class with a discussion of that country. I use Paraguay as an example of a nineteenth century, traditional, "sleepy" society, what Latin America <u>used</u> to look like before the onset of modernization in such other countries as Argentina, Brazil, Chile, and Venezuela, but which in Paraguay still exists. Only the earliest stirrings of modernization had occurred there. If you like backward, traditional, quasi-feudal societies, Paraguay is the place for you. Novelist Gabriel García Márquez should have located his fictional "Macondo" in traditional Paraguay, not in far more modern Colombia.

We also visited the Pantheon of the Heroes, a monument to the country's history (like Poland's, I would later discover) of quixotic leaders, hopeless battles, seemingly endless martyrs, and disastrous wars and military campaigns. The Pantheon is the centerpiece of the Plaza of Heroes where we would sit with Kristy, allow her to play, and watch the Paraguayan world go by. Guaraní vendors were selling Indian feather headdresses as well as bows and arrows, artisans displayed their pottery, and itinerant merchants sold everything from patent cures and aphrodisiacs to miracle knife sharpeners. Iêda was particularly impressed by the gorgeous, hand-made (again a mark of a traditional society) lace blouses, napkins, and tablecloths, and we bought several samples to carry with us.

Paraguay's Indian population is known as the Guaraní; the country is predominantly mestizo, a mixture of European and Indian. The currency, a popular softdrink, and the major hotel—among many other things—are also called "the Guaraní." Ninety-five percent of the population speaks both Spanish and Guaraní, making Paraguay the only country in Latin America where the native Indian language is widely spoken by all classes. There is a small white elite, often Hispanic, Argentine, Brazilian, German or foreign born. Historically the country often felt ashamed of its Indian background and mixed social heritage; now, in an age of diversity and multiculturalism, it takes pride in its Indianness. Modernization is beginning to take hold.

While Iêda and Kristy rested in the afternoon, I went out to the U.S. Embassy to talk to officials there. Through Kantor, I also had contacts in the opposition Liberal and Febrerista parties, but I quickly discovered that all my contacts were in exile and it was dangerous to inquire about them. I toured Asunción extensively by getting on a bus in the center and riding all the way out to the end of the line, then paying another fare (20¢) and riding back—a cheap way to see the city. I also learned from that method that almost all the paved roads in the country ended at the city limits of the capital city; the rest of the country was still primitive and all but inaccessible.

A highlight of the visit was a trip to the Chaco with Paraguayan government officials—actually, from the Ministry of the Interior, the Paraguayan secret police—but don't tell my human rights-advocating friends about that! The Chaco, which takes up two-thirds of the country and is still largely unpopulated, is an incredible emerald-green jungle; one of the least spoiled places on earth. My Paraguayan friends told me we were going jaguar hunting by horseback—again not something that I should tell to my animal rights activist friends—but for reasons that were unclear those plans did not work out and we had to be content with a brief automobile tour. But even then it was fantastic: animals, birds, reptiles, flora and fauna that I had never seen before in my life and probably never would again.

Uruguay

From Paraguay we flew downriver to Montevideo, Uruguay. There is a riverboat that one can take from Asunción downstream about six hundred miles to Buenos Aires, just across the estuary from Montevideo, a two-day excursion that is both beautiful and great fun; but on this trip we didn't have time for that. The plane ride took only an hour and a half.

By the time we got to Uruguay it was downright cold. Our summers are, across the equator, their winters; while we had not noticed the change in Brazil and Paraguay, Uruguay is considerably farther south. We of course knew about the reverse seasons but hadn't realized how cold it would be and we weren't well equipped in the way of clothes. Our first task therefore was to buy a new sweater for Kristy—all wool (one of Uruguay's traditional products), very warm, and so well made and tightly-knit that eventually it was worn extensively by all three of our children. Iêda figured out that if we needed a yearly wardrobe of sweaters, suits, dresses, and coats, the savings from buying them all in Uruguay would more than pay for the round-trip air fares.

While we were there in the month of July, Uruguay was cold, wet, windy, and rainy—not the best weather for tourism. I still have images of Uruguay of old men dressed in hats and heavy (wool, of course) overcoats slurping their soup in dimly-lit and poorly heated cafes. Everyone looked cold and, frankly, a little bit down on their luck. It reminded me of what a much poorer than now, pre-World War I Europe must have looked like, or that I have seen in newsreels: small bars and cafes, inadequate lighting or heating, people bundled up in out-of-date overcoats, and soup as the main course, getting steadily thinner and more watery as the week wore on.

And, of course, that is a correct image of Uruguay. It had few Indians at the time of the conquest, and so it is a predominantly European society, mainly Spanish and Italian. And, while Uruguay flourished in the nineteenth and early twentieth centuries, mainly on the basis of the export of its traditional products (beef, hides, leather goods, wool, mutton), in more recent decades the terms of trade had shifted and Uruguay had fallen on harder times. Its prosperity earlier in the century had enabled Uruguay to develop South America's first social welfare state, but now it could no longer afford the generous benefits it had been paying out. Hence my image of old, often pale, European-looking men drinking their thinning soup in poorly-heated cafes. Probably quite a number of them had gout and tuberculosis as well.

This snapshot is not very attractive, but actually Uruguay is one of the really nice countries in Latin America—in a way, like Costa Rica. It is more prosperous than most of the other countries, more literate, and more middle class. It has not had the problem of integrating large numbers of Indians into the national life. Its history is less violent and less militaristic than that of the other countries, and from the beginning of the twentieth century to today, for over a hundred years, Uruguay has been (almost) continuously democratic. Its major breakthroughs came under President José Batlle y Ordoñez, elected in 1903 and to a second term in 1911, who settled the last of Uruguay's nineteenth century civil wars, put in place a system based on parity and co-participation to share power with the opposition Blanco Party, firmly established the system of democratic politics, and initiated Uruguay's progressive welfare state.

Montevideo is a pleasant city, clean and European-looking. Down the road about eighty miles is the beautiful, world-renowned seaside resort of Punta del Este. When we were there, Montevideo had a population of about 750,000, half as big as Caracas but considerably bigger and more sophisticated than the Central American and Caribbean capitals, or Asunción, we were more familiar with. At the same time, it was considered a bit provincial by the standards of Buenos Aires, Rio, São Paulo, or Mexico City.

We liked Uruguay a lot, despite the rain, the cold, and the down-on-its-luck appearance. Its people were personable and friendly—not pretentious like the Argentines. At the same time it was cosmopolitan, a successful country socially, politically, and economically. Iêda liked it, especially now that we had a child, because it was clean and well-kept.

We spent most of our time in the Old City, built on a peninsula that juts out into the Rio de la Plata and that divides the river estuary from the Atlantic Ocean. The Old City is surrounded on three sides by water; we liked to stroll along the succession of ramblas that border the city. We stayed in a pensión near Independence Park; from there we could easily tour the central area where the palace, cathedral, markets, and museums were located. The city spreads out east, west, and north from the Old City, rising from sea level to the hills where the newer, nicer residences and shopping centers are located.

I was fascinated by the politics of Uruguay. There were several things that fascinated me. First, I was interested in the system of parity and co-participation, which sounded remarkably like Venezuela's Punto Fijo or Colombia's National Front: an organic as distinct from pluralist way of organizing society and politics that, now in a democratic context, had some striking parallel to the systems of authoritarian corporatism I had already studied in the Dominican Republic, Mexico, and Brazil (see Chapter 6). Second, I was interested in the question of how a once-prosperous country with an advanced welfare state handled the politics of cutting back on its welfare system once its economy could no longer afford to support the advanced measure put in place earlier. The answer: not very well, resulting in what was called a "creeping coup" and in 1973 a full-scale military takeover that led to an interruption of Uruguay's long democratic record—although when we were there in 1966 no one saw a coup coming.

Third, I was fascinated by Uruguay's political party, electoral, and political system. Uruguay is a highly organized society with clearly defined interest groups and a two-party system, organized around the Blanco and Colorado parties. But the two parties are in turn further subdivided into lemas and sublemas (factions) which in effect give Uruguay a multiparty system based on proportional representation.

The lemas and sublemas can be made up of ideological factions, political machines, clientelistic networks, or individual party leaders. The system encourages division and fragmentation. Further adding to the division is the fact that, to prevent dictatorship, Uruguay had for a long time a plural executive ("government by committee") consisting of nine persons who represented the main lemas and sublemas. This was a wonderful system so long as the economy is booming to achieve parity, co-participation, and co-government; but after Uruguay's economy went into a slide, the political system mainly produced gridlock, indecision, and paralysis. Uruguay could not effectively deal with its problems, which then led to polarization, a guerilla movement, and the military coup which produced (uncharacteristic for Uruguay) political repression.

So off I went in search of the lemas and sublemas. Batlle had succeeded in building the Colorado Party into a majority political organization by mobilizing the working and middle classes of Montevideo behind a strong reform agenda, but as the steam ran out of his program opposition to his leadership arose within the party and anti-Battle factions (sublemas) were formed. I had received from my old mentor Kantor contacts to the democratic-left sublemas within the party, but as I interviewed their leaders I found that both the lemas and sublemas had turned into gigantic patronage machines, very corrupt, clientilistic organizations, with leaders awarding their friends and supporters by giving them cushy government jobs and multiple entitlements which the country could no longer afford. Uruguay, which because of its advanced social welfare system was variously referred to as the "Sweden" or "Switzerland" of Latin America, was going broke; and its paralyzed political system was incapable of dealing with the problems. This was Sweden or Switzerland run amuck, awash in corruption, special favoritism, and gridlock. As the military in the next few years began its "creeping coup," aimed at weeding out corruption and straightening out the political system, I was not entirely surprised.

In one of the most democratic countries of Latin America, democracy had produced not pluralism and liberalism in the American sense, but conflict, corruption, paralysis, and such fragmentation that it verged on national disintegration and near-civil war. We would later see the same or similar processes in Argentina, Chile, and, more recently, Venezuela. It got me for the first time to thinking that democracy in Latin America was not the end-all and be-all of the political process; instead democracy, in its inorganic forms, seemed to produce a gradual national unraveling that led to sclerosis, paralysis, and breakdown.

Argentina

It was only a twenty minute flight across the Rio de la Plata from Montevideo to Buenos Aires. For reasons that only our travel agent knew, we arrived in the middle of the night. This is not something you want to do when traveling with a small child, especially since we had no advanced reservations. Plus, the tourist information booth at the airport was closed at that hour, and our taxista into the city informed us that one of Argentina's largest interest groups, the Rural Association, was holding its annual convention that week and there were no hotel rooms available. So there we were in this giant city, with our baby in our arms, and no place to stay. Fortunately the taxista took pity on us and promised not to abandon us until he had found us a room. After three or four hotel stops in the downtown area, he informed us that he had found us a room, just off Calle Florida. But it was the presidential suite at the then princely price of $95.00 per night. I snapped it up, wanting to take care of my family first but recognizing my faculty research grant would run out quickly at these rates. The next day that same hotel managed to find a regular room for us, at the regular price.

Buenos Aires is an incredible city; with about seven million residents at that time (one third the Argentine population), it was the ninth largest city in the world. It is a very sophisticated city, a city that consciously imitates the European cities of Rome, Paris, and Madrid and likes to think of itself as the "Paris of Latin America." It is also a beautiful city in the central area (but not in the outlying slums!) of broad boulevards and parks that remind one of Haussmann's city plan for Paris, of magnificent theaters and public buildings, of great opera and culture. Buenos Aires produces great classical music, has a magnificent literary tradition, has wonderful shopping and dresses in all the latest styles—from Paris of course! It is also a royally screwed-up city: Buenos Aires has more psychoanalysts per capita than any other city in the world, more even than (Woody Allen's) Manhattan!

During our first days in BA as it's popularly called, we took a grand tour of the city. The first day we took in the downtown area exploring the Plaza de Mayo, the presidential Casa Rosada ("Pink House"), the cabildo or town hall where the Argentines rose up against Spanish colonial domination in 1810, the Cathedral, the Congress, and the Banco de la Nación Argentina. On another walking expedition we went up to the famous Teatro Colon, the Opera House, the Obelisk. Walking still farther afield we visited the old immigrant district where the tango was invented, La Ricoleta with its elegant residential and shopping districts, and San Martín with its first class hotels and boutiques.

Just ogling, strolling, and people-watching in Buenos Aires is a joy—just like in a European capital. The people in the downtown area (El Centro) are elegant—or at least appear to be, appearances being all-important. We would stroll down Calle Florida (of course!) and then back up San Martín: to see and to be seen. Many Argentines had beautiful, tailored wool suits and elegant coats—often furs. The women are very fashion conscious, dressing with a Parisian flair, with just a touch of bleach in their hair to provide blond streaks, and wearing there hair long like a lioness. Iêda discovered that one could shop for a variety of fur styles in one of the many boutiques, and then be transported by limo (with champagne!) out to the suburbs to be measured and fitted, and have the completed, tailored, customized coat delivered to our hotel the next day. It's like the process by which tailored suits are made in Hong Kong or Singapore. Although we didn't buy, we discovered that even on my lowly assistant professor salary Iêda could have had an absolutely beautiful, hand-made fur coat.

In BA we met for dinner our graduate school colleague Paul Lewis who was writing his dissertation on the Febrerista Party in Paraguay—all of whose leaders were in exile in Buenos Aires and Montevideo! Paul had gotten his MA at Florida and had overlapped with Iêda and me, but he then transferred to the University of North Carolina at Chapel Hill to get his Ph.D.; he ended up taking the Tulane job that I had also explored. Argentina is of course famous for its luscious beef and steaks, thick, juicy, tasty, range fed, and very cheap. For Paul and his wife Ann, Iêda, and me, the total bill—four persons, with wine, steak dinners, first-class restaurants, everything included—was less than $8.00. That's total, not per person. Wow, did we eat well in Argentina!

We had arrived in Argentina at an interesting moment (July, 1966). The ineffective but democratically-elected, Arturo Illía had just been replaced by a military regime headed by General Onganía. It was a familiar pattern and dilemma in Argentine politics: the labor-based but quasi-fascist Peronist movement had been overthrown and kept out of politics by a succession of three military regimes. But how can you run a country if you exclude 40-45% of the population from participation in the national political life. Yet whenever the military bowed to political pressures and allowed the Peronists to run, they inevitably won the election which then triggered another military coup. That had happened both in 1962 and now in 1966. The present government of Onganía, however, had vowed to stay in power to reform the entire political system, introduce honesty and probity (perish the thought!) in the handling of public funds, and also reform morality by turning the lights up in Argentine nightclubs. But the reforms failed, the country fragmented and polarized, virtual civil war broke out, and the military regime was forced to use even greater repression. Thousands were killed in the most gruesome ways. It was a formula for disaster.

Even though Argentina is the most developed country in Latin America, the most literate, the most modern, the most middle class, it is also deeply divided, fragmented, and prone to breakdown. It does not at all conform to our social science cum policy notions that the more developed a country is, the stabler and more democratic the country tends to be. This paradox, this contradiction—a rich, developed, sophisticated country yet thoroughly unstable and periodically unraveling—is at the heart of the Argentine psychosis—and why it has so many psychoanalysts. For the Argentines themselves are mystified by the questions of why such a favorably endowed country is unable to govern itself.

Many factors are involved; I will focus on only three of them. First, it is precisely because they are so richly endowed that many Argentines feel they don't have to work or put forth effort. Let's call it the "Saudi syndrome." Here's a country with the world's richest agriculture in the <u>pampa</u>, loam soil so deep that anything will grow and you can drive a plow for 1200 miles and never hit a stone. In addition there is iron ore, oil, manganese, natural gas—all the resources one needs to become a developed country. But if that is so, why work? And if the country goes bankrupt, as it does periodically, even in the midst of all this natural wealth, it must be the fault of corrupt, venal politicians or exploitive multinational corporations, never the fault of the Argentine people. Argentina is therefore the home par <u>excellence</u> of the old Spanish get-rich-quick mentality, the attitude of live a gentlemanly life but <u>never</u> soil your hands with actual work, the sense that this world owes them a living and will beat a path to their doorstep but that no effort on their part is required.

The Argentines are a haughty people, thoroughly unloved by their fellow Latin Americans. While individual Argentines are often nice, pleasant, and hospitable, the overall Argentine political culture tends to be self-centered, egoistic, elitist, and selfish. Argentines are, and think of themselves, as the most "European" of the Latin American countries. That is a racial code word for white. The Argentines tend to look down on their mestizo and mulatto neighbors elsewhere in Latin America. They are superior, condescending, and racist. They cannot comprehend why they, a <u>European</u> country, should be plunked down in this God-forsaken, mongrelized wilderness called Latin America. For this reason, the Argentines are thoroughly despised by all their neighbors.

The Argentines seek to maintain a first-world standard of living on a third world income. They want to be a tropical South American Sweden, Denmark, or France but their per-capita income places them closer to Bolivia or Paraguay. Argentina has a vast welfare system and an elaborate system of entitlements (many Argentines receive income from 5-6 entitlements at once) but it cannot afford them. It is a system dominated by corruption, patronage, and sinecures— not just for individuals but for vast groups of people. Organized labor, business, the Church, the military, students, professors, journalists, artists, film-makers— <u>everyone</u> is on the public payroll in one way or another, usually multiple times. Argentines habitually live way beyond their means; to pay for this vast extravagance they print bundles, even wheel barrows full of worthless paper money, borrow heavily abroad, and then depend on the IMF, World Bank, or U.S. to massively bail them out, which occurs about once every decade. Without such bailouts, the economy collapses and usually the political system as well.

One final consideration bears mentioning. Like the other Latin American countries, Argentina is an organicist and a corporatist polity, not a pluralist one. The theory needs to be elaborated, but I am convinced that development within such an organicist/corporatist framework leads not to greater democracy and pluralism à la the U.S. but instead to segmentation, fragmentation, polarization, morbific politics, and ultimately to paralysis, gridlock, and national breakdown and disintegration if not civil war. As the most "developed" of the Latin American countries, Argentina has proceeded further down this conflict-prone path than any other nation. It is a scary thought because, if correct, it means all the assumptions of historic development theory (Rostow, Lipset, Deutsch, Almond et. al.) and of the U.S. foreign aid program (pour in economic aid and democracy and stability will automatically and universally follow) are wrong, fatally flawed.

Chile

From BA we flew westward across the pampa, toward the Andes (the world's second highest mountain range, after the Himalyas) and Chile. From the Argentine side, the ascent is gradual and peaceful; but when on later trips I flew easterly from Chile to Argentina, the ascent is so steep that I was sure we were going to crash into the mountains before gaining enough altitude to clear them. From any direction, descending into the Central Valley of Chile is rather like that of landing and taking off in Costa Rica: the Valley is so compact and the surrounding mountains so high that you have to do a looping, circling route to get down to ground level. If you succeed in dodging the peaks, it is a spectacularly beautiful view, with snow-covered mountains all around and a lush, green valley below. Need we say that Chile has some of the most spectacular, all-year skiing of any country in the world and, don't forget, our summers are their winters: July and August are the height of the ski season.

On a map Chile looks like a geographical extravaganza, a string bean stretching some twenty-nine hundred miles (almost as long as the U.S. from east to west), tucked in along the west coast of South America in that narrow stretch between the Andes and the Pacific Ocean. But in fact—and again the parallel with Costa Rica comes to mind—eighty percent of the population and virtually all of the industry, banks, government, and society are tucked into the central area, and are particularly concentrated in the capital of Santiago. One of the main reasons for democracy's success in both Costa Rica and Chile is precisely because these two countries were so well integrated. Even before the onset of modern communications and transportation, these two countries were knitted into a functioning nation-state because most of their effective life was concentrated into a single, small, interpersonal geographic region.

Of all the Latin American countries, Chile is the one that bears the closest resemblance to a continental European political system. One suspects that is why so many American and European scholars go to and study in Chile. It seems familiar to them. They think they are at home. It appears to be like France. They think they understand its politics. It conforms to their prejudices. It seems to fit their ideological models. And many Chileans abet these notions by claiming to be the "most European" of the Latin American countries.

When we arrived in 1966, Chile was governed freely and democratically under the Christian-Democratic presidency of Eduardo Frei. Chile at that time had basically a six-party system arranged neatly and ideologically along a left-right spectrum as in the French parliament. On the left were the Communists and Socialists, with the Socialists on some issues more radical than the Communists. In the Center were the Radicals (also patterned after the French Radical Party, including its anti-clericalism) and the Christian-Democrats, then the largest single party. On the right were the Liberals and Conservatives: traditional, nineteenth century elite parties. Not only did the party system reflect the Left-Right European pattern but the political culture (educated, participatory), the interest group system (closely tied to the parties), and the state-bureaucratic system were predominantly European-style as well. Chile appeared to be a stable, functioning, democratic state.

But these appearances disguised some troubling features under the surface. For one thing, the Chilean economy was in bad shape; like Uruguay, Chile also had an advanced, elaborate, European-style welfare system which it could no longer afford and which its politicians failed to face up to. Second, Chile's history was not quite so peaceful and democratic as supposed: in the 1930s it had been governed under the dictatorship of Carlos Ibañez who brought back Chile's dormant authoritarian tradition and also introduced corporatism into the country. Third, the Left groups in Chile were pursuing when we were there (pre-Salvador Allende) some totally irresponsible strategies: land seizures, factory sabotage, political strikes and disruptions, pro-Castro and pro-Soviet policies. Fourth, there were powerful groups in Chilean society—fascists, reactionary clerics, corporate groups, most importantly a politicized Army—that this "European country" interpretation of Chile ignored. I understand and agree with the interpretation of Chile as more European than most of the other Latin American countries, but that should not disguise the other features in Chilean society that are not particularly democratic and may be even anti-democratic. Already in 1966 we were able to observe the division, fragmentation, and polarization in Chilean politics that would lead to breakdown, near-civil war, the Pinochet coup d'etat, and mass repression a few years later.

If one only concentrates on the "European" character of Chilean politics, therefore, one misses a lot. For Chile is also and at the same time a "Latin American" country. We may be happier focusing on those aspects that make Chile appear European, but that is not a complete picture of the country. It also has coups, authoritarianism, elitism, organicism, and corporatism—perhaps not as much of these traits as other Latin American countries but present nonetheless and which we ignore at our peril. Moreover if our interpretation is that Chile is basically or perhaps only a "European" country, then what happened in 1973— the Pinochet coup, the repression that followed—is only explainable as the result of "outside forces:" the CIA, Nixon, Kissinger, the Pentagon, U.S. policy. But that is not an accurate picture either: I have had numerous Chilean military officers and business elites claim to me that they are resentful of the fact that all the credit for the coup went to the CIA, when they are perfectly capable of overthrowing their own government by themselves, thank you.

What we are saying here is that while Chile has the outward (and many inside) appearances of a French-style democracy, it also has other forces coarsing through its history that are closer to the troubled histories of Spain or Portugal. And that one ought not to emphasize exclusively the one to the total exclusion of the other. As Iêda and I toured Santiago in the summer of 1966, all these conflicting currents were on display.

We had a fine time roaming around the center of Santiago. In the Plaza de Armas, the symbolic heart of Chile as well as its political, social, religious, and commercial center, we observed vendors selling religious icons, street performers swallowing fire, and older men playing chess in the southern corner of the park. Nearby is the cathedral, twice destroyed by earthquakes and once by fire, and rebuilt in the classical style in the 18th century. The National Congress, the central Post Office, and the Audiencia (now the National Historical Museum) are all nearby. A few blocks away is the Moneda Palace, the nerve center of the Chilean government. When we were there in 1966, Chile was still so peaceful (at least on the surface) that we could walk unescorted into the courtyard of the Moneda.

We stayed in a comfortable <u>pensión</u> that served excellent meals and fine Chilean wine, for which the country has more recently become famous. But it only served instant coffee, not the real thing. In fact in all of Chile, we never found a single decent cup of coffee, which bothered my Brazilian-born wife. Can one imagine a Latin American country that does not serve real coffee?

We explored the environs of Santiago but, even though I am an avid skier, did not have the time to go up into the Valle Nevado ("Snow Valley") or to the ski resort of Portillo east of Santiago for the superb summer skiing. Plus, our daughter, still under two years old, had caught a cold and we began to think we might have to cut our trip a little short. She didn't have a fever and was only sniffling; if truth be told, it was mainly her parents who were beginning to run out of steam from this long trip. But we still had one more stop.

En route to the airport we had one more adventure. A call came in to the taxi driver from our pensión claiming we had stolen a towel. The driver stopped long enough to search our bags and then reported back that we had no stolen towels. I wrote this off as a simple mistake (they had misplaced the towel) on the part of the pensión. But Iêda saw more sinister motivations. She believes it was the secret police looking for an excuse to search our bags. Could this have been a foretaste of what would occur systematically and much more brutally under Pinochet?

Peru

From Santiago we started our return trip home. Taking off from Santiago with the Andes to the east and the Pacific Ocean off to the west is always spectacular. You fly north, over the water but up the coast; looking out the right-side window the spectacular Andes with their snow-capped peaks are clearly visible in the distance for some five hundred miles. There seems to be no pollution here at all—although Santiago, located in the valley, has a pollution problem as bad or worse than Los Angeles. Proceeding up the coast, next comes the Atacama Desert, Latin America's largest and home to some of Chile's vast mineral deposits.

As we head toward Lima, the plane flies farther out over the Pacific and the Andes recede from view. It's about 1400 miles, a little over three hours. When we arrive in Peru, it's a completely different world from the one we had just been in.

Peru is divided into three main areas which support completely different lifestyles and even civilizations. First is the coastal plain. That's where the airport, Lima, Trujillo, all the major cities, and the European or Hispanic part of Peru is located. Then come the mighty Andes, the heart of the ancient Inca civilization, what John Wayne would call "Indian Country." Finally there is Amazonian Peru, over the Andes reaching eastward toward Brazil, hot, tropical, and jungle territory, home of primitive Indian tribes, largely unpopulated and undeveloped (except now for coca), stretching over two thousand miles all the way to the Atlantic. One of my old biology professors at the University of Michigan wrote a fascinating book about this area titled "East of the Andes and West of Nowhere."

Rather like Guatemala, Bolivia, Paraguay, Ecuador, and maybe Mexico, <u>the great issue</u> in Peruvian politics has always been, over five hundred years, how to integrate that great Indian mass, the majority of the population, into national life—politically, socially, culturally, economically. <u>No</u> government ever in Peruvian history—colonial or independent, left or right, military or civilian—has ever succeeded in doing so, although there have been many abortive plans. Without such integration, Peru can never be complete, or successful as a nation.

Historically, the whites, the Europeans, lived in Lima and along the coast, while the Indians lived in the highlands. But during the course of the twentieth century, as part of the larger process of urbanization, more and more Indians had been moving to the coast and to the capital. Lima was now surrounded by Indian squatter settlements or <u>calampas</u>; this migration pattern is literally changing the face of the country. I am not a Peru specialist but I have traveled there frequently, averaging maybe once every five years since that first visit in 1966; and at every one of these intervals Lima looks more "Indian" and less "European." In other words, the Indian civilization of the highlands is slowly (not so slowly) moving down to the coastal plain and supplanting, or growing up alongside, the European civilization of the capital, thus reversing or rolling back the pattern of settlement that goes back half a millennium. Some Indian movements (such as the murderous Tupac Amaru and the Sendero Luminoso) want to go so far as to roll white, western, Christian, European civilization back into the Pacific from which it came. Meanwhile the indigenous groups here and elsewhere in Latin America are increasingly asserting their <u>rights</u> as against the central government, rights the assertion of which are often even more complicated by the fact that they cross national boundaries.

Along with Mexico, Peru was one of the two main centers of Spanish colonial rule in the Americas. Both were viceroyalties, the highest rank in Spanish colonial administration. Because both were the centers of the main pre-Columbian Indian civilizations in the Americas (Aztec and Maya in Mexico, Inca in Peru), they offered ample opportunity for spreading the Christian faith. But perhaps there were more prosaic reasons for Spain thinking of these two as its most valuable American colonies: both had vast wealth in gold and silver, and both had abundant, virtually endless native labor supplies to exploit.

The most ambitious and imaginative program in all of Peruvian history to integrate the Indian population into the national life was that of the Alianza Peruana Revolucionaria (APRA). Founded in 1924, APRA was the granddaddy and inspiration of all the democratic left parties in Latin America. It had a social-democratic agenda, advocating revolutionary change but using democratic elections as the only legitimate route to power. However, even though it was by far the most popular party in Peru, its route to power was consistently blocked by the Peruvian oligarchy using the military as its counterrevolutionary agent. Whenever APRA won an election or even showed signs of doing so, the Army would annul or cancel the election. Rather like the military and the Peronistas in Argentina, except that in Peru: (1) the Apristas were clearly the majority party regularly winning up to 60% of the vote, and (2) this cycle of Aprista electoral victories and military annulments went on for over fifty years, from the 1930s through the 1980s. You can't have democracy on that basis; Peru was not a democracy.

The founder and leader of the Apristas was Víctor Raúl Haya de la Torre. Extremely intelligent and charismatic, Haya had been a presidential candidate several times but had consistently been denied the presidency by the army and the oligarchy. The last thing these oligarchs wanted was to see Peru's Indians become educated, mobilized, and integrated into the national life. From the oligarchy's point of view, it was better to keep the peasants poor, illiterate, and downtrodden. That way they would not become "uppity." But Haya had always championed the integration of the Indians into the national life, and for his efforts he had been repeatedly jailed, even becoming a famous case in international law when he once sought and was granted political asylum in a foreign embassy in Lima but the Peruvian government nevertheless refused to allow him safe passage to the airport to leave the country.

My old mentor Harry Kantor had befriended Haya while he was in exile, had thoroughly studied Peruvian politics, and had written his doctoral dissertation (later book) on the program and ideology of the Aprista movement. APRA had also served as the inspiration for many like-minded democratic-left parties in Latin America: the Febreristas of Paraguay, Acción Democrátíca in Venezuela, the PLN in Costa Rica, the PRD in the Dominican Republic, and others. So, armed with a letter of introduction from Kantor, I made an appointment to see Haya and to visit APRA headquarters.

It was one of the most amazing interviews and visits I've ever had. First of all, APRA headquarters is not just a party office; it is a whole block-wide complex. Second, there I found not just classes in agrarian reform, labor organization, and peasant mobilization but also technical classes in appliance repairs, electronics, and hair-cutting (for both men and women). Third, the headquarters had all the appearance of a radical movement that had been under siege for decades, including monitors, guards, and, on one wall, the mounted bars of the jail cell in which Haya had once been a prisoner. Finally, there was Haya himself: barrel-chested, domineering, intellectually sharp despite his advancing years, and wanting to question me (about the DR and Central America) as much as I wanted to interview him. It was one of those rare moments when you know you're in the presence of a great man, somewhat larger than life.

As had occurred in the DR and Central America with leaders of other democratic-left parties, young APRA organizers took me around Lima and into the countryside. The party organization was impressive! It was Peru's best-organized and most unified political force. APRA had won the 1962 election but had been denied power by the military. The next year the armed forces had staged new elections won by its favored candidate, Fernando Belaúnde Terry and his Popular Action Party. When we were there in 1966, Belaúnde was still in power but already the campaigning for the next election had begun. APRA had made common cause with the supporters of General Manuel Odría in Congress to block Belaúnde's reforms, a marriage of convenience (since Odría had earlier been responsible for keeping APRA out of power) that discredited the party in some voters' eyes. But Haya told me that the party needed to make this alliance in order to enhance its possibilities of winning the next election. Whether that would have proved a sound strategy we will never know since in 1968 a reformist Peruvian military took power again and steered Peru in some radical new directions that permanently altered the political landscape.

We didn't have time for a lot of sightseeing in Lima, as our trip was drawing to a close. One night we traveled out to the upper class neighborhood of Miraflores for dinner. And since Lima was once the administrative center of the viceroyalty, it has a regal history as the "city of the kings" that lives on in its Plaza Mayor, the presidential palace, and the cathedral. Lima also has a lively intellectual life, considerable sophistication among the elite families (even Haya traces his history back to the conquistadores who arrived with the Pizarro brothers in 1535), and a vigorous street life, not least in the hundreds if not thousands of "informal" businesses that line the main streets.

But once one leaves the center Lima is not a pretty city; its many adobe slums inside and surrounding the city give it a gray ugly, appearance. Moreover there is constant fear: fear that some day all those majority indigenous peoples up in the mountains will swoop down, whether in the form of Sendero Luminoso or some other rebaptized organization, and reclaim the city and the country for themselves, sweeping that thin veneer of white, Catholic, Hispanic, European civilization back into the sea.

Wrap-Up

We flew home directly from Lima, the end of our scheduled excursion "around the horn" of South America. We flew over the Andes and refueled in Trinidad, before heading up on the last leg to New York.

What a trip! We had seen most of South America in an intensive, eye-opening eight-week span. It was not meant to be a trip involving large blocs of original research—we didn't have time for that—but a get-acquainted venture meant to introduce me to the area and to provide grist for my teaching on <u>all</u> of Latin America. But the trip had important intellectual advantages for me as well, not only introducing me to new countries but also broadening my intellectual horizons. I was particularly intrigued by the presence of organicism and corporatism—ideas that had fascinated me in the DR, Mexico, and Central America as well—in so many forms, varieties, and types of regimes: the Punto Fijo of Venezuela, Peronism in Argentina, the cogovernment arrangement in Uruguay, the Stroessner regime in Paraguay, Christian Democracy in Chile, and now the Apristas in Peru. When combined with the research I was doing on the Vargas regime in Brazil and the Catholic labor movement there, these insights would fundamentally change how I viewed Latin America. And, all modesty aside, my writings on these subjects would have a big impact as well on the professional body of Latin Americanists and their interpretation of the area.[3]

NOTES

1. "From Fragmentation to Disintegration: The Social and Political Effects of the Dominican Revolution," America Latina, X (April-June, 1967) 55-71. Reprinted in Eugenio Chang—Rodríguez, The Lingering Crisis (New York: Las Americas, 1969), and in Richard Fagen and Wayne Cornelius (eds.), Political Power in Latin America (New York: Prentice—Hall, 1970.

2. "The Dominican Fuse," The Nation (February 11, 1968) 12-16, as well as the rejoinders in subsequent issues.

3. "Toward a Framework for the Study of Political Change in the Iberic-Latin Tradition: The Corporatist Model," World Politics, XXV (January, 1973) 206-35.

CHAPTER 6

BRAZIL—1966, 1968, 1970, 1972

We had previously skipped over the Brazil part of our 1966 trip, indicating that visit deserved a chapter by itself. So let us return now to Brazil, flying into Belém from Venezuela, then going on to Rio de Janeiro, Belo Horizonte, and São Paulo, before flying on to Paraguay.

The reasons Brazil deserves special treatment are that we spend a lot of time there, my wife Iêda is Brazilian, we have extensive family there and wonderful access and connections. From the mid-1960s on we traveled there at least every other summer, with Iêda going there even more often to do research and visit her family. And, if truth be known, there was a time during this period when, given the access and extensive family connections, I thought seriously of becoming a Brazilianist, of specializing in Brazil. In the end, I decided not to do that, but in the meantime we spent some marvelous times in Brazil and I carried out some research projects there that changed my whole way of thinking about Latin America.

Belém

Flying over the Amazon jungle is an incredible experience. It is the world's largest rain forest. From the air it seems to form an endless carpet of green—no towns, no roads, no lights—sliced only by the curving contours of vast rivers. As we flew south from Venezuela, we crossed the equator—the first time for me. Generated by the steam and heat of the rain forest at the equator, vast billowing clouds and storm centers rise to fifty or even sixty thousand feet. It is impossible even for commercial jetliners to fly over these storms. As one crosses the Amazon basin, lightning from these huge cloud patterns seems to envelop the plane. Even the huge 747s bounce around in this buffeting as if they were matchsticks. I don't think I have ever been so petrified on a plane ride as when crossing the Amazon—especially right in one of these violent thunderstorms.

The Amazon's statistics are impressive. It is the world's largest river—by far. One can go on it by oceanliners for nearly 2000 miles, across the continent to Iquitos in Peru. The force of the river is so powerful that it carries fresh water fully one hundred miles out into the Atlantic Ocean. Many of its tributaries, all unknown to Americans, are bigger than the Mississippi. The basin of the Amazon covers four million square miles and extends to eight other South American countries. Brazilians are fearful that the U.S. Pentagon has plans to seize the Amazon or dam it up, thus creating a gigantic inland lake useful for trade and commerce no doubt, but depriving Brazil of half its national territory. It will not happen!

The Amazon rain forest produces a third of the world's oxygen supply and about 20% of the world's fresh water. Colleagues often ask me why Brazil seems hell-bent on developing ("paving over") the Amazon since it provides the rest of us with the air we breathe, but they do not understand Brazil's nationalism and its overweening desire to develop. Why should Brazil remain poor and underdeveloped, Brazilians ask, for the sake of giving us a lifetime of oxygen; and in any case aren't we Americans the world's largest polluters? Under international pressure, Brazil does in fact, at least formally, often bow to these demands, but informally Brazilians farmers, loggers, miners, and land speculators continue to exploit the area's vast resources. And the area is so huge—roughly half the size of the entire United States—that it seems unlikely to be exhausted within any of our lifetimes.

The Amazon contains 500,000 catalogued species of plants and animals. Many areas remain unexplored, and there are still stories of lost tribes, Amazon women, unearthly creatures and gilded cities—El Dorado. Much of life centers on the river and its vast inland waterways, some of which are so wide that one cannot see across. In exploring the markets of this area I have seen what must amount to every conceivable fish, animal, creature, root, flower, poison, herb, and aphrodisiac known to man. Many—especially the eels—we are probably better off not sampling or knowing too much about. You can also buy, live, many varieties of man-eating piranhas, either for cooking (ugh!) or to bring home to release in your local backyard pond!

We landed in Belém, near the mouth of the Amazon, at 4:00 in the morning. Belém in those days was a city of only 150,000; now its population is over a million. It lies on the south bank of the Guamá River, a little down the coast from where the Amazon empties into the sea. It is barely above sea level and only three longitudinal degrees below the equator; even at that early morning hour it was over 100° and 100% humidity outside, and absolutely stifling in the unairconditioned airport immigration area. By the time we got out of the building my clothes were completely soaked through with perspiration. We have a running joke in our family from this experience: because Iêda is always cold, she insisted on sleeping under a blanket in our hotel room even on the equator and right at sea level In that steamy, 105° "jungle outpost."

We have another early memory of this visit. This was my first time in Brazil and, naturally enough, Iêda wanted to show off her country in the best possible light. So after napping for a couple hours after our overnight plane ride, we went down to the hotel restaurant for breakfast, and I quickly discovered a dead fly (or bicho) in my coffee cup. When I politely mentioned this to the waiter, he took up the cup, examined the bicho, blew it out of the cup onto the floor, and then proceeded to fill that same cup with coffee and handed it back to me. Ugh! I don't want to drink out of a cup that had a dead fly in it. Iêda was appalled. This was not the first impression she wanted me to have of her country.

Belém is a port city, serving both riverine and ocean-going traffic. Strategically located, it was first settled by the Portuguese in 1616, who saw its value as a military outpost and a gateway to the Amazon. Like the city of Manaus a thousand miles west upriver, Belém was subject to the boom-'n'-bust cycles of the Amazon. It prospered during the rubber boom of the late-nineteenth century, but after the rubber trees were spirited out of Brazil by the British and replanted in Malaysia, the entire Amazon area went into an economic tailspin. Wood, minerals, and tourism are now reviving the area. From Belém you can take a riverboat cruise up the Amazon and through its immense tributaries.

Belém is the capital of the state of Pará. Right at sea level and only a few degrees off the equator, it is hot and sticky all the time, even at night. If you're going to tour the city or the river, it's best to do it early in the morning. The rest of the day is too hot to function.

As a port city, Belém has everything imaginable. That means sailors, transients of various kinds, tourists, prostitutes, an incredible social and racial mix of people. It reminded me, on a much larger scale, of Puerto Barrios in Guatemala. Both are hot, steamy, tropical, right at sea level. Both have gone through cycles of boom and bust, based on the exploitation by outsiders of local resources. Both, à la Graham Greene, have the scent of rot and spoilage in the air—both literally because everything tends to spoil in that searing tropical sun, and figuratively in the sense that buildings, marriages, families, public administration, and government all seem to wilt in the punishing heat and humidity. Everything, buildings as well as institutions, are affected by rot and putrification.

Young and adventurous, we were determined to see the city despite the stifling heat. But it doesn't take long before you're completely drenched with perspiration. And in the mid-1960's, there was almost no air conditioning. Nevertheless, we wandered around the streets of the city, determined to see it all. The Cathedral da Sé, built in the 1770's, is a mix of baroque, colonial, and neoclassical styles; it was constructed during one of the Amazon's periodic booms. The Forte do Castelo was the original fort built by the Portuguese, to ward off foreign interlopers and as a base for exploring the Amazon. Right downtown are the Our Lady of Mercy and Saint John the Baptist churches, designed by the same architect who designed the cathedral and built in the same era. My carpenter's eye immediately noticed that in all these historic buildings, severe wood rot has set in; it would take another thirty years before restorations were begun—almost too late.

We walked down to the river to explore the sights and sounds. Some of the streets are still lined with mango trees, but these are disappearing. At the riverfront it was sheer bedlam: noise, smells—a cacophony of visible, auditory, and olfactory impressions. Small riverboats were loading and unloading, people were everywhere, it was raucous, the smell of rotting fruit (all those dropped mangoes) and fish was everywhere. It seeped into your clothes along with the heat and perspiration. Here, there are varieties of fish, snakes, eels, animals, fruits, and tubers that I've never seen before. Of course, there is no refrigeration or even ice, so the smells are pretty overwhelming. It's a place you want to visit once but probably not again.

We had gone to Belém because I had insisted that we couldn't go to Brazil without seeing the famous Amazon. But once there and having seen the sights, we discovered that we couldn't leave. There were only two flights a week from Belém to Rio. We were stuck there whether we wanted to be or not. So we spent three days roaming around in that steam heat—not a place, I decided, that I would want to live permanently.

Belo Horizonte

We eventually flew from Belém to Rio de Janeiro, landing at Brazil's Galeão international airport. We were met there by Iêda's brother Hegel, a medical doctor (bone specialist) who was both a professor of medicine at the Federal University of Minas Gerais and had his own private clinic in that state's capital of Belo Horizonte. Iêda's family is full of medical doctors: another brother who is a neurosurgeon in Chicago, two nieces who are cancer specialist in Brazil, their husbands also doctors, and a younger brother who is a veterinarian. Rather than touring Rio at that time where Iêda has more, but not immediate, family, Hegel whisked us off by car to Belo Horizonte. Although we had been married for going-on three years, this would be my first opportunity to meet my wife's family.

It should be said immediately that when I go to Brazil and stay "en familia," I am treated like visiting royalty. I am wined, dined, cared for, protected, shielded from bad things, and enveloped in a multi-layered cocoon that is the Brazilian family system. I never have to cook or do dishes, never mow the lawn, and live a life of leisure. A car and driver are often put at our disposal, appointments are arranged for me, only the best food is prepared, I am chauffeured off to wherever I want to go, and maids are put at our disposal. In part this is the Brazilian extended family and its generous hospitality at work; in part it is Brazilian nationalism, wanting me to see only the good parts of Brazil and never the bad. As an independent American, I sometimes find all this family attention, pampering and protection a little confining, even smothering; at the same time it's kind of nice to be enveloped in family attention and to have all roads paved and flowered before me. Brazil can be a difficult place for outsiders and foreigners to live and do research, but when I am there, because of the family connections, access is guaranteed and all doors swing open.

That is one reason why I flirted during this period of my life with becoming a Brazil specialist. Through the family, I have marvelous access and connections. One of Iêda's uncles, Wanor Oliveira, (much more on him below) was an old-time politician and patronage operator at local, state, and national levels. I could swear he knew everyone in Brazil, and he took it upon himself to show me, a visiting foreigner, the ropes. I don't think Uncle Wanor ever understood my profession as a professor of political science (he had been trained in law; at this time political science was still an unknown discipline in Brazil), but he took me under his wings and was determined to show me everything about Brazilian politics and to introduce me to everyone he knew. I don't think I ever enjoyed myself more than when I was out on the political circuits with Uncle Wanor.

In addition, I was literally married to Brazil. The noted Columbia University anthropologist Charles Wagley used to say that if you truly wanted to understand Brazil, you had to marry a Brazilian. He and I had both done so—he into a landholding family from the Northeast, me into a professional family (Iêda's father was a high school principal in Belo Horizonte). I have always felt that being married to a Brazilian gave me insights into the all-important Brazilian family system, the patronage network, the behavior of the middle class, the professional and political elite that few people had. So why not take advantage of these family circumstances to become a full-fledged Brazilianist.

Belo Horizonte is only about two hundred miles north of Rio. It is the capital of the state of Minas Gerais ("General Mines"—famous for its gold, iron ore, and diamonds) and the third largest city (after São Paulo and Rio) in Brazil. It is more traditional and conservative than these other two, less sophisticated and less international. Though in the U.S. this drive would take about three hours, on Brazil's windy roads—and pre-expressway—it took most of the day. We climbed first to Petrópolis where the Brazilian monarchy and then elite families and politicians took refuge from Rio's summertime heat, then through Juiz da Fora where Iêda's father (and later president and family friend Atemar Franco) had come from, next Santos Dumont (named after the Brazilian version of the Wright Brothers but whom Brazilians claim beat the Wrights as the "first in flight"). Approaching Belo Horizonte ("Beautiful Horizon") over the mountains from the south, we saw how the city got is name: surrounded by mountains, tree-lined avenues (most of which have since been cut down), and gorgeous views in all directions (now, unfortunately, like Santiago or Mexico City, obscured by thick pollution).

Our destination was the home of Iêda's older sister, Edna, and her husband Paulo on Lake Pampulha on the western outskirts of Belo. That is where we would be staying while in Belo. They had a beautiful home, designed and built by Paulo, overlooking the lake. Their neighbors included ex-mayor, ex-governor, and ex-president Juscelino Kubitschek (who was also the godfather of Iêda's high school graduating class and whose wife worked with Iêda's mother on social programs for the poor—see what I mean about family political connections!), a social club (with pool and tennis courts) where Paulo was a member, a church designed by world famous architect Burle Marx, and across the lake Belo Horizonte football stadium where I spent many evenings learning the fine points of Brazilian-style soccer—then the world's best.

Paulo worked as an executive for the Bank of Brazil in an office building in downtown Belo. Soon I started riding into town with him in the early morning to explore the city and do research, returning by bus in the early afternoon. The house he had built could be described as a Brazilian version of Frank Lloyd Wright: ranch style, blending into the environment, overhanging eaves, open space, cantilevered balconies, tiled patios, very graceful. Paulo and Edna had three children all of whom earned doctorates: one in medicine, a second in engineering, the third in computers. They were a superior family and, in the tradition of Brazilian hospitality, gave Iêda, Kristy, and me the master bedroom with our own private bath and a balcony overlooking the lake. They normally had one maid who had been with them for decades and was almost one of the family, but for the duration of our stay and to help out with cooking and cleaning, they brought in a second maid.

From this description it sounds like Edna and Paulo were wealthy. But they were not. They had built their house themselves. Paulo's job, though white collar and therefore by definition middle class, was not very well paying. And yet, in the tradition of Brazilian hospitality, which is quite like that in Russia, they felt they had to show us a good time, give us more than everything we needed, and leave a good impression. For example, even though I repeatedly offered, Paulo would never allow me to buy soccer tickets, fill his tank with gas, or pay for all the food we were consuming. As a matter of pride and hospitality, he would always pay for everything.

I also learned, en familia, the fine points of maids. Some work, others loaf. Some are honest, others steal. Some are there only briefly to find an excuse to take you to court, which under Brazilian law favors the poor. Some practice spiritualism or voodoo, others not. If you're so unfortunate to hire a maid that practice voodoo, it means she works very few days because she celebrates Catholic, national patriotic, and voodoo holidays, leaving only a scattering of work days. Plus you can't fire a voodoo-practicing maid or she'll put a hex on you, your plants, or your children. While not all Brazilians believe this, they are wary enough that they will hire a second maid to do the work rather than firing the voodoo-practicing one.

What a time we had! Paulo and his family were exceedingly gracious, way beyond the call of duty. Their children were all bright but exceedingly polite; we used to have two-on-two soccer games on Paulo's balcony overlooking the lake. Iêda's mother (my mother-in-law!) was a gem, very intelligent, a good sense of humor, always accommodating, never pressing me too hard, always managing things efficiently so our visits went smoothly and pleasantly. Iêda's father was also exceedingly intelligent but quieter and sometimes withdrawn; not long after this visit he was diagnosed with Alzheimer's disease.

Hegel and his wife Eleanor and their three children (also polite) invited us to their house for dinner. Uncle Wanor and his wife Gina came up from Rio and took us to his club. His daughters, cousins Carmen and Sónia, were young and fun-loving Cariocas. We later had swinging Sónia as a guest at our house in Amherst. In those days the New England Patriots ran their summer camp in Amherst. The first day she was there, I took Sónia down to see the practice. She was mightily impressed. Since this was her first visit to the U.S., she inquired if all American men were built like that: muscular, three hundred pound behemoths. To string her along, I said yes. Even today, Sónia remembers this episode and is still impressed by American men.

Paulo drove us to <u>Ouro</u> <u>Preto</u>, the gold-mining town that had once made Portugal the richest colonial power in the world. He and Edna took me to an auction and craft fair in Belo where we arranged to have a gorgeous mahogany wood carving custom made (so that it would just fit in our biggest suitcase) depicting all the spectacular churches in Ouro Preto, themselves steeply climbing the mountain from which the city's famous "black gold" came. Iêda's mother masterfully supervised the household, often putting on three full meals a day and, for my benefit, cooking them American style—always complete with three or four desserts. Younger brother Elio invited us out to his small farm in Sabará, another historic town outside of Belo where Iêda's mother and father also had a house and where Iêda's mother built and administered a combination school, medical clinic, and social service center.

I learned that both Paulo and Hegel, in addition to their city homes, had farms out in the country—Paulo a small one of about twenty acres close to Belo and Hegel a giant estate of thousands of acres east of the city that included the highest mountain in the state of Minas. As a doctor, Hegel always carried antibiotics in the car and distributed them widely, knowing that among poor people everyone in Brazil had a disease that the medicine would surely help to cure. This was his way of being a distributor of "patronage," in his case in the form of medicines.

Because of Paulo and Hegel, Iêda and I became interested in buying land in Brazil (still very cheap at that time) and explored several large estates north of Belo in the Sete Lagoas and Reprêsa Tres Marias areas. But there are great difficulties in foreigners buying land in Brazil and, though it was beautiful country, we decided it was too far to commute on weekends. However when we got back to Amherst, we began looking at farm and wooded land in the Berkshires of Western Massachusetts, made our first purchase in 1969 which we then kept adding on to, and became rather like a Brazilian <u>fazendeiro</u> (landowner). The trouble is, there are no peasants to work and care for the land in Western Mass as there are in Brazil; we had to do that ourselves.

Every day I would take long walks or runs along and even all the way around Lake Pampulha, studying the spectacular architecture of the fine homes there— gathering ideas that we later incorporated when we built our own Amherst house. I also went into central Belo every day. It is (or was) a beautiful city, with a large central park, broad avenues filled with flowers, and clean streets. I went up to the neighborhood where Iêda had grown up and her family had lived, two blocks from the square that fronted the governor's mansion and from the Isabella Hendrix School where her father was headmaster and she, her sisters and brothers had gone to school. It was a Methodist School and hers a Methodist family—unusual in Catholic Brazil—and I'm sure the Protestant religious background importantly shaped the values and strong work ethic of Iêda and her family. Isabella Hendrix was recognized as the best school in Belo Horizonte, with the result that Catholic and Jewish families also sent their children there, adding to its diversity and multiculturalism.

Living on the salary of a schoolteacher made Iêda's family middle class in social terms but poor in economic terms. They never owned a car, which affects her self-confidence in driving still today. They never had bicycles and the toys that American kids enjoy, and had to make their own toys and improvise their own games. They devised traps to catch birds—and then cooked and ate them besides. As budding surgeons (Iêda had also taken and passed the medical school entrance exam, before winning a scholarship to come to the U.S. which altered her plans), Hegel, Edir, and Iêda occasionally operated secretly on the animals that wandered into their yard, much to the consternation of neighbors who sometimes found their pets permanently missing. On one notorious occasion (and a major family secret) the dog on which they were operating jumped off the operating table and ran away, with some crucial parts missing. The two older brothers (who often tried to get their little sister in trouble—is this a universal trait?) and Iêda received a stern warning and punishment from their parents over this one.

On that first visit to Brazil, while Iêda stayed with Kristy at her sister's house in Belo Horizonte, I took a side bus trip up to the new capital of Brasilia. I love to travel by bus in the Third World; you see and experience so much more than if you travel by plane or even by private car. The trip, which took all day, was reminiscent of my busito trips through Central America: bumping along on only partly-paved roads in a small van, stops in dingy cafes with no or primitive sanitary facilities, friendly people everywhere, small-town sidestreets where we picked up and let off passengers, a sea of humanity, animals, and unknown crops that crowded the streets and often managed somehow to get loaded onto our crowded bus.

Brasilia to me was a disappointment. There was some spectacular architecture—already showing signs of decay due both to the tropical climate and shoddy construction—in this planned and artificially created capital, just opened in 1960, located in the vast interior and designed to lure Brazilians away from the coastal cities and to develop new frontiers. Already vast slums had grown up in the area surrounding the city. Brasilia itself seemed barren and without life; it still had none of the clubs around which much of Brazilian social life swirls. Uncle Wanor explained to me that even though the government had <u>formally</u> moved to Brasilia, almost all politicians and government officials only flew up there on Tuesdays, spent two days in the capital, and then flew back to Rio on Thursdays for a long weekend in their "real" homes.

While in Brasilia then and on later occasions, I went to the university and met with David Fleischer, an American political scientist like me who had also married a Brazilian. We got along well, had a lot in common, became good friends and stayed in touch over our forty-year careers. Unlike me, however, David stayed in Brazil, settled there, taught on a permanent basis at the University of Brasilia, and looked like and <u>became</u> more Brazilian than American. While at the University, I also met other members of the newly-created Political Science Department (as distinct from law), lectured there, and received an invitation to join the faculty. Back in Belo Horizonte a few days later, I also met with the new Political Science Department at the Federal University of Minas Gerais. All this was part of my effort to build up contacts in consideration of making Brazil my longterm research specialization.

The Research Agenda

I was thoroughly fascinated by Brazilian politics. In 1966 a military regime was in power, having taken over from the corrupt, demagogic, leftist government of João Goulart in 1964. Like the Argentine generals, the Brazilian generals had vowed to stay in power until they had reconstructed and reformed the entire corrupt, patronage-based political system; but unlike the Argentines, the Brazilians were skillful and good at it. They rooted out corruption, were determined to provide good, honest, public administration, and to develop the country. At least initially, the regime used only limited coercion; this was not a violent, repressive, human right abusing regime. It was not Pinochet.

I was especially interested in the organic, corporatist, patrimonialist features of the Brazilian system. I had seen these traits in other Latin American political systems; now in Brazil I was observing them both historically and, in updated forms, in the Getulio Vargas (1930-45, 1950-54) regime, in military regimes as well as civilian ones, in regimes of the left as well as regimes of the right. I was preparing to launch a full-blown theory of Latin American politics based on these corporatist—organicist themes which would stand in contrast to the American model of liberal-pluralist development. Although it drew on other sources (Mexico, the DR, Venezuela, Chile, Argentina, Uruguay), Brazil was the launching pad from which the theory emerged.

On that first trip to Brazil in 1966, I collected boxes full of newspapers, journals, books, and government publications related to these themes, which brother-in-law Paulo forwarded to me thanks to the Banco do Brasil mailing room. When I returned in 1968 and then again a couple years later, I came equipped with major research grants from my university's Labor Research Center (thanks to director Ben Seligman who had a longtime interest and experience in international and comparative labor movements), the National Endowment for the Humanities (NEH) and the National Institute of Health (NIH-for research specifically on the politics of population policy). My project in 1968 focused on the Brazilian Catholic labor movement. The research included case studies of the Catholic labor movement in Belo Horizonte and Rio as well as research at the central headquarters of the movement on top of the mountain (Santa Teresa) in Rio.

What an experience—never to be repeated—that was. Obviously I used Belo Horizonte as my main case study because I had my family and family connections there. First I scouted out the premises of the Catholic labor movement, on a side street in Belo. Then I walked in, cold turkey, with no letter of introduction and no connections (as I had with democratic-left groups in Latin America), and introduced myself to the low-level functionary in charge. All the <u>wrong</u> ways to do research in Latin America. Nor, am I Catholic—Iêda tells me that Brazilians can tell the difference between Protestants and Catholics in about five seconds. The functionary of course sent right away for her superior— a priest! While I am not Catholic, I have studied a lot of catechism in my lifetime and knew the writings of Saint Thomas Aquinas backward and forward. Could I bring this off and win the confidence of the priest?

We had a long chat. He must have been satisfied. He said he needed to consult with his board of directors, whose permission to study the organization came within a few days. Meanwhile I could begin work in the organization's library.

What a treasure trove! My experience, having done this kind of research on several occasions, is that often officials of an organization do not know what kinds of materials are in their own libraries and archives. Moreover, they are too busy and with insufficient time and inclination to take the time to check. One can often find out more in the library of an organization than one is supposed to find out or that its directors expect you to find out.

So there in the library of the Catholic <u>Círculos Operários</u> ("Workers' Circles," as they were called) of Belo Horizonte I found a complete collection of books on the history of the Catholic social movement about which I had never read in detail before, a rich selection of books on the history and sociology of the Church in Brazil, most of the major works on the determinative Vargas regime in Brazil and its relations with labor, business, and other groups of both left and right, picture albums depicting the history of the Catholic social movement in Brazil, and the annual reports of both the national and the local Workers' Circle movement. In addition and at least as valuable, I found files of private letters, internal memos, budget figures, and position papers detailing the relations of the Church and its labor movement with government officials, the state, private interest groups, and individual sponsors. Naturally I did not tell my clerical overseers that there was far more in their own library than it was prudent of them to allow me to see. The holdings were so rich that I could write most of my monograph there in the library and supplement these materials through interviewing of church, government, and labor union official.

So there I sat in the library for several weeks running, investigating every aspect of the Catholic labor movement. The library had a window that overlooked the assembly hall, so when new people walked in—usually recognizable from the photo albums I kept handy—I would hurry down to meet, talk to, and arrange to interview them. After a few days the staff and I were on friendly terms, and they must have assumed, since I was there every day, that I had the approval of the higher-ups. Often, when the priest wasn't there, I would ask them for additional information which they were pleased to supply. What a con man I am!

Occasionally I overheard snippets of conversation from senior administrators and members of the board of directors gesturing and talking among themselves, questioning what this <u>Americano</u> was doing there, but no one ever confronted me or demanded to know exactly what I was up to. Confrontation is not the Brazilian style and no one likes to precipitate a crisis; meanwhile I was spiriting documents out overnight in my briefcase to make copies on the Banco do Brasil copier and then returning them the next day, and even using the Círculos' own Xerox machine to make copies of other documents right on the premises. Probably these activities are not all in accord with "The Researchers' Code of Ethics" (there is no such code), but I did not purloin any documents and returned all of the ones copied to their original files. I do confess in the research to a degree of sneakiness, deviousness, and perhaps misrepresentation of what I was about.

Out of this research came an article and later a full-fledged monograph on the Catholic labor movement in Brazil. Despite the quite critical nature of the report of one of their own organizations, a Brazilian Catholic publisher also issued a Portuguese language edition.[1]

More important, this research helped serve as the basis for the elaboration of the more general and theoretical "corporative model" of Iberian and Latin American politics, the first iteration of which occurred the same year (1969) as the case study of Brazil was published.[2] In this model, which had a major impact on the field of Latin American politics, I indicated that Latin America was following a completely different model of social and political organization than was the case of the liberal-pluralist model of the U.S. That model was organicist, patrimonealist, elitist, corporatist, and often (but not exclusively) top-down and authoritarian. The model suggested an entirely new way of thinking about Latin America and argued by implication that U.S. assistance and development policy toward the region were based on a set of wrong assumptions. The elaboration of this model challenged and shook up the field of Latin American studies and its assumptions; it was also very controversial. And though it drew from other countries, Brazil was the primary country on whose developmental experience the model was based.

Rio de Janeiro[*]

Rio de Janeiro has to be one of the great cities of the world. It is spectacularly beautiful, with wide Guanabara Bay opening onto the Atlantic Ocean, steep mountains rising sharply off the sea, offshore islands that frame the sunrise, some of the most beautiful beaches in the world, and spectacular architecture tucked into the crevices and waterfront areas between the mountains. In addition, the Cariocas, as the residents of Rio are called, are pleasant, friendly, genuinely nice, and fun-loving people, and, as in California, they never feel guilty about going to the beach instead of to work.

As you come into Rio from the airport or, as we did on that first visit, driving from Belo Horizonte, you pass along the southern edge of Guanabara Bay. A spectacular suspension bridge across the Bay connects with the satellite city of Niteroi on the other side. You can then continue along the Bay aptly named Perimeter Avenue, passing by the old (Santos Dumont) airport; or you can turn into the city, proceeding down President Vargas Avenue into the historic Centro. There you will find the National Library, the History Museum, the Fine Arts Museum, the Municipal Theator, the Candelária Church, and the old U.S. Embassy—still used for U.S. government offices but now with the main embassy

---

[*]   I have also spent time in Brazil's other great city São Paulo. But I do not know São Paulo as well as I know Rio (although Iêda does) and—probably my own fault—I do not find São Paulo as exciting or interesting as Rio.

moved to Brasilia. In our various visits to Brasil I spent many afternoons roaming around the historic center of the city.

But on our first trip, our driver (Uncle Wanor's car, and driver) opted at our urging for the more spectacular beach route. Rounding the turn past Santos Dumont airport and the Museum of Modern Art, the road opens onto an eight-lane, ocean-front highway, with many parks and vast, gorgeous, open beaches and panoramas, that proceeds southernly through all the main luxury living areas of the city. The first beach is the circular Gloria Beach with the luxurious Gloria Hotel at the end of the curve; next come the Flamengo and Botafago Beaches—both beautiful and with expensive, high-rise apartment buildings lining the streets to the west. Proceeding through the tunnel, one comes out at the famous Copacabana Beach, then Ipanema (where the "Girl from Ipanema" song originated), then Leblon. These are the main beaches, each a mile or so long; but tucked in between are smaller but no less glorious beaches—Urca, Vermelha—that the tourists seldom see. Also tucked in here is the famous Brazilian Superior War College (ESG), attended by both the civilian and military leadership of the country where I have visited and lectured on several occasions.

But our introduction to Rio's beaches was not over yet. Past Leblon and going further south, where the backdrop of mountains that frame Rio's beaches and residential areas comes right down to the ocean, Avenida Niemeyer snakes along the edge of the mountain. To the east is the Atlantic Ocean with waves and spray washing up on the rocks below the road, to the west and climbing the mountain is Rochinho, one of Rio's most famous and spectacular slums, home to some 200,000 people and made famous in a variety of the films about drugs and violence in Brazilian favelas.

The road returns to sea level again at São Conrado, a natural amphitheater set in the mountains but with its own beach, the beautiful Intercontinental Hotel where I happened to be staying during the 9/11 terrorism attack on the U.S., the expensive Gávea Golf and Country Club, Pedra Bonita Mountain from which Rio's hanggliders take off to float over the sea, and a luxury shopping and residential center where many of the political, economic, and social elite live.

We had one more beach to go. Continuing on Avenida Niemeyer, once more climbing over the mountains where the lanes of the highway were constructed on top of each other to save building space, through some tunnels of solid rock until at the last tunnel the road opens up to a spectacular view. There is a river below, mountains to the west, and in front of us an eleven-mile stretch of pure white sand and gorgeous ocean, one of the most beautiful beaches in the world and then almost completely empty: the Barra da Tijuca. This would be our base during our many stays in Rio. Research in such an ocean-front setting is hard to take, right? Who could not love Rio in that beautiful beach location?

A word of explanation is in order. Iêda's Uncle Wanor had two apartments in Rio. The first, his main home, was centrally located in Villa Isabel. But he also had this beach apartment at the Barra. It was located on the fourth floor of a six story apartment building that faced the beach. At the time, it was one of only a handful of buildings along the beach; the Barra then was not the crowded, rather garish suburb it has since become. The apartment had three bedrooms, a kitchen, a dining area, a maid's quarters, a large living room and open patio that faced the ocean, and a garage in back. But because the time of our visits to Brazil—usually July and August—was Brazil's winter, Wanor and his family considered the beach apartment too cold. For me, however, growing up in Michigan, the temperature in the ocean at that time was about what it was like in Lake Michigan in August: about 70° and "just right." So while Wanor and his family stayed in Rio, coming out to visit us on weekends, he let us use the beach apartment. I'm sure we had the nicest living arrangements of any foreign visitor in Rio.

Our party consisted of Iêda's mother along to help us out with babysitting and to supervise the household, and a maid, really another family member brought along from Belo Horizonte to cook and help clean. What a life! During the week we were there by ourselves, able to write, do research, and engage in immediate family activities. On weekends Wanor and his family, assorted cousins and relatives, and even our friend Paul Lewis and wife Ann from Gainesville and North Carolina came out for lunch or a visit. But even then, Iêda's smart and shrewd mother, knowing that it was tiring for me to be surrounded by relatives, even kind and well-meaning ones, all of the time, served as an effective policewoman, shielding me from excessive obligations and providing us with times of privacy— all but impossible in Brazil's social and family-enveloping environment.

During the week the Barra was empty of tourists and other visitors. I would get up early just as the sun was rising over the ocean, and go for long runs on the beach—extremely strenuous exercise when your feet sink into the wet sand. Tiny crabs scurried across the sand as the waves receded and burrowed into it as the waves washed out. Kristy and, later, Howard, loved to chase and catch them, throwing them into a bucket which, even though they were only an inch round, we would clean and cook. We would see jellyfish washed up on the beach and whales out to sea humping over the waves. After busy weekends, we would find flowers, bottles of wine, and pots of rice and beans on the beach—offerings by Brazil's many practicing spiritualists to the gods. If the tides came in and took these gifts with them, it was a sign the gods were happy and the person offering them would be blessed. Even though Brazil has many poor and hungry people, we never saw any of these foods tampered with or taken; Brazilians know better than to anger the gods.

At midmorning, when Brazilians usually arrived at their offices, I would hop the bus that stopped right in front of the apartment house and go into the city. Back along Niemeyer Avenue to Leblon where there was a central bus area and I had to change vehicles. Late in the afternoon or early evening I would return along the same route—unfearful then of what has now become a near-epidemic in Brazil: crime and violence. In those days Columbia University Professor and Brazil specialist Ronald Schneider had an apartment in Leblon (not as nice as ours!) and we visited him there. Then, along all those spectacular beaches again for appointments in Botafogo, Flamengo, or the Centro.

On various days I visited the Ford Foundation offices in Rio, the Getulio Vargas Foundation (a major research center and think tank), the National Library, and the U.S. Embassy. As part of my research on labor relations, I did work at the Labor and Social Security Ministry, as well as at the headquarters of the Círculos Operários (which also housed a Catholic research center) in Santa Teresa. When Iêda and I later did research on the politics of family planning in Brazil, we visited hospitals, schools of medicine, various interest groups, the Health Ministry, the Office of Demography and Census, as well as, over several weeks, the Brazilian family planning agency BEMFAM. We also got together with many friends and Brazil specialists from the U.S.: Warren Dean, Charles Wagley, Lawrence Graham, Kenneth Erickson, Riordan Roett, the Schneiders, many others.

Recall, this was the period when I was trying to decide whether to become a full-time Brazilianist or not! I was exploring research possibilities and building up contacts—a process my Brazilian relatives thought was hilarious because I seemed to be in the "contacts" business. But back to the point: just the names above suggest that becoming a Brazilianist would involve some pretty strong competition. Ron Schneider was working on a project on contemporary politics very close to my own interests, and he was way ahead and knew much more than I about the subject; Ken Erickson was doing his dissertation on labor relations and the corporatism theme; Warren Dean knew the social and economic history cold; Riordan Roett was a specialist in development; Larry Graham was writing about the state and public policy. At that time Brazil was, thanks to the NDFL program that had paid my way through graduate school, becoming saturated with serious scholars many of whom knew more and had spent far more time in Brazil than I. Over time I decided: (1) to stick with my own research specialty, the Catholic labor/social movement; (2) to stick with my specialization on the

Dominican Republic where I could be a "star" (and almost only) scholar in a much smaller country; and (3) to write, based on my already extensive travels throughout the Caribbean, Central, and South America, on general, theoretical themes—i.e., the corporatism model.

In addition to my wife and the good fortune of being married into a Brazilian family, my other great advantage in Brazil was Uncle Wanor. Wanor, a lawyer had grown up in the embrace of the Republican Party of Minas Gerais, an old-fashioned and patronage-based party that in its glorious days back in the 1880s had helped lead Brazil's struggle for republicanism and against the monarchy. Wanor was himself a patronage politician and seemed to know everyone in the country, at local, state, and national levels. At that time he was director of CADE, the Couselho Administrivo de Defesa Económica (the Administrative Council of Economic Defense), a federal agency that combined the functions of the American Security and Exchange Commission (SEC) and the Anti-Trust Division of the Justice Department. This was an important office in Brazil that paid a good salary and carried prestige; it also helps explain the two apartments and the car and driver that he sometimes put at our service. Wanor's daughter, cousin Sónia, also worked at CADE as a librarian. He was very helpful in setting up interviews for me with Brazilian government officials

Uncle Wanor would frequently invite me to go along on his political excursions. What an experience! He was himself a politician (several times unsuccessful in running for elected office) and a back-slapper. He knew everyone from the president on down. When Uncle Wanor walked into a room, heads turned and he was immediately recognized everywhere he went. There would be many <u>abracos</u>, back-slapping, and inquiries after family and friends. Job and favor-seekers would gather around him. He was deft at putting people off, sounding positive but never quite committing himself, promising the moon but knowing he could not deliver all that was wanted. Wanor was an artist in practice of the aphorism that when a Brazilian says yes, he means maybe; when a Brazilian says maybe, he means no.

When Wanor walked into a government office and smartly slapped (with a loud snap) his calling card down on the desk, clerks and functionaries would scramble to do his bidding. He didn't have to actually hand out the patronage, but everyone knows that CADE in its anti-trust functions had the power to make or break almost every business deal. Except there was one time that I recall that his method didn't work. Iêda, as a Brazilian citizen, needed a document from the secret police that she was: (1) not a prostitute, (2) not a communist, and (3) had paid her taxes—or else she would not be permitted to leave the country. It's hard, as one can imagine, to prove these negatives; and as far as the taxes were concerned, she had left Brazil at the age of seventeen to pursue university training in the U.S. and therefore had never in her life had any income on which to pay taxes. But how to prove this. Anyone who knows Latin America can appreciate the difficulties—and the paperwork—that would be involved. So we enlisted lawyer Wanor and his political connections to help us out.

I was with Wanor when we went to the secret police (SIM) headquarters. As usual, Wanor slapped his calling card down on the desk, demanding attention. But no one moved, some sneered. Recall, the current government was a military regime that intended to introduce honesty and probity into the public administration; it did not operate by the old patronage rules—and that was especially true of the secret police. Wanor was extremely frustrated; I don't think he had ever before run into a situation where the (and his) old patronage rules did not apply. Eventually we did get the papers we needed but had to wait our turn like everyone else; for once, Wanor's "connections" and patronage way of operating did not work. It was a sign of the new, more modern, more efficient Brazil—but over time (even under the military regime) and in most other government offices the country slipped back into its bad old patronage ways.

What a time we had in Brazil in those years of 1966, 1968, 1970 and 1972! We had a gorgeous apartment right on the beach. We had a wonderful family that enveloped us warmly, seemed to know everyone in the country and the inside scoop about then, helped us enormously with contacts and appointments, and yet also was sensitive and sensible enough to leave us alone, give us privacy when we needed it, and keep unwanted relatives and others away. It was also a wonderful experience for our small children, to be included in a loving extended family, to have that beach to run and play soccer on, and to have nice, polite, bright cousins to play with.

The Barra da Tijuca was a great place. We could both relax and also work very hard. We swam a couple times a day. We had great tans from the beach—and because it was so isolated and deserted, never had to worry about theft. We had a built-in babysitter, a built-in maid, and relatives that went way out of their way to do favors for us, make us comfortable, and give us a good impression of Brazil. At the end of the day when I returned from the city center, Iêda and I would go down to a neighborhood tavern for beer (Brahma) and a dishful of (fish, nuts, crab, olives) appetizers. It was in many ways an idyllic existence. But we also needed eventually to go on to other things. And those other plans would soon take us away from Latin America and toward Europe as a major research enterprise.

NOTES

1. Howard J. Wiarda, The Brazilian Catholic Labor Movement: The Dilemmas of National Development (Amherst: Labor Relations and Research Center, University of Massachusetts, 1969); Portuguese edition published as O Movimento Operário Católico Brasileiro (Rio de Janeiro Centro João XXIII, 1974).

2. Howard J. Wiarda, "Toward a Framework for the Study of Political Change in the Iberic—Latin Tradition: The Corporative Model." First presented as a research paper at the Mershon Center, Ohio State University, 1969; later presented at the American Political Science Association Annual Meeting in 1971; and published in World Politics, XXV (January, 1973).

CHAPTER 7

PORTUGAL AND REVOLUTION, 1972–74

By 1966 I had lived, traveled, and done research in fifteen of the twenty Latin American countries—plus Puerto Rico. I had had excellent political, historical, and area studies training on Latin America at the University of Florida and, when coupled with my travels and research in the area as a young professor, thought I had acquired a good general knowledge of and orientation to the area. In addition, my wife and her family, from Brazil, gave me, I thought, particular insights into that most basic and fundamental of Latin American institutions: the family, in both its nuclear and extended forms.

In all this travel and research, several features particularly fascinated me. Wherever I had gone in Latin America, whether in Left or Right wing regimes, whether under civil or military governments, whether in one-party, two-party, or multi-party systems, the same basic, underlying, systemic characteristics seemed to leap out at me. These included a strong role for the unitary Latin American state (as distinct from the checks and balances of the U.S.), an organic or integral conception of public authority, the functional or corporatist conception of society, an emphasis on group rights as distinct from individual rights, elitist and hierarchical rule, and a top-down authoritative if not authoritarian conception of government. So many common features in such a great variety of regimes, I reasoned, could not be merely coincidental. Hence I determined to get to the bottom of these phenomena, to their roots and origins. And that meant a research project that would take me back to the mother countries of Spain and Portugal.

But which of these countries to choose? In making that decision, which was actually quite arbitrary on my part, my earlier research in the Dominican Republic and Brazil came into play. Never having been in Iberia before, I imagined Spain would be rather like Brazil: a larger, complex country with multiple centers of power, difficult for any one scholar to master in the one year's time that I had available. Portugal, I imagined, to be more like the DR: a small, compact country, with one major city and center of power, where everyone knows everyone else and everyone else's business, a country that one could really come to know in one year's time. Hence the decision went to Portugal—although the same research on organicism and corporatism could just as well have been done in Spain. In 1971-72, therefore, I began seriously studying and reading everything I could find on Portugal and the corporatist regime of Antonio Salazar. For Salazar's regime was often seen in the literature to be the purest, most complete and institutionalized extant example of a functional, corporatist state. I also began sending out grant applications to support a year's research abroad.

In Preparation

After having taught at the University of Massachusetts for six years, I had earned a year's sabbatical. My university, like most major research universities, gives you the choice of taking a half year off at full pay or a full year at half pay. In the four sabbaticals that I have so far earned over my lifetime, I have always taken the full-year option, supplementing the reduced salary with research grants that have enabled us to avoid absorbing a salary loss—and that have frequently enabled us actually to come out ahead.

This was to be, like all my sabbaticals, an especially ambitious research year. For since spending a year, 1969-70, at Ohio State University's Mershon Center for Education in National Security, Iêda and I had become interested in the issues of family planning and population control, what we called "the politics of population policy." At Mershon we had been members of an interdisciplinary faculty seminar focused on population policy and chaired by law professor Mary Ellen Caldwell. This was more Iêda's research area than it was mine, but I was interested as well, and it was a then very current, hot, and fascinating area of public policy. Iêda approached it more from a women's/child health care perspective while I, more skeptical, and less committed to the policy goals involved, saw it as a wonderful illustration of how the Latin American public policy process, and the role of outside donors and actors in it (the U.S., population agencies), worked or failed to work. Plus, since population policy was then such a hot issue (after Paul Ehrlich's <u>Population Bomb</u> and Robert McNamara declaring it the World Bank's number one priority), there was generous funding available for research on family planning.

Hence Iêda and I (it was mainly her initiative) applied for and received a generous, three-year research grant from the National Institutes of Health (NIH) for the period 1972-74, renewed again for 1976-78. Our project involved a comparative study of the politics of population policy in three countries that we already knew well: the Dominican Republic, Venezuela, and Brazil. The grants provided us with a way to get back to some of our favorite countries, while also involving me in a new and exciting policy area. Meanwhile, I had applied for and received a senior fellowship for 1972-73 from the Social Science Research Council/American Council on Learned Societies (SSRC/ACLS) for my project on corporatism/organism and whether these and other features constituted a distinct model of Iberic-Latin American politics, a project to be carried out in Spain and Portugal as well as Latin America.

In terms of travel and logistics, it was a very complicated year. First, I went off to the Dominican Republic in the spring of 1972 to do my case study of the larger population policy project. There I discovered: (1) that the DR saw the issue in purely national terms as compared with the global perspective of the population agencies; (2) that the DR felt it needed more people to combat nextdoor Haiti's always looming threat, rather than less; (3) that because of its Catholic tradition, the DR would be very leary of going too far on this issue; (4) that the international population agencies often practiced deception in dealing with the issue, talking about "family planning" but really meaning population control; (5) that these same agencies engaged in a stealth campaign of hiding the funding and sponsorships as they commenced these population campaigns; (6) that local interests and sensitivities were ridden roughshod over in the course of pursuing population controls; (7) that the U.S. government and international lending agencies were neck deep in all these campaigns but hiding behind the figleaf of "purely privately-sponsored" activities. It was a shameful program, badly conceived and executed, full of deception and shady undertakings that, if the issues were not so serious, deserved to fail. I enjoyed exposing some of these lies and false starts, which became very controversial, in my writings.[1]

In the fall of 1972, Iêda went off to Venezuela to do her case study. I stayed behind with our two children, Kristy and Howard. But since our Amherst house had been rented as of September 1, the kids and I stayed for a time in our newly-acquired summer cottage up on Norwich Lake west of Amherst in the Berkshires hilltown of Huntington. Kristy even went to school for a time that fall in Huntington; I did the cooking and household chores. But by the end of September it was getting very cold up there. Our water heater had conked out so we had to bathe in the lake. In the frigid water, Kristy cut her knee wide open on a submerged rock and I had to rush her to the hospital for stitches. And while our cottage had a heater, it worked poorly and the cottage had no insulation, with the result that my children were constantly complaining about the cold. What kind of father can put up with his children getting hurt and being cold? So we altered our plans, I made airline reservations as quickly as possible, and the first week of October we flew off to join Iêda in Venezuela.

Iêda had by then largely finished the Venezuela part of our population policy research, so after a week more in Caracas we went on to Brazil. Skipping Belém and the Amazon this time, we went first to Belo Horizonte for a week and then settled in once more at the beach apartment at Rio's Barra da Tijuca. In Brazil our research on family planning was aided by the fact that so many in Iêda's family were doctors, on the medical school faculty, or <u>in</u> the medical schools as students. Plus, Iêda's mother had endless friends and contacts in the health and social care areas, Uncle Wanor set up our interviews in the health ministry and other government agencies, and, it turned out, the head of the largest Brazilian "Family Welfare" agency, BEMFAM, was a family friend and distant cousin. Of course; that's how things work in Brazil!

Our research on family planning was parallel to the earlier work I had done on the Catholic labor movement. The issue was national but we focused on some narrower case studies—primarily in Belo and Rio—that we could really examine in detail. Once again, our use of the library of the organization we were studying yielded unexpected treasures: private correspondence, memoranda, and reports that detailed the entire, inside, private history of BEMFAM including its relations with outside donors—materials that, had the directors known were there, would never have been shown to us. And once more, we were able to use family and personal connections to gain access to people and organizations to which no one else could get access.

The Brazil research raised even more troubling issues about the politics of family planning than had our work in Venezuela and the DR. Brazil was/is very nationalistic; like the DR it wanted <u>more</u> people to fill its vast empty spaces (the Amazon basin) and developmental potential, not less. It suspected the U.S. had a plan through population control to keep Brazil underdeveloped and prevent it from becoming a major power. Once again, in a Catholic country, the abortion issue was explosive politically. The international population agencies, the World Bank, and the U.S. government all had conspired on a stealth plan to bring family planning to Brazil but to disguise it under the cover of a label that was otherwise unassailable, "maternal and child health care." Meanwhile, we discovered that the Brazilian agencies and some of the personnel in these nefarious plans not only despised the international (especially American) donors but, at the same time, were using the big grants from Planned Parenthood, the Pathfinder Fund, the Ford Foundation, the United Nations, and others to live a lavish lifestyle. We documented these tensions, conflicts, and even illegal activities in a series of reports—although the larger, book-length comparative study that we were planning remained only in draft form.[2]

By the end of November we had finished the Brazil part of our research and most of the overall project dealing with comparative population policy. We flew back to Amherst the week of Thanksgiving. Since our house was rented and occupied, we stayed in the home of our best friends, Marcia and Sheldon Goldman, who had gone to New York for the long weekend. Essentially in Amherst all we did was briefly catch our breaths, exchange one set of research materials (population policy) for another (corporatism), and exchange our summer-in-Latin-America clothes for our winter-in-Portugal wardrobe. At the end of that Thanksgiving weekend we flew off to Portugal, another leg in what would prove to be a very complicated and difficult research year.

In Portugal

We landed in Portugal, after an overnight flight, on the morning of my birthday, Sunday, November 30, 1972. The plane approaches Portugal from the west, flies over the coast and up the Tejo (Tagus) River, and banks sharply before landing at the undersized Lisbon airport. My first impression of Portugal was from the air and it was a favorable one: clean, neat, whitewashed villages in the area just north of Lisbon—probably Obidos and other impeccable towns like it. The villages looked attractive and that was part of the "charm" of Portugal: a quasi-medieval society seeking to turn the clock back to an earlier era as part of Salazar's vision of a stable, well-ordered, Catholic-corporatist society. But beneath the orderly, whitewashed façade, I would soon discover, were high levels of poverty, illiteracy, malnutrition, and underdevelopment, and the most rigid, ossified, pre-World War I society in all of Western Europe.

Of course, when you fly to Portugal overnight from the U.S., you land very early in the morning. We landed about 8:00 a.m., cleared customs before 8:30, and caught a cab to haul the many suitcases for a family of four. At that hour, and on a Sunday morning, the streets were deserted; we sped to our residence and the taxista, happy to collect extra fees for the baggage and in a hurry to be rid of us, deposited us and our suitcases on what appeared to be a deserted sidewalk at #32 Rua das Janelas Verdes. There was no sign out front, no door in sight, and no one on the sidewalk to tell us if we were in the right place. I was sure we had been given the wrong address, and with all those suitcases and a tired family in tow sitting there on a deserted sidewalk, our Portuguese excursion seemed to be getting off to an inauspicious, even dismal start.

I had been given this address and a recommendation by Larry Graham, a former fellow graduate student at the University of Florida who had also started out as a Brazilianist but had similarly begun to do research on Portugal. Leaving my family there on the sidewalk with the suitcases, I began to explore further, quickly discovering that behind the wall and to the side was a long stone stairway leading up. We gathered the suitcases and climbed, still not sure this was the right place. At the top were doors leading into a seventeenth century former convent, and finally a sign identifying this as Residencia York House. We had the right place after all.

It was a guest residence frequented by British and American scholars doing research in Portugal. There are only thirty six rooms: each has been marvelously restored and individually furnished. It is scrupulously clean and well cared for; meals are available in the comfortable dining room/patio garden area. It is atmospheric and small but with an intensely loyal clientele. Fortunately they had our reservations and gave us a room even at that early hour, but only after we pleaded that our children (us too!) were extremely tired from the overnight plane trip and needed to sleep.

We slept 'til noon, woke up refreshed, had a very late breakfast at the residence, and then went out exploring. Lisbon on Sunday is quasi-deserted as many residents head to the beaches at Cascais and Estoril. Rua Janelas Verdes is part of an older section of Lisbon, west of downtown, in the Lapa neighborhood, on one of the many hills overlooking the Tejo River. The Red Cross Hospital and the Museum of Ancient Art are located nearby; the parliament and the Bairro Alto neighborhood are within easy walking distance. We stayed at York House for a week while looking for an apartment.

We had four priorities before I could begin my research: obtaining an apartment, buying a car, getting our children in school, and opening a bank account. Finding a furnished apartment in Lisbon in those days was almost as hard as finding one had been earlier in Santo Domingo. There were very few available, the few available did not advertise in public want-ads, and most arrangements were done personally and by word of mouth. Most foreigners who worked in Lisbon found houses out in the luxury areas of Cascais and Estoril, which we could not afford. For three days we looked at a succession of dreary, dark, poorly and semi-furnished, and often water-damaged apartments mainly in the northern part of the city. I did not want my family to live in any of these places.

Finally I located a place out in the suburban Restelo area west of the city, above Belém. One goes out along the Tejo River to the Monument to the

Discoverers and the Jerónimos Monastery, turns north up the Rua dos Jerónimos, curves right at the soccer stadium on Rua Goncalves Zarca, and then left on Rua Tristão Vaz. This was a newer section of five and six story apartment buildings but with more light and open space (for the kids to play) than in central Lisbon. The apartment was furnished but not luxuriously, had two bedrooms (the children would have to be in one room) and two baths, a living room, dining area, kitchen, open-air balcony, and a maid's quarters which I used as my writing office. It was clean, carpeted, and had no obvious problems. It was so much better than anything I had seen previously that I snatched it up immediately.

That proved to be a mistake—at least in the short run. The apartment had two main problems: the plumbing and the electricity. Neither problem showed up until we had rented the place and moved in, by which time it was too late to change apartments. The plumbing problem involved a terrible smell in the bathrooms which we never fully got rid of despite several visits by a plumber, except by massive doses of Comet and Lysol. Iêda was convinced it was unhealthy and that our children would get sick, but they never did and over time the Lysol and Comet seemed to cover over the problem.

The electricity was more complicated. The apartment had been cheaply and inadequately wired. You could have the TV on or the water heater, but not both at once. You could have two weak lightbulbs on but not three. You could have the water heater on and one lightbulb but not two. Any such overload would result in explosions in the fuse box above the entry door, sparks shooting out, and all the power going out. During the first two weeks there I must have visited the landlord's office in the downtown Rossio at least every other day. He wanted my dollars and would send an electrician out to do the repairs; the man would replace the fuse but that night it would blow again. Finally, more substantial repairs had to be made that enabled us to have two machines on at once, or three lights, or one machine and two lights—but never more that that. On that basis we limped along and survived for the next nine months. Of course when spring came and the days got longer, the light and heat problems seemed not so severe. On such slim threads of hope and optimism are renting a place abroad often based.

We spent another week furnishing the apartment. It had the basic furniture but not bedding, pillows, blankets, towels, or kitchen items. In the process of buying these necessities we learned a lot about Portuguese society and the functioning (or lack thereof) of the economy. First of all, most goods were in short supply; second, many sizes were unavailable; third, domestically produced goods were often shoddy; fourth, imported items were prohibitively expensive.

All this was a product of the fact that in a corporatist, mercantilist, protected economy, as under socialism, prices, wages, and production were all set by the state, not the market. This led to shortages, poorly-produced goods, and often irrational prices. Service was similarly virtually nonexistent; no transaction could be accomplished quickly and efficiently. It was like living in the Soviet Union.

Eventually we learned to do our shopping across the border in Badajoz, Spain, not exactly a vibrant metropolis but infinitely better than shopping in Portugal. For in Badajoz there was a big Corte Inglés department store, with large selections, abundant goods, cheap prices, efficient and knowledgeable clerks, and the ability to take travelers' checks, credit cards, even personal checks. Since we had to renew our Portuguese visas every sixty days anyway, we came to look on the trip to Badajoz as an opportunity to go to an efficient and rational economy as compared to an inefficient and frustrating one.

Once we had the apartment more or less straightened away, we went in search of a car. Our idea was that we would spend the workweek in Lisbon but that on weekends we would regularly get out of the city to explore historic and beautiful rural Portugal. As we had done in the Dominican Republic—but using a borrowed Peace Corps Jeep. Not knowing a thing about the local used car market, we again relied on the want ads in the newspapers. It's hard to chase down cars in a city where we didn't yet know addresses or neighborhoods, and where we didn't understand prices or the culture of bargaining.

After three days of looking, we bought a gem of a used VW Beetle (considered a working class car) from the <u>porteiro</u> (custodian—a working class position) of a large Lisbon apartment house. I had it checked out by a neighborhood garage and paid U.S. $1000.00 for it. That car served us flawlessly for our entire time in Portugal, taking me to work every day, on our weekend expeditions around Portugal, and on longer trips to Spain, France, and Switzerland. In pre-revolutionary Portugal, as we sped along rural roads in our little Beetle, peasants would doff their hats and bow their heads as we passed by, obviously recognizing one of their betters! At the end of our time period in Portugal, we sold that car to another foreign researcher coming into the country for the first time—for $200.00 more than we had paid for it.

With our living situation settled and a car to take us around, we began to look for a school for our children. There were several choices: the French School, the English School, the American School, and a school run by Irish Dominican nuns. The French School was all in French and our children spoke only Spanish and Portuguese, so that was out; the headmaster of the English School was so excessively authoritarian and grouchy to the children during our visit that we wanted no part of it; and the American School seemed to be full of snotty rich kids. That left the Irish Dominican nuns' school, Saint Dominic's. At first, with my Calvinist background, I was reluctant to send my kids to a Catholic school, but as usual Iêda was more perceptive than I. She right away perceived the commitment and dedication of the nuns. And in fact it turned out to be the best school our children have ever attended, better even than the vaunted Amherst schools. The principal was committed to the school and extremely hard-working, the teachers were devoted to her and to the children, parents were involved in many school activities, and the learning environment was superb: orderly, disciplined, and yet kind and loving. Not only did our kids learn a lot in that school but the entire experience was enjoyable besides. The school turned out to be one of the best parts of our stay in Portugal. To attend the school, Kristy had to be fitted with a uniform, which could only be purchased at the firm of Edoardo Martins. The process required numerous visits, great inefficiency, and a month of grief before we got the uniforms: another example of the inefficiency and irrationality of the Portuguese economy.

Opening a bank account was the final preliminary item on our agenda, prior to beginning the actual research work. We had come to Portugal with cash, travelers' checks, and cashiers' checks, planning to open a savings and a checking account with the substantial cashiers' checks. So we visited one of the big downtown banks, the Banco Pinto e Sotto Mayor. We filled out the applications, turned over our cashiers' checks, and waited. And waited and waited and waited! Days and weeks went by without anything happening.

Over time I learned two things. First, the Portuguese banks were holding companies, conglomerates, family empires; small private accounts like mine were of no interest to them. Second and even more preposterous, the banks maintained a list of officially acceptable cashiers' checks signatures. Since my checks had been signed by a "mere" branch manager (not David Rockefeller!) the Portuguese banks would not accept them. Meanwhile we had begun to run out of readily available cash and travelers' checks and could not pay the next month's rent. It was another example of the rigidity, formality, and old-fashioned character of Portuguese institutions. Eventually we withdrew the still pending cashiers' checks from the bank, used some of our scarce cash and travelers' checks to open our accounts, and cashed the cashiers' checks in Badajoz. In my interviews I would soon learn more about the functioning of these banking grupos in Portugal.

The Research Agenda

Settling into Portugal took about a month. It is the stiffest, most formal, most bureaucratic, most traditionalist and old-fashioned, most inefficient, most difficult to operate in country I have ever lived in—until, that is, I lived in a former communist country in Eastern Europe, where the rules and bureaucracy are even worse. Over the years, since we return there often, Iêda and I decided that Portugal is a great country to visit as tourists—great food, great wines, great scenery, great history—but not to live in. Interestingly our closest Portuguese friends, though on nationalistic grounds loathe to admit this, privately tell us the same thing, lamenting the endless bureaucracy and immense amounts of time wasted on what should be simple transactions.

Once we had made the apartment livable, gotten a car, gotten our kids in school, and, finally, opened a bank account, it was Christmas time. Lisbon was pretty at that time of year. We bought a small Christmas tree (really a branch) and decorated it with a few fragile ornaments and paper items our children made in school. Iêda learned about the markets and which neighborhood vendors sold the best, freshest products. Even as the winter cold came on, we would head down to the Rossio, the city center, to shop and stroll with other Portuguese families. I bought a beautiful, all-wool, hand tailored, made-in-Macão overcoat which I still have and still looks like new. We would stop off for coffee, ice cream, deserts (Balas de Berlin), and/or a beer at the Café Suica—then the most elegant place to see and to be seen. Those were happy days; Portugal was looking up.

Sitting in the Café Suica was a great place to observe and watch the (Portuguese) world go by. There were few tourists on the streets. The Portuguese themselves tended in these pre-revolutionary days to be very formally and austerely dressed. Older women, because their husbands often died early (of gout, liver disease, heart problems, tuberculosis) tended to be almost uniformly dressed in black. Younger women tried to introduce a bit of color but somehow lacked the flair that French, Italian, or Spanish women have. I noticed that the older generation tended to be quite short and that even the men, at 5'3" or 5'4", wore elevator shoes. We used to joke about Portuguese men wearing high heels—until I learned more and discovered that during World War II that generation had been so deprived of food by the German/Nazi U-Boat blockade that they grew up malnourished and undersized. Another lesson in not joking about people's physical features! The much better-nourished younger generations in Portugal are a striking contrast in height to their elders.

Between Christmas and New Year's we took a long car trip in the newly-acquired VW Beetle to Spain, France, and Switzerland. This was part of our effort (see Chapter 8) to take advantage of our year in Portugal to explore Europe more broadly. It was a rich but harrowing trip (details below); it was also our last bit of vacation before the kids went off to school and I began my research work in ernest.

Right after the first of the year I began to go regularly to Portugal's National Library to do my research. That was an adventure in itself. As with all things Portuguese, the process was extremely bureaucratic, formalistic, and arduous. This was not a library like I was used to where you could just walk in and borrow a book. I had to present my passport, a letter from the American Embassy vouching for my character, and a letter from my university saying I was a bona fide scholar. The approval took several days to process; meanwhile, you cool your heels by waiting.

The library itself was a modern and impressive edifice with rich archival holdings. But inside, it was also bureaucratic and forbidding. Public access to the stacks was forbidden. Instead, upon entering, one used an elaborate form to present a list of books requested to the front desk. Within a half hour or so, the books would be delivered to your desk. But what if you didn't know the title or author? What, even more importantly, if you wanted to explore unknown but related titles shelved in the same section? Then you were out of luck. Fortunately I had to come to Portugal equipped from my U.S.—based research with a vast bibliography; and the footnotes in those sources helped with other great finds.

After a while we learned via the grapevine that the book requests we turned in every day were also examined by the PIDE, Portugal's dreaded secret police, to see if we were looking at forbidden or sensitive materials. I therefore concentrated on the historical part of my research first going back to the middle ages, assuming that would be "safe." I also learned to scribble the title and author in unreadable hand writing, leaving only the call number clear and assuming—correctly—the police would be too lazy to look up the actual book. In a funny twist, I even met one time the PIDE's secret spy within the library, over coffee and rolls in the library's cafeteria. He was as I expected: an old, broken-down bureaucrat, a time-server who had little real interest in what we were reading, not a jack-booted gestapo type. In fact, this was fairly typical of the Salazar regime: not vigorous fascism as was sometimes alleged but sleepy, tired, and old-fashioned. The PIDE agent and I had a pleasant exchange about Portuguese versus Brazilian (from which we had just come) soccer.

The library had incredibly rich holdings. Here is where I found all the materials later used in my book on the relations of contemporary corporatism to its Roman, Christian, and medieval historical and cultural roots. Here is where I found the materials on the early formation of the Portuguese and Spanish state system and the historic pattern of corporatist state-society relations. Here also I found French, Italian, as well as Spanish and Portuguese books on the ideological conflict between liberalism, socialism, and corporatism ("the three great isms," as the title of one of my chapters put it) in the nineteenth and twentieth centuries. And here I found unexpected and incredibly rich materials on the corporatism of Salazar's Estado Novo: the debates over the early corporatist constitution and labor laws, debates over what form corporatism (state or authoritarian versus societal and participatory) should take, entire journals devoted to the evolution of the corporatist regime, its changing legal and political bases, doubts and internal criticisms of it, its internal crises and the gradual evolution away from corporatism. All of this wealth of materials went into the major book I wrote, Corporatism and Development: The Portuguese Experience.[3]

The scholars using the National Library all worked in one great central hall, and I soon noticed that there was a handful of other Americans and English-speakers around. At the coffee bar and as we milled around early in the morning waiting for our requested books to be delivered, we soon became acquainted. The group included Douglas Wheeler, a historian from the University of New Hampshire who considered himself the "dean" of Portugal scholars in the U.S.; Sidney Greenfield, an anthropologist from the University of Wisconsin who was, related to my work, researching the origins of patrimonialism in Portugal; and Richard A.H. Robinson, a British historian from the University of Birmingham who was writing a history of twentieth century Portugal, also overlapping with my work. Thrown together by accident in dealing with the library inefficiencies and bureaucracy, we soon became fast friends, went to lunch together everyday, and shared information and sources.

Our lunches were an interesting dynamic. As the (self-appointed) dean of Portuguese studies, Wheeler, who was a bit of a stuffed shirt, demanded deference and an acknowledgment of his superiority from the rest of us, which we refused to give him. He was also a "dusty archives" historian, devoid of theory or models, believing the documents would "speak for themselves." Greenfield and I, as social scientists, scoffed at this, told Wheeler that he couldn't understand Portugal without using models or at least acknowledging his hidden or disguised models, and in effect said he didn't "understand" Portugal at all. For the "dean of Portuguese studies" this was too much to take and he would go stalking off—only to return again the next day. Robinson took a third position, as a dusty-archives historian but one who used social science models in his research. It was stimulating conversation, and in the process we all learned a lot and traded valuable bibliographic information.

As I learned more and my files filled with notes, and as I gained greater self-confidence in knowing how to operate in Portugal, I began to supplement this historical and archival research with interviews. As in the Dominican Republic dissertation research, I would spend mornings in the archives, head home for lunch, and then go in late afternoon-early evening for interviews. What an eye-opener into Portuguese society that proved to be! First, most of my interviews were very formal affairs and, in keeping with other aspects of the society, exceeding stiff and ritualistic. Second, they had to be arranged and choreographed in great detail, with letters sent in advance, my own credentials examined and explored, etc. One could not in Portugal simply "drop into" an office and expect to come away with any information; rather one had first to be "received," often with elaborate protocol and, to an American, a tremendous waste of time. Part of this was Portuguese formality but part of it was lingering fears of police-state retribution if they said the wrong thing.[*]

The interviews were fascinating, and I learned at least as much there as I did working in the archives. First, I discovered that many of the original architects of the Salazar corporatist state put in place in the early 1930s, such as Pedro Teotónio Pereira and J. Pires Cardoso, were still alive and willing to talk. Mostly idealistic members of Catholic youth and professional groups in those days, they were now in their 70s and 80s and, at that age, eager and willing to lay it all out to a sympathetic foreign investigator. Second, I found that there were still some academic and/or private centers for corporatist studies, in a couple instances still publishing a journal about corporatism and often with rich archives that rivaled those in the National Library.

Third, I interviewed high government officials to find out how corporatism and the Estado Novo <u>actually</u> functioned, as distinct from the founding laws and constitution of forty years earlier. Many of these public officials held private sector jobs simultaneously (no conflict of interest in Portugal!)—often in the banks that I'd already figured out were really holding companies. So there I was, for example, in the executive offices of the Banco Pinto e Sotto, ironically the same bank that at minor clerk levels was unable to accept my cashiers' checks for

---

[*]   As a visiting foreigner and a political scientist, we became convinced that our apartment telephone was being tapped because we often heard strange noises on the line. That was confirmed one time when, in a heated conversation with Greenfield over the merits and demerits of two Portuguese soccer teams, our "listener" could not restrain himself and, obviously himself a rabid fan, actually broke into our discussion to denounce what we were saying about his team! Another example of the comic-opera as distinct from police state nature of the regime by the early 1970s.

week after week. There and in other banks and corporate offices I was ushered into plush waiting rooms, with maybe a Velásquez on one wall and a Goya on the other. There would always be a <u>LeMonde</u>, usually unread, on the coffee table. Many of these buildings were a bit shabby on the outside but their inner courtyards were filled with Jaguars and Mercedes, and the interior furnishings were expensive and tasteful. It was in these banks/holding companies that real money and power rested in Portugal, and in the incestuous relations between government and these private companies. I had a never-to-be-forgotten chance to see them from the inside.

Fourth, I discovered that Portugal had a separate Ministry of Corporations, later renamed the Ministry of Corporations and Social Assistance as its functions became more like those of other European social assistance ministries. I had no contacts there and I just brazenly walked in one day and asked if the Ministry had a publications office and a library. It did, and I was quickly introduced to Maria Fernanda Sousa Fernandes, the chief librarian. She was pretty, pleasant, and extremely helpful in making ministry library and printed materials available to me. Her husband also worked in the ministry as a young lawyer, and he was also helpful in my research. Once again I discovered in the library private papers and documents extremely helpful to my research that, if they'd known were there, the ministry should not have allowed me to see.

Apparently someone did tell ministry higher-ups that there was a foreigner and a stranger doing work (snooping around?) in the ministry archives, and I was soon visited by ministry officials. My "interrogator" turned out to be Dr. Antonio da Silva Leal, director of the ministry's Center for Social and Corporative Studies. I must have passed his examination; indeed he was flattered, like others I had interviewed, that someone was actually interested in his subject matter. Silva Leal largely put the facilities, materials, and personnel of the ministry at my disposal, and of course I as usual used that opportunity to poke into offices and matters that I should not have poked into. Research in a closed, authoritarian regime like the Portuguese is tricky stuff but it can yield rich dividends.

A high point of my interviews was the one conducted with Prime Minister Marcello Caetano, who in 1969 had succeeded Salazar. Caetano had been a young student leader in the 1930s and one of the main architects of the corporatist state. He had later fallen out with Salazar but then made a comeback and was now prime minister. To gain an appointment with the prime minister, I had to specify beforehand what areas I wished to speak to Caetano about. To be safe, I wrote down "the early history of the corporatist movement," assuming that was neutral, bland, and old enough to get the appointment; hopefully the interview might expand into other areas as well.

But when I met with Caetano in the São Bento Palace, he spent about five minutes on corporatism and then turned immediately to the difficult issue of Portuguese Africa, at that time engulfed in three distinct guerrilla wars. Caetano told me that he wanted to grant some degree of autonomy to the African colonies but was blocked from doing so by conservative President Admiral Américo Thomaz, the military, and the big banks with vast holdings in Angola and Mozambique. He said that if he took even the slightest step toward granting autonomy to the colonies, he would be overthrown "just like that" (and at that he snapped his fingers to indicate that it would be instantaneously).

My own assessment, and that of the American Embassy, was that Caetano did have a window of opportunity, he was much more popular than Admiral Thomaz and "the bunker" (as defenders of the old regime were called), and he could have moved on both Africa and the domestic reform agenda if he'd had the courage and political skills to do so. But Caetano stalled, temporized, and frittered his opportunity—and his popularity-away. It's always easy to say in hindsight but had Caetano listened to us, Portugal might have avoided the revolution and social upheaval that followed exactly a year later in 1974.

Exploring Portugal and Portuguese Politics

As we began to feel more at home in Portugal and got used to operating within the confines of behavior of an authoritarian police state (however farcical at times), we began to expand our contacts, our activities, and our travels. We reached out to new friends and acquaintances. We even got involved in the domestic politics a bit. After our early frustrations, we came to enjoy Portugal and Portuguese ways and even invented a vocabulary ("Portuguese gridlock," a "Portuguese moment") to describe the dumb, frustrating things that happened to us.

While both Iêda and I made friends among both Portuguese and in the international and ex-patriot communities, living in Portugal was sometimes very difficult for us. First, Portugal is a quite stiff and formal society; especially under the austere and authoritarian Salazar regime, people kept their social distance; some could be stand-offish; and it is relatively rare for outsiders to be invited to see the inside of Portuguese homes and family life. Second, there is a strong strain of anti-Americanism in Portugal, a lack of respect for American universities and academic degrees, and a certain resentment toward what are perceived to be "rich" Americans. I personally experience these resentments, condescension, stand-offishness, and formality-verging-on-rudeness on numerous occasions.

As a Brazilian, Iêda had a particularly hard time in Portugal. She was often treated as someone "from the colonies," "from the tropics," probably racially impure, of obscure social origins, undoubtedly "inferior." Now it happens Iêda is the smartest, nicest, and most intelligent person I have ever met (no prejudice here on my part); with her educational background and Ph.D. she need not take a backseat to anyone. But with the <u>porteira</u> (caretaker) in our apartment, with vendors, with service personal, and even among some university-educated elites she was often treated as a second-class person. It was shameful behavior on the part of too many Portuguese—and puts the lie to the notion that Portugal is somehow less racist and less prejudiced than other colonial countries.

A good place to start the discussion of our Portuguese social and political life is right in our own neighborhood of Restelo. Up on the hill overlooking the Tejo river, the Monument to the Discoveries, and the Gerónimos Monastery, Restelo had clear skies, fresh breezes, and open space. My four year old son Howard and I used to go down to watch the boats on the river, especially the small, family-size freighters with their cars on the deck, and dream of traveling the world on a permanent sabbatical. Nearby was the coach museum (horse-drawn carriages) and the Belém Palace (once a royal residence) where we also visited as a family.

Across the street from our apartment was an open park where Howard, Kristy, and I played soccer every evening. A block up from the apartment was a steep hill good for climbing where Howard found a "secret place" to make his "fort." On top of the hill were two ancient windmills, left over from when our neighborhood was still a rural area, from whose heights we could look west all the way to the Atlantic Ocean.

Two blocks down from us was the big soccer or fútbol stadium. In those days Portugal had world class teams of which the best was Bemfica whose star player, Eusebio, came from Mozambique. One of the stories current was that the reason Portugal hung onto its colonies past its time was to preserve the flow of soccer talent from the "overseas." Howard and I went to several games though, if truth be told, both of us were bored by soccer; a good American college football rivalry (Michigan-Michigan State) has much more excitement and is a better "show" (bands, style show, cheerleaders, television, crowds, receptions, tailgate parties, plus the game) than any European soccer match.

Around the corner from us and a block down was the Ministry of Overseas (Ultramar)—that agency responsible for administering the colonies. I am not an Africa expert and had never been there, but in 1973 and living in Portugal one could not but be fascinated by the colonial situation. Portugal claimed, with some validity, it was different from other colonial powers, more open to racial miscegenation (as in Brazil), more relaxed and easy-going in dealing with native peoples. But the relationship was also exploitive and should have come to an end years before since it was not possible for such a small country to fight three guerilla wars at once (in Angola, Mozambique, and Guinea-Bissau), especially after the guerrillas got SAM missiles from the Soviet Union and began to kill Portuguese soldiers with disturbing regularity. Portugal is a small, closely-knit nation where everyone knows everyone else, and the sight of those increasing numbers of body bags lined up on the Portuguese docks was just devastating to the Portuguese soul.

So I dreamed up a research project that would take me to Africa. I proposed to study the effort of Portugal to transfer its corporatist laws and system to the "overseas." In preparation for the research I even found in Angola a journal dedicated to corporatism, a considerable amount of laws, social assistance programs, and institutions focused on corporatism, and even a fascinating philosophical cum policy debate on whether corporatism was applicable in nonwestern areas. To my surprise, the project was accepted and funded by the Portuguese government and I was scheduled to travel there in the spring of 1974. The government promised no interference with my research; I would not even have to go on television and proclaim what "great" colonizers the Portuguese were. Understand, this was only one year prior to the revolution and yet the Portuguese still in 1973 were so confident of their position in Africa that they were willing to let me, an impartial scholar, go there to observe and study with no strings or conditions attached. Unfortunately, just as I was ready to go, the Portuguese Revolution occurred, the colonies were precipitously and without preparation granted their independence, Portuguese Africa exploded in even greater violence and civil strife, and my trip had to be cancelled. It would take almost thirty years before I was able to make that trip to Southern Africa.

Across from the Overseas Ministry and just above the soccer stadium, two blocks from our apartment, was a gorgeous area of beautiful, single-family homes, the nicest residential area in all Lisbon. As a student of architecture, I used to take long weekend hikes through this neighborhood again gathering up ideas for my own future house; Iêda and I would take shorter walks there in the evenings as spring dawned. President and Admiral Thomaz also lived there and we would often pass him on our evening strolls. Much to our surprise, the President had no or minimum security; we would say hello and nod our heads as we passed in the street. In that same neighborhood and whom we also met on the streets at night lived Jimmy Roosevelt, son of FDR, and Robert Anderson who had been a cabinet member in the Eisenhower Administration.

Slightly farther afield we socialized with some of the U.S. families assigned to NATO's Iberian Atlantic command (Portugal was a member, mainly because of its bases in the Azores but Spain was not) established in 1971 and headquartered in the neighboring suburb of Oeiras. Our kids' school was also in Oeiras and we made good friends there too among the teachers, principal, and parents. Portugal in those days was a haven for ousted European royalty and Latin American dictators so among the children at the nuns' school was a grandchild of dictator Fulgencio Batista of Cuba, the great grandchild of ex-king Umberto of Italy, and a great, great grandchild of former Queen Victoria of England. As good Americans, our kids were not impressed with royalty types and knew them just as José or Mary.

The Greenfields and Wheelers lived farther out in Estoril and Cascais and were good and gracious friends even after our spirited luncheon exchanges. Our best friends were an Italian family from a neighboring apartment house whose kids went to school with ours and caught the same schoolbus every morning. The parents, our age, had been born in Ethiopia during the period of Italian conquest in the 1930s and, like us, were very much internationally oriented. Iêda and she became quite close friends during our period living there.

We (or at least I; Iêda was pregnant by now, and it was a difficult pregnancy that made it difficult for her to get around) also socialized through my growing list of political friends. While we lived in Portugal, a new newspaper, Expresso, had appeared which was by far the freest, most free-wheeling paper in the otherwise censored press. Expresso writers and editors pushed right up against the limits of the censorship in publishing the best available analytic and investigative stories covering all aspects of politics. I interviewed Expresso's editor, Francisco Pinto Balsemão, and we became good friends. He later became Prime Minister and, in that capacity, I saw him in Washington. Balsemão introduced me to his chief writers, a number of whom briefed me on contemporary political issues. Some of these were also involved in opposition politics.

Other opposition groups were centered in the academic and professional communities. I became close to several members of the CENDES (Center for Economic and Social Studies) study group and was invited to some of their get-togethers. The first time I went I was expecting a small social group; instead I found several hundred of the country's leading artists, scholarly, and journalistic communities. These reminded me of the agapes thrown by the PRD in the DR in 1964-65. Opposition political parties were still illegal in Portugal, so the opposition had organized as a "study group" instead. But it was really a political party, specifically the nucleus of the Social Democratic Party (PSD). And just as in the DR ten years earlier, the CENDES meetings were both to serve as a way of rallying the opposition <u>and</u> of demonstrating to the regime that the opposition was a sizable force that had to be taken seriously.

The degree to which Portugal had liberalized under Caetano may be surprising to those who think of the rigid authoritarianism of the Salazar regime. The censorship had become much more relaxed, the secret police were much less repressive, and liberal reforms in the areas of education and social policy were under way. Opposition groups were forming more or less openly in anticipation of the regime coming to an end; opposition candidates both civilian and military were beginning to plot their campaigns; even the underground Socialist and Communist parties had begun to step up their activities. The political pot was stirring, yet in the face of this Caetano continued to temporize. He neither repudiated the older Salazar regime or its corporatism and authoritarianism, nor did he come around to embrace liberalism and democracy. A popular joke at the time captured the temporizing this way: "you can always tell Caetano's car in traffic because it signals left but turns right."

While the political system was astir with rumors and political comings and goings, no one anticipated the revolutionary upheaval that would engulf Portugal the following year. Portugal was considered far too traditional, too Catholic, and too conservative for that. The scent of change was in the air but not revolution.

We left Portugal (more on that below) in July, 1973, only nine months before the revolution exploded. But in February, 1974, only two months before the revolution, I was called back to Portugal by the State Department to advise on political developments. Rumors of coups and coup plotting were in the wind, lots of political balls were up in the air. The Caetano government managed to snuff out one of the coup attempts but it missed another, even larger one, as well as the social upheaval boiling underneath. The image I used then, as in the DR in the months before the 1965 revolution, was that of a juggler (the president or prime minister) trying to balance a variety of balls or spinning bowling pins that had been tossed into the air. As they came down, he caught one or two of them. But he lost sight of the others, and one of them came down and hit him on the head.

Winding Up

That spring, once the weather got better and I had the research for my book on Portuguese corporatism well in hand, we began traveling around Portugal more and more. We went to Obidos for a day, a beautifully preserved and whitewashed city that still looks like a medieval town. We went up to the mountain town of Sentra where the English poet Lord Byron stayed for a time. We toured Mafra and the incredible royal palace located there. We traveled to

Coimbra to visit the historic medieval university and its gorgeous library, after which I patterned my own office library—complete with book-laden balconies— in our home in Washington, D.C. We went to Oporto and up the Rio Dão River to see (and sample) the famous Portuguese wine industry.

On longer trips we went to Evora, an historic town that was often a battleground between Christians and Moors, later between Spain and Portugal. On my own I went to Santa Comba Dão, the small town where Salazar was born, not to worship at his birthplace by any means (by then I had figured out the negative aspects of corporatism as well as its positive features), but to get a feel for the place where the main character in my book grew up. With our friend Manuela Semidei from Paris we toured the southern areas of Portugal, the Alemtejo and the Algarve, home to many British retirees and, at Sagres, where Prince Henry the Navigator established his fifteenth century school for sailors which enabled Portugal for a time to emerge as one of Europe's great powers and perhaps the greatest seafaring nation of all times.

On these trips we usually stayed in what the Portuguese call <u>pousadas</u>: historic castles that had been lovingly restored and converted into modern overnight residences. The rooms were gorgeous, the food and wine excellent, and the prices reasonable considering the elegant surroundings. Our children loved these Pousadas because most of them had deep, dark, scary dungeons just like in the bedtime stories we read to them, and in some, guests could actually stay in one of the restored dungeon rooms.

On one last trip I went on my own around the north or Tras-os-Montes (Over the Mountains) area of Portugal: Guimarães, Braga, Chaves, and Braganca. This is a mountainous area of Portugal near the border with the Spanish province of Galicia. It is from this area that many historic Portuguese stories about witches, werewolves, and mysterious happenings originate—rather like Transylvania in Romania. It is in this area also, which largely escaped the Moorish Islamic invasion, that the basic and best values of Portuguese political culture are thought to have originated: Catholicism, industriousness, toughness against the odds, hard work, perseverance, a certain stubbornness that sometimes seems to defy all rationality. The North is said to be the home of the real, authentic, and true Portuguese values, all of which seemed to go by the wayside in the revolution of 1974. Or did they?

The reason I went on my own to Tras-os-Montes was that Iêda was pregnant, it had been a complicated pregnancy, and we didn't want to take any chances by taking an extended trip on rough roads into a remote area of the country when there were no doctors. Little did we know then just how difficult the actual delivery would be. When labor started our gynecologist, Maria Elena Freitas, informed us that she had hepatitis and would be unable to deliver the baby. Worse, she hung up the phone and "disappeared" without giving us the name of another doctor or arranging for us to be admitted to a hospital. That set off a desperate, several-hour search on my part during which we were turned down for admission, even in this situation of emergency, by three different hospitals. It was one of the most exasperating and dangerous three hours we have ever experienced. Over the years in Portugal we have come to call these incredible lapses of judgment and good sense "Portuguese moments." It is, and is meant to be, an ironic term.

When we finally found a hospital in Oeiras that would accept us, the nurses were unpleasant and we could not persuade the doctors to take a look at Iêda. The staff and nurses refused to accept the flowers I had sent to Iêda or to provide water and a vase. The doctor who finally consented to see her let her suffer in labor for two days with the baby in a dangerous breach position before finally and reluctantly consenting to induce birth. It was the most miserable health and hospital care we have ever experienced in forty years of wandering the globe. More "Portuguese moments!"

But our troubles were not yet over. We had decided to name our baby Jonathan. Jonathan is a good Biblical name, an Old Testament name; he was a friend of King David who helped save David's life and even gave his own life for his friend. What better name could there be! But not to the Portuguese. Like a good father and in accord with the law, I went down to register baby Jonathan at the civil registry in Oeiras. There I encountered one of those aging, septuagenarian, stubborn, unbending Portuguese bureaucrats of the kind made famous in the Nobel Prize-winning fiction of José Saramago. The clerk had a big black book of officially acceptable Portuguese names; he spent a laborious half hour looking through it, and finally announced to me that we could not name our baby Jonathan. I immediately pulled out my billfold assuming that the turndown was really a preliminary to a solicitation for a bribe.

But the ancient clerk explained "Oh no, senhor, you don't understand; I don't want your money.[†] He went on to explain that the reason we could not name our baby Jonathan was that in Catholic Portugal only saints names were deemed

---

[†]   One of Portugal's landmarks is the Gulbenkian Museum, surely one of the world's most beautifully-displayed and viewer—friendly private museums. It is named for Caloueste Gulbenkian, an early twentieth century Armenian businessman who was known as "Mr. Five Percent" because for a long time he received 5% of the proceeds from every barrel of oil exported from Iran. The story is that when Gulbenkian visited Portugal, the first three people he tried to bribe refused to accept his money. Gulbenkian was so impressed that he determined to leave his considerable fortune to Portugal. Hence the Gulbenkian Museum.

acceptable. If we wanted to name him "João (John), that was acceptable, but not Jonathan—even if it was a Biblical name. Later, since I am a professor of comparative politics, I investigated this further. It turns out that other historically Catholic countries, such as France or Italy, also have books of officially acceptable names. But there the issue has either been challenged in the courts or else parents proceed to name their babies whatever they want (like our friend Manuela; actually from Corsica, which explains her name) regardless of the law. But not in stiff, formal, legalistic Portugal. On the other hand, when we got back in Amherst, I overheard a conversation of a father and son in which it became clear that the son had been named Oedipus. What a terrible name with which to burden a child—rather like that Johnny Cash song about "A Boy named Sue." Perhaps the Portuguese system of officially acceptable names had some merit after all.

In desperation I asked the clerk what we could do. The long and short of it was: I had to go to the American Embassy and get a letter from the ambassador saying it was acceptable to the United States government if we named our baby Jonathan. The letter then had to be notarized with the official embassy stamp, then rolled and tied with an official red ribbon, then wax dripped on the knot, and then the Embassy's stamp affixed again to the wax seal—presumably so we would not tamper with or seek to forge the ambassador's signature! All this took three days of back and forth—more "Portuguese moments." Finally, armed with this formidable document, I returned to the civil registry. My "friend" the aged clerk took a half hour to read what was a two-sentence letter. At last he approved; we named our son Jonathan!

There is one final (we feared more) twist to this tale. We were by then, my research complete by July, 1973, preparing to leave the country, but since the baby was so young we could not get him to wake up enough to open his eyes for the required passport photo, whose requirements included that the passport bearer's eyes had to be open. We tried everything from popping a balloon, to shouting loudly, to propping the eyes open with matchsticks. Nothing worked. Finally the photographer himself clapped his hands loudly right over Jonathan's nose, his eyes popped open, and the photographer successfully snapped his picture—just before the eyes closed back down again.

Armed with the pictures, we quickly got Jonathan included on my passport and left the country. We feared that there might be some last-minute bureaucratic glitch that would prevent the authorities from allowing our Portuguese-born baby from leaving the country, but that never materialized. We also worried that as a Portuguese citizen Jonathan might someday years later be traveling in Portugal and find himself impressed into the army to be sent to fight the guerrillas in Southern Africa; but the 1974 revolution leading to independence for the colonies meant that fear would not be realized either.

En route home, we stopped off (but did not stay) in the Portuguese Azores Islands, one-third of the way back across the Atlantic from Europe toward America. The Azores are gorgeous, volcanic outcroppings, bright green like Ireland with whitewashed villages, still unspoiled by tourists, and yet very poor even by Portuguese standards. The last is the reason so many Portuguese immigrants to the U.S. are from the Azores and less so the Mainland. As the only islands (besides Iceland) in the mid-Atlantic, the Azores also have strategic value for the U.S., particularly in those years of the 1970s as a refueling station for U.S. military aircraft on the way to the Middle East, and provide the key reason for Portugal's admission to NATO even while a regime similar to Salazar's, that of Franco in Spain, was not admitted.

In subsequent years we would return almost yearly (and sometimes more than that) to Portugal, which came to rival the DR and Brazil as the country we most often visited. But while in Portugal during that eventful year of 1972-73, we also took the opportunity to take some grand tours of the rest of Europe as well.

Epilogue

When the Portuguese Revolution broke out in April, 1974, we were back in Amherst, having returned to teaching in the fall of 1973 and to writing my book on (Portuguese) corporatism and development. I had gone back to Portugal in February, 1974, two months before the Revolution, to advise the Embassy on political developments (the coup plots underway), but because of teaching obligations was unable to stay for more than a short visit.

As the Revolution first destroyed and devoured the old regime of Caetano, Thomaz, the secret police, corporatism (officially abolished) et. al., and then as the Revolution swung radically to the left with the Communists making a push for power, a number of Portugal specialists myself included were called to Washington to advise the State Department. My recollection is that there were two meetings that I attended; among the other invitees were Douglas Wheeler from the University of New Hampshire, Lawrence Graham of the University of Texas, Kenneth Maxwell of Columbia University, Philippe Schmitter of the University of Chicago, Gerald Bender of UCLA and John Marcum of MIT—the latter two being Africa experts. We were asked to prepare papers on what we saw as the future of both Portugal and Portuguese Africa. As a specialist on Portuguese political culture, my paper was the only one that predicted that Portugal would eventually return to its more conservative, Catholic, corporatist, and bureaucratic roots. That prediction proved to be an accurate one. The trouble was it took about ten years to happen; meanwhile Portugal seemed, to use an expression of that time, to be fast going down the tubes.

Within a few months of the Revolution I had also been contacted by the Institute of International Relations at the University of South Carolina. The Institute was headed by Richard ("Dixie") Walker and was one of the main university-based international affairs research centers in the U.S. The Institute asked if I would undertake an investigation and prepare a study of the Portuguese revolution and its foreign policy implications. Of course I agreed. The project included research in Portugal and then a presentation of the results at a major 1976 conference in London—all paid for by the Institute.

En route to London I stopped off in Portugal to update my research materials in the light of the Revolution. One of my interviews was with the newly-named ambassador to Portugal, Frank Carlucci. Part of the interview was conducted in the big armored Buick that had been imported to Lisbon for Carlucci's use in a dangerous and revolutionary situation. But the Buick was so wide that it could not fit through many of Lisbon's narrow streets and, if a terrorist were so inclined, could have been blocked and ambushed by as little as a bicycle or motor scooter. At one point Carlucci and I abandoned the car and proceeded on foot with no security.

It turned out I had arrived in Portugal just in time to become involved in a foreign policy dispute between Carlucci and his secretary of state, Henry Kissinger. Kissinger believed that Portugal had already been lost to communism, had told then Portuguese Prime Minister Mario Soares that he would be the next Kerensky (the Russian prime minister in 1917 replaced by the Bolsheviks), and was contemplating both CIA and NATO actions to reverse the far-leftward trajectory of the Revolution. In contrast Carlucci, on the ground in Lisbon, believed Portugal was not lost, had faith in the moderate elements and that the U.S. should aid them, believed that Portugal's conservative and Catholic traditions would eventually reassert themselves, and argued that Portugal was quite capable of finding its own murky solutions to its own messy problems. I sided with the Carlucci arguments.

Normally an American ambassador in the field finds that it's suicide, a career-ender, to take on his own secretary of state, and does not do so. But Carlucci had his own formidable resources. He had been head of OEO (Office of Economic Opportunity), had his own friends in the Nixon and Ford White Houses, and had been a Princeton college roommate of Defense Secretary (the first time) Donald Rumsfeld. In addition, he was a skilled political and bureaucratic infighter.

Since I had just completed a major research project on Portugal, knew the country, and had interviewed most of the leading military and political officials, Carlucci and the Embassy sought out my advice. My job was to provide the Carlucci team with information that they could use in their bureaucratic/political battle with Kissinger. It was not that I was formulating policy options for decision-makers; rather, I was assisting one side in an already existing, insider political battle where the stakes were high.

And if truth be known, that is mainly how academics or think tank scholars do in fact influence policy—when they influence it at all. It is not that U.S. government agencies want policy options from scholars; instead they want facts, data, and arguments to support a position that they have already reached. In this case, eventually the Carlucci argument prevailed, I had a strong hand in advancing it, and it proved to be the correct course of action.

This was my first real experience at high level policy-making. The entire process was so fascinating that it whetted my appetite for a greater and ongoing policy role. Hence in 1976 I got deeply involved in the presidential campaign really for the first time, and after the 1980 election I parlayed my academic and policy work into a full-time and more-or-less permanent Washington career. It all really began with the Portuguese Revolution.

Reluctantly leaving Lisbon after this heady experience, I went on to my conference in London. There I met for the first time Brian Crozier, James Theberge, Lawrence Martin, Richard Starr, Richard Allen, and other first-rate, high-level strategic thinkers. It was a heady experience, even though I did not share the political views of the more conservative members of this group some of whom actually supported the Kissinger position that the communists were taking over Portugal. Nevertheless I learned a lot about policy-making from these encounters and experiences which whetted my appetite for more. In the meantime my book on Portuguese corporatism was published and so were the papers and monograph I prepared for South Carolina and the several Portuguese conferences I attended.[4] All this paved the way for a complete reorientation of my work and thinking during a two-year stint spent at Harvard University where I retooled as a foreign policy analyst to complement my comparative politics specialization.[5] But first, there were more foreign travel and research projects, and many more adventures abroad.

NOTES

1. Howard J. Wiarda, "The Politics of Population Policy in Dominican Republic," in Terry McCoy (ed.), <u>Dynamics of Population Policy in Latin America</u> (Cambridge: Ballinger, 1974) 293-322.

2. Howard J. Wiarda, "The Politics of Population Policy in Brazil," unpublished manuscript, 1972.

3. Howard J. Wiarda, <u>Corporatism and Development: The Portuguese Experience</u> (Amherst: University of Massachusetts Press, 1977).

4. Wiarda, <u>Corporatism and Development: The Portuguese Experience</u>; <u>Transcending Corporatism? The Portuguese Corporative System and the Revolution of 1974</u> (Columbia: Institute of International Studies, University of South Carolina, 1976).

5. For the Harvard experience, see Howard J. Wiarda, <u>Universities, Think Tanks, and War Colleges</u> (Princeton, N.J.: XLibris/McGraw Hill, 1999) Chapter 6.

INDEX VOLUME I

978-0-595-39710-5
0-595-39710-7

www.ingramcontent.com/pod-product-compliance
Lightning Source LLC
Chambersburg PA
CBHW020411290526

45785CB00002B/502